Liberalism and Prostitution

OXFORD POLITICAL PHILOSOPHY

General Editor
Samuel Freeman, University of Pennsylvania

Oxford Political Philosophy publishes books on theoretical and applied political philosophy within the Anglo-American tradition. The series welcomes submissions on social, political, and global justice, individual rights, democracy, liberalism, socialism, and constitutionalism.

Imposing Values: An Essay on Liberalism and Regulation
N. Scott Arnold

Liberalism and Prostitution
Peter de Marneffe

LIBERALISM AND PROSTITUTION

Peter de Marneffe

UNIVERSITY PRESS

Oxford University Press, Inc., publishes works that further
Oxford University's objective of excellence
in research, scholarship, and education.

Oxford   New York
Auckland   Cape Town   Dar es Salaam   Hong Kong   Karachi
Kuala Lumpur   Madrid   Melbourne   Mexico City   Nairobi
New Delhi   Shanghai   Taipei   Toronto

With offices in
Argentina   Austria   Brazil   Chile   Czech Republic   France   Greece
Guatemala   Hungary   Italy   Japan   Poland   Portugal   Singapore
South Korea   Switzerland   Thailand   Turkey   Ukraine   Vietnam

Copyright © 2010 by Oxford University Press

Published by Oxford University Press, Inc.
198 Madison Avenue, New York, New York 10016
www.oup.com

First issued as an Oxford University Press paperback, 2012.

Oxford is a registered trademark of Oxford University Press

All rights reserved. No part of this publication may be reproduced,
stored in a retrieval system, or transmitted, in any form or by any means,
electronic, mechanical, photocopying, recording, or otherwise,
without the prior permission of Oxford University Press.

Library of Congress Cataloging-in-Publication Data
deMarneffe, Peter, 1957–
Liberalism and prostitution / Peter deMarneffe.
  p. cm. — (Oxford political philosophy)
ISBN 978-0-19-538324-9 (hardcover); 978-0-19-992594-0 (paperback)
1. Prostitution. 2. Liberalism. 3. Paternalism. 4. Civil rights. I. Title.
HQ115.D43 2009
345'.02534—dc22   2009003016

Printed in the United States of America
on acid-free paper

For my teachers

Acknowledgments

The first draft of this book was written when I was a Fellow in Ethics at the Edmund J. Safra Foundation Center for Ethics at Harvard University, 1997–1998. I thank the Center for support, and Arthur Applbaum, Paulina Herlinde-Studer, Lisa Lehman, Richard Miller, Sebastiano Moffetone, Richard Pildes, and Dennis Thompson for comments on early drafts of chapters 3, 4, and 5.

My research on prostitution laws began when I was a Rockefeller Fellow at the University Center for Human Values at Princeton University, 1993–1994. Debra Satz, another Fellow at the Center that year, was working on her article "Markets in Women's Sexual Labor." Debra and I disagreed about the available justifications for prostitution laws, and I started to read more about prostitution to see if my beliefs were defensible. This began the process that led to this book. I thank Debra for stimulating to me to think harder about prostitution laws, and I thank Tony Coady, Kent Greenawalt, Amy Gutmann, Alan Houston, George Kateb, Arthur Kuflik, Stephen Macedo, Thomas Pogge, and Yael Tamir, for many stimulating discussions about liberty and liberalism during my time at Princeton.

My scholarly research on liberty and liberalism, individual rights, paternalism, and government neutrality began with my doctoral dissertation, "Liberalism and Education," written under the direction of John Rawls and Thomas Scanlon at Harvard. I am grateful for all I have learned from these two great teachers. I also thank the Spencer Foundation for a Spencer

Fellowship for Research in Education, which supported my final year of dissertation research.

The manuscript that I wrote at the Safra Center in the late 1990s was about rights and paternalism, focused on the policy issues of drug and prostitution laws. After writing a draft of this manuscript, I was asked by Cambridge University Press to write a book with Douglas Husak for and against drug legalization. Since my views on drug legalization (against) have now been presented in this other book, this book focuses on prostitution laws. I thank Doug Husak and Cambridge University Press for the opportunity to clarify ideas on rights, paternalism, and government neutrality that are developed here.

A number of people read drafts of this manuscript and I thank them all for their helpful comments, in particular Scott Anderson, Sam Freeman, Doug Portmore, and Tim Scanlon. In October 2008 I presented material from this book at the Program in Ethics and Public Affairs Seminar at the University Center for Human Values at Princeton University, and I thank all the participants for their comments, particularly Liz Harman, my commentator. I also thank Stephanie Attia at Oxford University Press for preparing this manuscript for publication. For access to many of the publications cited in this book I thank Christie Hansen and the Interlibrary Loan staff at Arizona State University.

Contents

Introduction	3
1. A Paternalistic Case for Prostitution Laws	12
2. Government Moralism	45
3. The Permissibility of Paternalism	65
4. Individual Rights	107
5. Government Neutrality and Perfectionism	133
Conclusion	154
Notes	163
Index	187

Liberalism and Prostitution

Introduction

Prostitution is commonly characterized as a "victimless crime," especially by those who believe it ought to be legalized. Opponents of legalization counter that prostitution is not victimless: it is harmful to those who do it, and it is often forced on a person by economic need if not by an abusive pimp. To many, however, the characterization of prostitution as victimless remains convincing. Why is this? One reason is that most prostitution appears to be voluntary. Another reason is that not everyone who does this work is obviously harmed by it. In this book I consider whether prostitution laws might be justified nonetheless, and I conclude that they might be. Given a set of defensible empirical assumptions, prostitution laws in some form are morally justifiable even if most prostitution is voluntary and not all prostitutes are harmed by it.

There are different arguments for prostitution laws. They have been defended as necessary to protect or affirm traditional sexual morality, to protect wives and children from adultery and its consequences, to reduce the spread of sexually transmitted diseases, to protect women as a group from gender discrimination, and to foster respectful intimate relationships between men and women. In this book I focus on a different argument, which is that prostitution is harmful to those who do it. Contemporary feminist critics maintain that prostitution is inherently dangerous; that it commonly results in lasting feelings of worthlessness and self-hatred; that it typically interferes with the ability to form stable, trusting, mutually respectful intimate relationships; and that it typically results in the loss of important social, educational, and economic opportunities. I take these claims seriously. If prostitution laws function to reduce these harms, I believe this is sufficient justification for them, at least in some form.

Laws that are justified as protecting those whose liberty or opportunities they limit are commonly characterized as *paternalistic*. Many have thought that government paternalism is wrong. I reject this view. Some forms of paternalism are clearly wrong. For example, it is clearly wrong for the government to coerce apostasy for the benefit of a person's immortal soul. It is not wrong, however, for the government to prohibit dueling or gladiatorial contests for the benefit of those who might otherwise be tempted to engage in them, by prize money, a sense of honor, or fear of humiliation. Some have claimed that it is essential to liberalism to hold that paternalism is always wrong. I reject this view as well. A liberal theory of rights must recognize the great value of individual liberty. It must recognize that individuals have rights to important liberties such as freedom of expression, freedom of worship, and sexual freedom. It must therefore endorse a principle of antipaternalism that forbids the most intrusive forms of paternalistic interference with these and other important liberties. Some forms of paternalism, however, are consistent with these liberal commitments, including some paternalistic prostitution laws.

Liberalism does place constraints on what government policies can be morally justified, and some prostitution laws may violate these constraints. Perhaps laws that categorically prohibit the *sale* of sexual services, for example, cannot be justified consistent with a due respect for sexual autonomy. Perhaps laws that categorically prohibit the *purchase* of sexual services are an unjustifiable restriction of adult sexual freedom. Even if these policies are unjustifiable, however, other restrictions on prostitution might be justified. Laws that prohibit the purchase of sex from anyone under 21 might be justified, for example, as might laws that prohibit the operation of brothels. I believe that on certain defensible empirical assumptions these and other restrictions on prostitution can in fact be justified and justified compatible with the fundamental principles of liberalism.

In chapter 1 I state what I take to be the strongest paternalistic argument for prostitution laws: that prostitution is psychologically destructive and results in the loss of important opportunities, and that prostitution laws reduce this harm, by reducing the number of people who do this work and by reducing the amount of prostitution that is done by those who do it. In chapter 3 I defend the kind of paternalism involved, arguing that one may consistently endorse this justification for prostitution laws while accepting a general principle of liberty that rules out those forms of paternalism that liberal theorists of individual rights have found most objectionable. Against this possibility antipaternalists sometimes suggest that unless every form of paternalism is impermissible, every form of paternalism is permissible. Because they assume (correctly) that some forms of paternalism are impermissible, they conclude (incorrectly) that every form is impermissible. This kind of black-and-white reasoning is fallacious, and yet with respect to paternalism many seem to be convinced by it. For this reason I take time in chapter 3 to explain how one may consistently defend the kind of paternalism that defensible prostitution laws involve while opposing other, more objectionable, forms of paternalism.

Another common objection to prostitution laws is that they are moralistic. In chapter 2 I explain why, although prostitution laws might be paternalistic, they are not objectionably moralistic. Another objection to prostitution laws is that they violate the rights of individuals to sexual freedom. In chapter 4 I explain why, although it is true that we have rights to sexual freedom, and although some prostitution laws might violate these rights, some paternalistic prostitution laws violate no one's rights. Prostitution laws are also sometimes criticized as violating the principle of neutrality: that the government should be as neutral as possible toward different conceptions of a good life. So in chapter 5 I address this objection too. Although defenders of neutrality have made valid claims in defending this principle, these valid claims are perfectly consistent with paternalistic prostitution laws of some kind.

Liberal theorists of rights hold that individuals have moral rights to liberty; that certain kinds of government paternalism are morally wrong; that certain kinds of government moralism are wrong; and that the government should therefore strive for a certain kind of neutrality toward conceptions of a good life. I believe that all these claims are correct, at least on some interpretation. There is, however, a defensible interpretation of each of these claims—the best interpretation in my view—that is perfectly consistent with some paternalistic prostitution laws. As a consequence one may consistently identify oneself as a liberal, as someone who respects personal autonomy and values individual liberty highly, while supporting paternalistic prostitution laws in some form. Those who maintain that liberalism requires the legalization of prostitution are mistaken. These are the central claims of this book.

Some may question my focus on the issue of paternalism. There are nonpaternalistic arguments for prostitution laws. Why not focus on these arguments instead? Others may question my focus on paternalism for a different reason. Paternalism is wrong, they might hold, only because it interferes with our choices. Because prostitution is never really a choice, prostitution laws do not raise the philosophical issue of paternalism.

Against this last claim I assume throughout that prostitution is generally voluntary and consensual in the ordinary descriptive sense. I assume, in other words, that prostitution generally results from a deliberate decision that is based on a person's judgment that prostitution is the best thing for her to do in her circumstances, a decision that is generally not made in the face of direct threats of harm from others and does not generally result from ignorance of the nature of the transaction. This, I believe, is strongly confirmed by the available evidence, the testimony of prostitutes, and the observations of those who study prostitution.[1] Even those who explicitly challenge the assumption that prostitution is a choice often implicitly allow that it is.

For instance, the author of one recent book, after explicitly rejecting the characterization of prostitution as a "free choice,"[2] goes on to discuss the "decision" to enter and to leave prostitution, and characterizes the decision to stop as a "tough choice."[3] Moreover, he identifies a number of factors that typically lead prostitutes to quit, such as violent incidents, ill health, loss of children, imprisonment, a new relationship, development of an alternative career, disillusionment with working conditions, and the feeling that one has been doing this work for too long.[4] If prostitutes commonly decide to stop doing sex work for all these reasons, it makes little sense to hold that their decision to continue is not a choice. To be sure, there are horror stories of sexual slavery in which individuals are held against their will and forced to perform sexual acts in exchange for money. In economically developed countries, however, the documented cases of this kind of sexual slavery are rare.

Why, then, do so many critics claim that prostitution is not a choice? The most common argument is that the decision to engage in prostitution is made against a background of inadequate economic alternatives,[5] which is often true. The inadequacy of economic alternatives, however, does not show that prostitution is not a choice. The choice between working as a housecleaner, a bagger in a supermarket, a server in a fast food restaurant, and a prostitute is certainly not ideal, but it is still a choice. Few, if any, of us make our choices against an *ideal* array of alternatives. We all make choices nonetheless.

Given the apparently consensual nature of most prostitution, there are different positions that a critic of prostitution might take toward this choice. One is that whenever a mentally competent adult consents to do something, this automatically shields all the participants from criticism and penalties, and relieves others of responsibility to prevent the negative consequences, but that some activities that *appear* to be consensual are not *really* consensual and so the consent necessary to provide the relevant kinds of immunity is absent. When antiprostitution activists maintain that prostitution is not "a real choice," they sometimes appear to taking this position.[6] Because, however, most sex work appears to be voluntary, this position makes their argument against legalization less convincing. How, then, should they respond to the apparently consensual nature of most prostitution? They might hold instead that when a person consents to do something, this does *not* necessarily shield other participants from criticism and penalties and does *not* necessarily relieve others of the responsibility to do something about the negative consequences. If the activity is harmful to any of the participants, they might hold, others have a responsibility to discourage this activity, and criticism of and penalties for some of the participants might be warranted.

Any defense of prostitution laws, however, that takes this second position on the significance of choice is sure to draw the charge of paternalism. To understand why, it is helpful to consider a distinction we commonly make between the sexual consent of adults and the sexual consent of legal minors. Most of us would agree that because legal minors are not in a good position to assess what kinds of sexual activity are in their best interest and because sexual experiences with adults may be detrimental to them, it is legitimate for the government to discourage this kind of sexual activity with legal penalties, if only very mild ones. Although we commonly defend this position by claiming that legal minors "cannot consent" to have sex with adults, this is a legal fiction because many legal minors have the cognitive and volitional capacities generally sufficient to make meaningful agreements. They can agree to babysit, for example, or to walk the neighbor's dog for money, or to play a team sport, or to act in a school play. Consequently, when we say that legal minors cannot consent to have sex with legal adults we do not mean that they lack the cognitive and volitional ability to make agreements in general. We are instead expressing our unwillingness to treat their agreement as legitimating sexual relations with adults or as immunizing the participating adults from criticism and legal penalties. In contrast, many of us are inclined to hold that the sexual consent of a competent adult *does* immunize other participating adults from legal penalties and, perhaps, even from moral criticism. If we deny, then, that the decision of a legal adult to have sex for money immunizes others from criticism and penalties—clients, pimps, and brothel owners—it may seem that we are treating this person "like a child."

I believe it is the desire to avoid this charge of paternalism that leads many antiprostitution activists to deny that prostitution is a real choice. After all, if sex work is not a choice, then the government does not disrespect anyone's choices in seeking to deter her from doing this work. The available evidence, however, warrants the conclusion that most prostitution is voluntary and consensual. So if one is to respect the available evidence and yet oppose the legalization of the prostitution on the grounds that it is harmful to those who do it, one must defend the kind of paternalism that prostitution laws involve.

The argument for prostitution laws that prostitution is harmful to those who do it is not the only argument. Prostitution laws have also been defended as necessary to reduce crime, as necessary to reduce the transmission of disease, as necessary to protect women as a group from gender discrimination, as necessary to foster an environment that is conducive to respectful intimate relationships between men and women, and as necessary to protect the family. Why, then, do I focus on the paternalistic argument for prostitution laws instead of on one of these non-paternalistic arguments?

One reason is theoretical. It is commonly supposed that paternalistic policies are inherently incompatible with liberalism or with any view that takes individual rights to liberty seriously. I believe this is incorrect. In explaining why, it is helpful to focus on a particular policy that might be justified on paternalistic grounds. Here I focus on prostitution laws and argue that if the empirical assumptions of the paternalistic argument for these laws are sound, then prostitution laws in some form can be justified by a paternalistic argument, and justified compatible with a due respect for individual rights. If this is correct, it tells us something about the permissibility of paternalism and about the nature of liberalism.

Another reason to focus on the paternalistic argument for prostitution laws is that this is the argument that contemporary antiprostitution activists take most seriously. If one examines the written work of those actively opposed to the legalization of prostitution, it is clear that their primary concern is with the harm that prostitution does to the women who do it.[7] The paternalistic character of this concern may be obscured by the rhetoric of those who characterize prostitution as a form of "violence against women."[8] What makes this rhetoric seem appropriate is that prostitution seems to have negative psychological consequences similar to the negative psychological consequences of other forms of sexual abuse, such as rape and adult-child incest: a sense of loss of control; feelings of worthlessness, shame, and self-hatred; posttraumatic stress disorder; difficulty with intimate relationships; and so on.[9] The available evidence, however, taken as a whole, warrants the conclusion that prostitution is generally voluntary, at least in the standard descriptive sense identified above. So if there is a sense in which prostitution is a form of violence against women, it is not the ordinary sense of violence that implies the unwanted use of physical force and physical harm. If, however, prostitution is generally voluntary in the ordinary descriptive sense, then the primary argument against legalization that is made by antiprostitution activists is really this one: that if prostitution is legalized, more people will be harmed by work that they choose to do.[10] This is a paternalistic argument. Because it is now the argument most commonly made against legalizing prostitution, it makes sense to examine philosophically whether it can justify prostitution laws and, if so, in what form.

A related reason to focus on the paternalistic argument for prostitution laws is that it might actually be the strongest argument: it might have the greatest moral weight and be the most convincing to an impartial judge.

The paternalistic argument might also justify policies that nonpaternalistic arguments are unable to justify. To illustrate, consider the nonpaternalistic argument that prostitution laws are necessary to reduce crime. The only crime that appears to be highly associated with prostitution (other than prostitution itself and the related activities of solicitation, loitering, pimping, and pandering) is petty larceny.[11] A plausible explanation for this is that clients make easy targets where buying sexual services is illegal because these clients are unlikely to report these thefts to the police. If so, then the crime associated with prostitution would be reduced by legalizing prostitution, and therefore cannot be cited as a justification for more restrictive policies.

Consider, too, the nonpaternalistic argument for prostitution laws that they are necessary to reduce the public nuisance of streetwalking. Streetwalking changes the character of a neighborhood, making it seem seedier and so a more depressing place to live, thereby lowering property values. Solicitation on the street or in hotels, bars, and restaurants interferes with commerce, especially with establishments that aim to attract business from families. These are arguments for the regulation and zoning of prostitution, but not for more restrictive policies such as the prohibition of brothels, because legalized prostitution that is regulated and zoned would presumably do as well or better in protecting the relevant interests.

Other nonpaternalistic arguments might go further toward justifying the government in actively discouraging prostitution. Some have argued that toleration of prostitution fosters discrimination against women as a group.[12] Others have argued that toleration of prostitution encourages men to view women and sex in ways that make it more difficult for women to find and sustain emotionally satisfying and mutually respectful intimate relationships with men.[13] Here we must wonder, though, whether women as a group are more victimized by sex discrimination in nations where prostitution is tolerated, such as the Netherlands and Germany, than they are in the United States, where it is not. Are Dutch and German women less able than American women to find and maintain satisfying intimate relationships with men? It is not obvious that Dutch and German women are worse off in these ways than American women, and if the toleration of prostitution does not have these negative consequences, these arguments cannot justify prostitution laws in any form.

Another longstanding argument for prostitution laws is that they are necessary to reduce the spread of sexually transmitted disease. Defenders of legalization have argued that disease would be more effectively reduced by legalizing brothels and requiring regular testing of those who work there. Opponents of legalization reply that mandatory testing is ineffective because tests are not administered with sufficient frequency; testing sex workers leaves clients untested; and many prostitutes prefer to work outside of brothels. The transmission of disease is more effectively reduced, they maintain, by legal restrictions on prostitution that reduce the number of unhealthy transactions overall.[14] Even if this is true, however, it does not provide a *non*paternalistic argument for prostitution laws unless these laws can be justified as protecting unwitting third parties from contracting diseases from partners who have been with infected prostitutes. Because the rates of third-party infection are unknown and because, with modern medicine, most sexually transmitted diseases are not very serious, it is doubtful that significant restrictions on prostitution can be justified in this way.

HIV/AIDS is serious, but most researchers have concluded that prostitution is not a significant factor in its transmission, at least not in economically developed democratic countries such as the United Kingdom and the United States.[15] The available research indicates that although HIV is spread in these countries by prostitutes who are intravenous drug users, it is not spread by them significantly more than by intravenous drug users who are not prostitutes and it is not spread by prostitutes who are not intravenous drug users significantly more than by other sexually active people who are not intravenous drug users.[16] It is therefore doubtful that significant restrictions on prostitution can be justified by the nonpaternalistic argument that these laws are necessary to protect unwitting third parties from contracting HIV/AIDS.

I do not mean to dismiss every nonpaternalistic argument for prostitution laws. Perhaps one of the arguments I have just considered is sound. Perhaps some other nonpaternalistic argument is sound. Perhaps one of these arguments is sounder, normatively and empirically, than the paternalistic rationale for prostitution laws that I present in the next chapter. Even if this is true, however, it is useful to consider the paternalistic argument. Antipaternalists argue that if a government policy limits the liberty of a legal adult and this policy cannot be justified as benefiting *others* in some way, then this policy violates this person's rights. To assess this claim, we must consider policies for which the following might be true: although this policy limits the liberty or opportunities of a legal adult in ways that cannot be justified as benefiting others, this policy *could* be justified as benefiting this person *if* this argument were allowed to count in its favor. I argue that given certain empirical assumptions, prostitution laws in some form can be justified by the paternalistic argument for them even if they cannot be justified by any nonpaternalistic argument. If so, then some kinds of government paternalism are permissible in principle, and those who claim that paternalism is wrong in principle are mistaken.

This is primarily a study in political philosophy, not sociology, criminology, sexual psychology, or feminist theory. Fundamentally, this book is about whether paternalistic policies can be justified within a liberal framework that takes seriously the idea that individuals have rights to liberty. It examines this philosophical question by focusing on prostitution laws. Using the issue of prostitution to understand the implications of liberal theories of rights for government paternalism might seem callous. One writer has worried that theoretical discussion of prostitution obscures rather than highlights the harm caused by it, what she calls "the carnage: the scale of it, the dailiness of it, the seeming inevitability of it; the torture, the rapes, the murders, the beatings, the despair, the hollowing out of the personality, the near extinguishment of hope commonly suffered by women in prostitution." "To render this slaughter of women a matter to be assessed by analytic argument," she says, has at times seemed to her "an act of barbarism."[17] Mindful of this concern, I will do my best in the next chapter to identify the ways in which prostitution is harmful to those who do it. An honest evaluation of prostitution laws, however, must also acknowledge that individuals have important claims to liberty, including sexual freedom; that prostitution laws limit sexual freedom; and that some prostitution laws intrude into the lives of prostitutes and clients in ways that make their lives worse. Certainly we must pay close attention to the ways in which prostitution is harmful to those who do it, but we must also take seriously the legitimate claims of individuals to personal freedom and dignity, including the claims of prostitutes and their clients. Perhaps the analytic detachment of this book will strike some readers as cold and repellant. This kind of detachment, however, does help one to think more clearly about the moral justifiability of prostitution laws, to see through the fog created by the heated emotions on both sides of the legalization debate. We will never achieve full clarity on prostitution policy until we know much more than we do now about the causes and effects of prostitution and about the costs and benefits of various policy alternatives. We can, however, begin to think about how best to balance individual liberty and protection from harm from the liberal point of view, a point of view that takes seriously the idea that individuals have moral rights to liberty. This is my project here.

1

A Paternalistic Case for Prostitution Laws

The paternalistic argument for prostitution laws is that prostitution is harmful to those who do it and that prostitution laws reduce this harm by reducing prostitution. How, though, is prostitution harmful? Prostitution can be dangerous, but it would arguably be less so if legalized and regulated. Which harms would increase, then, if prostitution were fully legalized? In this chapter I identify psychological and social harms that prostitution causes and would cause even if prostitution were legalized. These nonphysical harms are harder to observe and quantify than physical harms, but they are no less real. Assuming, then, that prostitution laws reduce these harms by reducing prostitution, there is a paternalistic case to be made for prostitution laws in some form.

Even if prostitution is commonly harmful, it does not follow that prostitution laws can be justified as reducing this harm, because these laws might do more harm than good. We must therefore consider the costs of different policies and assess whether these costs might be justified by the benefit of reducing prostitution. In this chapter I distinguish three kinds of legal restriction on prostitution—prohibition, abolition, and regulation—and I argue that although prohibition probably cannot be justified by the paternalistic argument, abolition or regulation in some form probably can be.

In this chapter and throughout the rest of this book I focus on female prostitution. I do this primarily for three reasons. First, far more has been written on female prostitution and its negative effects than on male prostitution. Second, the vast majority of prostitutes are female and the vast majority of clients are male. Third, there is some reason to believe that the negative impact of prostitution on girls and young women is different from the negative impact on boys and young men, because of differences in male and female psychology and the different ways in which male and female sexual activity is socially stigmatized. Gender-neutral prostitution laws, however, apply both to female and male prostitution, and we must bear this in mind when considering the kinds of policy that might be justified by the paternalistic argument presented here. For the sake of simplicity I assume that male prostitutes are negatively affected by sex work in roughly the same ways that female prostitutes are. If so, then the arguments presented here can justify gender-neutral prostitution laws in some form. If not, we must consider whether unequal treatment by the law of male and female prostitution is warranted, but I will not pursue this complex issue here.

I. The Harm

There are different kinds of prostitution, some of which are less harmful and less risky than others. There is one kind, however, that is widely thought to cause lasting psychological damage. This is the kind in which the sex worker provides sexual services throughout the day or week to a number of men, some of whom she does not know at all, most of whom she does not know well. This work is commonly experienced as humiliating and abusive, and results in lasting feelings of worthlessness, shame, and self-hatred. This kind of work is also highly stressful, so stressful that some researchers report that it results in a posttraumatic stress disorder similar to that found in combat veterans.[1] This stress is created partly by the constant risk of violence and verbal abuse, but also by the fact that this kind of work demands an exhausting kind of emotional pretense. A successful sex worker must typically pretend to enjoy the company of her clients and to be sexually interested in and aroused by them even when they strike her as stupid, offensive, pathetic, or repulsive. As a result, those who do this work come to associate sex with emotional pretense and manipulation, exploitation and abuse, and, partly for this reason, doing this kind of work makes it difficult for sex workers to enjoy sex (with women as well as men) and to form stable, trusting, mutually supportive and respectful intimate relationships, both while they are working and well into the future once they have stopped.[2]

The claim here is not that all forms of prostitution are harmful in these ways. Nor is it that this kind of prostitution is always harmful in these ways or equally harmful to everyone who engages in it. The claim is simply that this kind of prostitution is *commonly* harmful in these ways and harmful largely in virtue of its duration or repetition. As Cecilie Hoigard and Liv Finstad put it, "Every trick is a scratch on the women's minds; as the sum of scratches increases, the consequences become increasingly destructive."[3]

The cumulative impact of prostitution is particularly relevant to understanding the psychological damage it inflicts due to how difficult it is to stop.[4] When a person begins to sell sexual services, she learns how to make money quickly. Because she can make more money in this way whenever she wants, she gets in the habit of buying what she wants, and there seems little reason to save. Although this person may sincerely believe she should stop because the work is bad for her psychologically, she may nonetheless continue to do it because it seems worth it to her to go out "one more time," given the alternative of having no money. Reasoning in this way, she does it over and over, even against her better judgment, thereby increasing the harm.[5] In this way, prostitution can be like an addiction—an addiction to the money and also, for some, to the excitement of being "in the game."[6]

Many young women who begin prostitution also have not finished school[7] and may have learning disabilities and emotional problems that make school and normal employment difficult for them. Other jobs do not pay as well and are more demanding of time and require commitment to a fixed schedule. A person who has worked as a prostitute may also feel vulnerable to shaming criticism from others in the "straight world," whereas she feels accepted and normal in the world of prostitution.[8] So having been "in the life," she may feel that she has more in common with others there than she has with those who are more conventional, which is another reason for her to continue to seek out her old associates.[9] For all these reasons, sex work is difficult to stop, a claim supported by the number of sex workers who say they hate their work and would stop if they could.[10]

When reflecting on the psychological toll of prostitution it is also important to bear in mind that many women start at a young age. Different studies identify different average ages of the first act of prostitution, but many put it at eighteen or younger, and some put it under sixteen.[11] Consequently, many girls turn their first trick at an age at which many of us are just beginning to learn about sex and intimate relationships, and just beginning to form our values concerning them. Assuming, then, that regular prostitution commonly follows not long after the first trick,[12] and that regular prostitution commonly has the negative psychological effects just described, it is reasonable to suspect that this kind of work will be even more destructive of a person's ability to form healthy, intimate relationships as an adult because of the early age at which it begins.

The argument so far is that there is a kind of sex work that commonly causes a psychological trauma from which it is difficult to recover. Psychological harm, however, is not the only negative consequence. Prostitution also typically results in the loss of valuable opportunities and has a negative impact on important relationships. Because prostitution is highly stigmatized—even in nations such as the Netherlands with permissive official policies—some employers will be unwilling to hire a former prostitute for certain jobs such as schoolteacher or day-care worker. A person might deal with this by hiding her past, but she will then continue to worry that her employer or coworkers will find out and hold it against her, creating anxiety.[13] Prostitution also limits the kind of people with whom a person can have honest, intimate relationships because not everyone will be able to accept that his or her girlfriend is currently or was formerly a prostitute.[14] Worrying how a partner might react a former prostitute might try to hide her past or avoid intimate relationships altogether,[15] but these are costly options. The secrecy needed to protect prostitutes from negative judgment also results in social isolation and feelings of loneliness and anxiety.[16] The fact that she will feel completely understood and accepted only by others in the world of prostitution may lead her to have relationships, such as the stereotypical relationship with a pimp, that are highly manipulative and abusive. Finally, if a woman has children during or after working as a prostitute, she is likely to worry about her children's feelings regarding it once they and their friends are old enough to understand. Will her children feel ashamed? Will they be subject to painful taunting at school? Must she then lie about her work or her past to her children, always worrying that it may come to light?[17]

Another negative consequence of prostitution, especially when started at an early age, is the related failure to accomplish the kinds of tasks and develop the kinds of abilities that form the basis for a stable sense of self-esteem going forward. If one is able to make money quickly by selling sex, one can use that money for clothes and drugs, which can make a person feel good in the short run. These quick boosts to self-esteem are fleeting, however. The psychological benefits of accomplishing tasks such as graduating from high school or college, or developing a skill such as a sport or playing a musical instrument, are greater and longer lasting and provide a firmer basis for a positive self-image. Furthermore, judging by their own testimony, most prostitutes do not feel proud of the skills needed to do this work well.[18] Nor do they generally feel uplifted by the fact that they are sexually attractive to customers. Perhaps this is because this work is stigmatized. Perhaps, though, this work is stigmatized because of how unpleasant it is to do. Whatever the cause, this kind of work, unlike many other kinds, tends to corrode self-esteem, not to build it. A further cost of doing sex work is thus that by providing money for the immediate gratification of clothes and drugs, it distracts young people from the tasks and activities that would form a firmer basis for self-esteem as adults.

Despite these negative consequences, prostitution may be an advisable choice for some people under some circumstances.[19] Making money in this way can offer young people a means of survival and some measure of independence from their families, which, if their families are sufficiently abusive, can be a good thing for them (given the bleak alternatives). If a woman has small children, it may be easier for her to find and pay for child care for the time it takes her to turn the necessary tricks than for a full-time job, and she may be able to do sex work near her home whereas she must travel long distances to reach other jobs. The available job alternatives may also be unappealing, such as boring and exhausting factory work.[20]

Finally, people have different attitudes toward sex and their own bodies and have different capacities for intimacy. Not everyone is equally vulnerable to feelings of shame and rejection by others. Bearing these possibilities in mind, it seems likely that the decision to work as a prostitute is advisable on balance for some women.

For most young women, however, this appears to be a very bad choice. Not only does it commonly have the negative consequences just described, but it also typically has no lasting benefit. Although many prostitutes report coming from middle-class families,[21] few achieve economic stability as sex workers and many characterize their financial situations while working as precarious.[22] Although many prostitutes dream of saving up enough to achieve some kind of financial stability and security, many of them spend the money they earn as soon as they get it, and very few save.[23] This is partly because prostitutes feel they need to buy clothes and makeup to attract customers, but it is also because they need to shop or use drugs as a reward for doing this work or as an antidote to the negative feelings it causes.[24] The failure to save is also due partly to the fact that a prostitute knows she can get more money in this way when she wants it.[25] Some sex workers, too, seem to regard the money they make through prostitution as tainted and undeserved, and so spend it as though they were trying to get rid of it as quickly as possible.[26] It is also important to bear in mind that, unlike in most trades, a prostitute's market value does not generally increase as she gets older, but declines.[27] Because, then, the benefits of this work are short-lived and the negative consequences are long-lasting, it makes sense to think that prostitution typically leaves a person worse off, not better off,[28] on balance, and that it is therefore an unwise choice for most young women. This seems true at least of most young women who work as prostitutes in economically developed societies that offer other ways to make enough money to live on.

If prostitution is typically an unwise choice for most girls and young women because it is typically harmful in the ways I have just described, and there are alternative ways to make enough money to live on, then it makes sense to defend prostitution laws as reducing this harm by reducing the number of people who do sex work and by reducing the amount of sex work that is done. If prostitution were completely legalized, demand would presumably increase, because there would be no legal penalties for purchasing sexual services, and supply would presumably increase to meet this increased demand, because there would be no legal penalties for selling sexual services or for operating a sex business. Relying, then, on the familiar principles of supply and demand, we can reasonably predict that prostitution would increase if fully decriminalized, and with it the associated harms.[29]

Like critics of drug laws, critics of prostitution laws commonly argue that the laws do not work. The most commonly offered evidence for this is that prostitution persists even though there are laws against it.[30] This argument is fallacious, though, because legal prohibitions *never* eradicate the harm they aim to reduce; they only *reduce* it. This is no less true of laws against murder, assault, and theft, and it does not follow that the criminal law is ineffective or that it ought to be repealed. The justification for laws against murder, assault, and theft remains that they reduce these crimes by enough to justify the burdens they impose, such as the costs of enforcement and the risk of wrongful conviction. If the same were true of prostitution laws, they would likewise be justifiable.

The "oldest profession" cliché suggests that it is futile to try to eliminate prostitution, from which some seem to infer that prostitution ought to be legalized. Petty thievery, however, is surely just as old a "profession" as prostitution, and yet it does not follow that petty theft should be legalized or that laws against it do nothing to reduce it. Disease and poverty are no more likely to be eradicated in the future than prostitution is; yet it does not follow that the government should do nothing about them. So it makes little sense to infer from the fact prostitution has existed for a long time and is unlikely to vanish that prostitution laws ought to be repealed.

The objection, however, that prostitution laws do not work would surely have less of a grip if there were nothing to it. Why, then, are some thoughtful and informed people drawn to this conclusion? I suspect it is because they believe that the costs of prostitution laws are greater than any likely benefit they provide, and that these laws therefore do not work well *enough* to justify the various burdens they impose. This may be true even if I have accurately characterized the ways in which prostitution is commonly harmful. Before we conclude, then, that prostitution laws can be justified as reducing these harms, we must consider their costs. But first I want to address two other objections that might be made to the paternalistic rationale that I have just presented for prostitution laws.

II. The Stigma Objection

The paternalistic rationale for prostitution laws is that prostitution is commonly harmful to those who do it, and that the government should therefore adopt some kind of restrictions in order to reduce this harm. Some readers, however, would surely challenge my assumption that prostitution laws reduce the harm of prostitution. Prostitution is harmful to those who do it, they would argue, primarily because it is stigmatized, and prostitution laws only increase this harm by reinforcing and perpetuating this stigma.[31] Assuming that the primary aim of prostitution laws is to protect people from the harms involved in selling sexual services, prostitution should therefore be legalized in order to eliminate this stigma and with it the associated harms.

The prediction, however, that prostitution would be destigmatized if legalized is empirically ungrounded. As one scholar has recently put it, "Research has shown that the legalization of prostitution does not diminish the stigma attached to prostitution."[32] More specifically, the available evidence suggests that prostitution remains stigmatized in Germany and the Netherlands,[33] where the sale and purchase of sexual services is decriminalized and where brothels are legal.

A defender of legalization might respond that prostitution remains stigmatized in the Netherlands and Germany only because prostitution is not fully decriminalized there. Prostitution will be *fully decriminalized* only where the criminal law treats prostitution in the same way that it treats every other trade. This is not the case in either Germany or the Netherlands. The Netherlands prohibits persons under the age of eighteen from working as a prostitute, which is higher than the age at which teenagers may legally consent to sex or be employed at other jobs without parental consent (sixteen). The Netherlands also does not issue work permits to non-European Union nationals for sex work, although it grants such permits for other kinds of work.[34] Germany, which permits the sale of sex by anyone sixteen or older, nonetheless prohibits hiring anyone under eighteen to work in a brothel, and prohibits "enticing" anyone under twenty-one to do so. Because prostitution is not fully decriminalized in either the Netherlands or Germany, it is arguable that the fact that prostitution is still stigmatized there is no objection to the prediction that it would be destigmatized with full decriminalization.

This possibility, however, also reveals an important stumbling block to destigmatization. Assuming that the age restrictions imposed by the Netherlands and Germany are justified as necessary to protect young people from harm, it would be morally objectionable to repeal these restrictions, because the law would then fail to protect these young people adequately. If it is morally objectionable to repeal these age restrictions, then full decriminalization is morally objectionable, and whatever stigma these restrictions cause is morally justifiable. Moreover, official destigmatization requires more than the decriminalization of the sale and purchase of sexual services. It requires, too, that the government treat prostitution as it treats any other trade. If, for example, the government requires a person to make a good faith effort to seek and hold a job as a condition of public welfare assistance, it must require women to make a good faith effort to seek and hold a job in a brothel as a condition of public assistance if no other jobs are available.[35] This requirement seems highly objectionable. Assuming, then, that the stigma of prostitution is caused by government policies that treat prostitution differently from other jobs, but that the government is justified in treating prostitution differently, the stigma will remain unless the government adopts policies that it should not adopt.

It is doubtful in any case that government policies are primarily responsible for the way in which prostitution is stigmatized. In general social stigma is not reliably correlated with illegality. Marijuana possession, for example, is illegal in most of the United States, but it is far less socially stigmatized than acting in pornographic films, which is legal. This suggests that the stigma attached to unconventional sexual activity is created not by the law, but by social attitudes toward sex and intimacy, attitudes that have been evolving for thousands of years in the presence of very different government policies toward prostitution.

To this an advocate of full decriminalization might now respond that we should change our attitudes toward sex and intimacy. The stigma of prostitution, she might suggest, is based on the mistaken belief that sexual activity is morally problematic in a way that other activities are not. Once we abandon this old-fashioned belief, the stigma attached to prostitution will vanish. The best solution to the "problem" of prostitution is for us to free ourselves of our irrational attitudes toward sex.

Consider, though, how radically our attitudes toward sex and intimacy must change in order consistently to believe that sexual activity is no more problematic than other activities. We must regard rape as a relatively innocuous form of physical assault, akin, say, to being nonconsensually wrestled and poked in the mouth. We must regard incest as just another form of physical closeness between family members. We must cease to regard child sexual abuse as a distinctive category of abuse. We must regard child prostitution as we view other kinds of child employment in the entertainment industry, like movie acting. We must cease to see anything objectionable about employers asking employees to perform sexual services as a condition of employment along with other services, like greeting clients or arranging office parties.[36] Leaving aside the desirability of such a radical change in our attitudes, it is extremely unlikely that it will occur, at least not in the foreseeable future. Moreover, there is nothing that any one of us could do to bring about such a radical change, nor any government policy that a free society could adopt and enforce that would accomplish this. So even if the stigma of prostitution were caused primarily by the belief that sexual activity is distinctively problematic, and even if this belief were mistaken, this would be almost entirely irrelevant to the practical assessment of prostitution laws here and now.[37]

It is also doubtful, though, that general beliefs about sex and intimacy provide the best explanation of why prostitution remains stigmatized in modern Western societies. I suspect that prostitution remains stigmatized in our society for a very different reason, because of the ways in which prostitution is commonly experienced and imagined.

"I do a lot of disgusting things every day," one sex worker reports. "Not all days are bad days, but there are those bad days, too. The act itself, intercourse, is very easy. At least as long as the client is okay. But sometimes, fortunately not every day, I meet a man I do not like. And then I have to force myself to smile, show a positive attitude and act like a high-class hooker. We have to look eager to please and appear sexually excited because that's what they expect. With some men, I have to close my eyes and think of the money, otherwise I would get up and run out of the room yelling, 'Keep your money and get out of here. I don't want to see you, don't touch my face.' Those are the bad times."[38]

Think about the people you interact with as a normal part of your job: students, colleagues, clients, patients, customers, and so on. Now think of those you dislike: those who strike you as cold, stupid, stubborn, unimaginative, self-important, superior, rude, contemptuous, and dismissive. Imagine that successfully doing your job requires, as a normal part, not only having sex with such persons but also flattering and trying to please them. How would you feel at the end of your workday? Nauseated? Disgusted with yourself and humanity? This is how sex workers commonly describe their feelings about their work. Some emotional pretense is required by most jobs. Few other jobs, however, require a person to pretend to be sexually interested and aroused by someone one finds boring or repulsive, or to appear to enjoy the company and agree with the opinions of people one finds idiotic and offensive.[39]

It is not only the exhausting emotional pretense that makes a sex worker's job difficult. A sex worker must constantly deal with people who show no concern or respect for her as a person.[40] One woman who briefly worked in a window in Amsterdam tells the following story. When a client's condom broke and she expressed anxiety to him about contracting AIDS, he simply laughed at her. "The worst part of it," she writes, "was that the guy was so fucking unconcerned—he just laughed and said I was a good fuck."[41] Sex can have significant consequences like pregnancy and AIDS. When the person with whom one is having sex is indifferent to these consequences or how they might affect you and your life, that person does not respect you and has no concern for your welfare. The experience of having sex with someone who has these attitudes understandably leads a person to feel revulsion toward this person, toward the interaction, and toward herself.

A further problem with sex work is that it makes it difficult to maintain important boundaries. Most of us express the view to others that they are not free to be physically intimate with us. If we have a partner, we are likely to express the view to outsiders that we are not sexually available. A sex worker, however, cannot maintain these boundaries consistent with her occupational role. Anyone—a teacher, a doctor, a mechanic, a hairdresser, a friend, a partner's friend, or any of her acquaintances—has at least a prima facie right to buy her services.[42] This reduces the kind of control she can have over her relationships and the quality of her social life, a kind of control that it is very important for most of us to have.

Presented as part of a defense of prostitution laws, these observations might prompt the sensible response that prostitutes have some control over their clients, and that if they find someone disgusting they are not required to serve him. It is therefore worth pointing out that pressure by pimps or by brothel managers substantially diminishes a sex worker's degree of control,[43] and that even for an independent worker it is often difficult to turn a client away once she has met him. Imagine finding yourself with a client you don't like. You've already expended the time and energy to make the connection, at a hotel, his place, or at your apartment. You need the money. You've already factored the fee into your finances. You've sold sexual services hundreds of times before. It will soon be over and you will have the cash.[44] If you turn him down, things could get ugly. "Hey, what's wrong with my money? You think you're too good for me, you worthless whore?"[45] At this point, you may think it is worth it to go through with it and get it over with. And you may think this over and over again in similar situations.

Advocates of legalization do not pay enough attention, I think, to the way in which prostitution is commonly experienced by sex workers when they suggest that it is just another job. They fail to put themselves in the prostitute's shoes and to imagine what this work is actually like. For this reason their arguments seem hollow and uninformed to antilegalization activists. It is also, I suspect, why advocates of legalization imagine that the stigma would vanish if prostitution were fully decriminalized. If, however, we focus on the repeated experience of physical closeness with people who repel you and who have no concern or respect for you as a person, the repeated experience of feigning intimate emotions one does not feel for the gratification of people one dislikes, and the difficulty of maintaining important boundaries, it seems doubtful that the stigma would vanish with legalization. If our jobs were like this, we would quit them as soon we possibly could. This, I think, is the primary reason why sex work is stigmatized.

In support of this conclusion it is worth reflecting on an attitude common among prostitutes. Although vehemently denying that there is anything *wrong* with what they do, they nonetheless express distress at the idea of someone they care about—a sister or daughter—doing this work.[46] Why would an experienced prostitute, who maintains there is nothing wrong with prostitution, be upset if someone she cares about were to do this work? The only plausible explanation, it seems to me, is that she knows what the *experience* of doing this work is actually like, and does not want anyone she cares about to have this experience. As long as prostitution is sufficiently unpleasant that those who do this work are distressed by the thought of someone they care about doing it, there is little reason to think that the stigma will vanish with legalization.

Perhaps it is worth adding that there is also some stigma attached to "having to pay for it." Men have different attitudes towards sex in general and paid sex in particular, but it is not uncommon for men to regard other men who patronize prostitutes as pathetic, incompetent, or psychologically disordered. Part of this may be due to an ideal of being sufficiently attractive that one does not need to pay for sex. I suspect, however, that much of it is also due to the fact that (even) men understand that when a woman sells sexual services, she is acting. She is pretending to be interested, pretending to enjoy it, for the sake of the money, when she probably does not.[47] This may be one of the reasons why the transaction is called a *trick*: the prostitute fools the client into thinking that she is attracted to him and is enjoying his company in order to get his money. For a man to enjoy this transaction, he must either deceive himself or be indifferent to the prostitute's inner life.[48] Because there is something stunted and undignified about being in either of these mental states, a man who is morally and emotionally mature is likely to regard this kind of transaction as beneath him. These attitudes have nothing to do with the *legal* status of prostitution, and as long as they persist, men will continue to look down on other men who patronize prostitutes, which will reinforce the stigma.

For all these reasons I find unconvincing the speculative claim made by advocates of legalization that prostitution would be less harmful to the sex worker if it were legalized because it would then be destigmatized. Sex work would certainly be less harmful if it were not stigmatized, but removing criminal penalties for adult prostitution would not alone completely remove the official stigma, and there is no reason in any case to believe that official policy is primarily responsible for the social stigma. I suspect that something close to the reverse is the case: the social stigma is caused by what we believe or imagine about the experience of doing sex work, and these thoughts lead us to support official policies that aim to discourage it.[49]

III. The Evidence

In stating a paternalistic rationale for prostitution laws I have now made a number of empirical assumptions. The central claim of this book is that *if* these empirical assumptions are sound, then prostitution laws in some form can be justified by this rationale compatible with a due respect for individual liberty, and so compatible with the fundamental principles of liberalism. Some readers might object, though, that even if my empirical assumptions are true, we are not justified in believing them. This would be a decisive objection if correct, because we should reject the case for any coercive government policy unless there is sufficient reason to accept the empirical assumptions on which it is based. Before going any further, then, I should say something about why I accept these assumptions.

These are the primary empirical premises of my paternalistic argument for prostitution laws:

1. Sex work is commonly bad for those who do it because it leaves them with lasting feelings of worthlessness, shame, and self-hatred, damages their capacities for healthy intimate relationships and limits their social and employment opportunities.
2. If the government adopts prostitution laws in some form, this will reduce the number of people who do sex work and the amount of sex work that is done, and so will reduce these harms.
3. Prostitution laws do not themselves injure sex workers by creating or maintaining a stigma that is responsible for these harms and that would otherwise vanish.

This is not the complete argument. A paternalistic defense of prostitution laws must also hold that whatever burdens are imposed by these laws can be justified as reducing the harm caused by doing sex work. This, however, is not an *empirical premise* of the paternalistic argument. It *is* the paternalistic argument, an argument that I make throughout this book. My primary aim in this chapter is to identify the harms that would increase if prostitution were fully decriminalized and to consider different policies that might be justified by this fact. The three empirical premises that I have just listed are the empirical grounds of my assumption that some harms would increase if prostitution were fully decriminalized. What, then, are my grounds for accepting these empirical premises?

I just gave my reasons in the previous section for accepting premise (3)—regarding the stigma of prostitution—and I will let the reader decide without further comment whether these reasons are convincing. In accepting premise (2) I rely on general principles of deterrence and individual rational choice that are commonly relied on in justifying criminal penalties in general, as well as on familiar principles of supply and demand. If these principles do not warrant the belief that prostitution laws reduce prostitution, then neither, I would argue, do they warrant the more general belief that criminal laws reduce crime. If this belief is unwarranted, then criminal penalties cannot be justified as reducing crime, and if they cannot be justified in this way, they cannot be justified at all. This is because, although retributive considerations might be relevant to assessing the appropriate punishment for committing a crime, the government is not justified in imposing criminal penalties by retributive considerations *alone*. On the other hand, if we are justified in believing that the criminal law generally reduces crime—enough to justify the costs of enforcement and the risks of wrongful conviction—then we are similarly justified in believing that prostitution laws reduce prostitution, at least to some degree.

Note that I have not yet claimed that these laws reduce prostitution *by enough* to justify the burdens they impose. I have claimed only that we are justified on the basis of familiar principles of supply and demand and rational choice and deterrence in believing that prostitution laws reduce prostitution *to some degree* and so reduce *to some degree* the harm that prostitution causes to the sex worker. Below I consider at greater length what kinds of policies might be justified as reducing this harm given the burdens that they impose.

What about the evidence, then, for premise (1), that prostitution is commonly harmful to those who do it? My description of prostitution and its harmful effects is drawn from a number of sources: research by sociologists, historians, and journalists, and the testimony of prostitutes. I have relied most heavily on the work of Hoigard and Finstad because it is the most detailed account of the harm caused by prostitution that I am acquainted with and because I find it convincing. Hoigard and Finstad may use overheated rhetoric in spots, but their description of the common negative effects of prostitution does not appear to me to be distorted by any specific ideological bias, and the conclusions they draw seem well supported by the research they present. Skeptical readers may suspect, however, that I am convinced by their negative portrayal of prostitution only because it was what I believed before I read their work. Perhaps Hoigard and Finstad are motivated by some kind of moralistic feminism or by a hidden religiously based view of sex, which distorts their findings. Why, then, should we trust what they have to say?

One reason is that so many writers on prostitution arrive at similar conclusions, and arrive at them from diverse intellectual backgrounds and orientations. Consider, for example, the conclusion of *The Lively Commerce*, a study of American prostitution in the twentieth century, published in the early 1970s. The tone of this book is detached and nonjudgmental. The authors' primary aim seems to be to present useful information to the curious reader. They do not seem driven by moralistic horror or feminist outrage. Their book does not have a distinctive political orientation. Its general outlook seems to be that of a nonpartisan, intellectually curious person with the broadly liberal, secular point of view that was once typical of well-educated Americans, Democrat and Republican. Yet this is what they write in their concluding chapter: "Respect for human beings and for the ideal of giving every person an opportunity to achieve, in John Dewey's phrase, the greatest quality as well as quantity of experience, is clearly inconsistent with condoning prostitution."[50] *Clearly*, they say. They do not cite any conclusive evidence. Why, then, "clearly"? Apparently they believe that anyone who is as informed as they are about prostitution and who evaluates the available evidence impartially will swiftly come to the conclusion that prostitution lowers the quality of life for the women involved.

Another reason to trust negative portrayals of prostitution and its effects on sex workers' lives is that this is consistent with what prostitutes say about their work, *even those who advocate decriminalization*. Consider, for example, the position on forced prostitution in the Statement on Prostitution and Human Rights, issued in 1986 at the Second World Whores' Congress by the International Committee for Prostitutes' Rights. Although this committee was constituted partly by working and former prostitutes who were firmly committed to a policy of decriminalization, it declares that forced prostitution should be recognized in international law as "a case of torture."[51] Why should this kind of forced labor be treated as torture if forced labor in general is not? The only plausible answer is that prostitution is traumatic in a way that other kinds of work are not and that those who have done this work know this.

Consider, too, what Margo St. James once had to say about the age at which women ought to be free to sell sex legally. St. James is the founder of COYOTE (Call Off Your Old Tired Ethics), a San Francisco-based prostitutes' rights organization that advocates decriminalization. When asked at a conference about the age issue, she answered, "If we're going to do the mental thing, we'd choose twenty-five because we feel that a young person should find their own sexual self before they're subjected to a lot of commercial lusting and leering."[52] St. James does not go into detail about the negative psychological impact of prostitution on persons younger than twenty-five, but clearly she believes that it has a negative impact. Otherwise she would not suggest an ideal age for prostitution that is any higher than the general age of sexual consent or legal employment. Coming from the best-known American sex worker advocate of decriminalization, this is significant, because it indicates that prostitution is psychologically damaging to young people in a way that other kinds of work are not.

Annie Sprinkle (a.k.a. Ellen Steinberg) is a sex worker who defends prostitution as a legitimate occupational choice, and who advocates a "sex-positive" view of prostitution that emphasizes the positive qualities of this work, for both the worker and client. Yet this is what she has to say about its common psychological effects: "I've known hundreds of erotic laborers and I've never known one to be immune from bouts of what I call Sex Worker Burnout Syndrome (SWBS, for short). It's one of the hazards—by-products if you will—of our titillating trades. The symptoms vary: depression, tiredness, problems in relationships, feeling like people want to drain your energy, feeling grumpy, low self-esteem, frustration, not wanting to be touched, a feeling of being trapped or stuck, being overly emotional, feelings of dissatisfaction with one's life, hopelessness, self-destructive behavior, and more. It can last anywhere from one day to years."[53] Most jobs give rise to some of these feelings to some degree. It is nonetheless revealing that sex-positive Annie Sprinkle identifies these as symptoms of sex work specifically, and says that she knows of *no sex worker* who does not struggle with them, and that they can go on *for years*.

Informed advocates of decriminalization, both sex workers and responsible scholars, argue persuasively that prostitution is not all bad, and that it is possible to avoid or minimize the worst aspects so as to make it more bearable. They do not typically deny, however, that prostitution is commonly harmful in the ways that Hoigard and Finstad identify. Consider, for example, the position of Wendy Chapkis, evidently known in some circles as a "celebrity apologist for prostitution."[54] Chapkis favors decriminalization and challenges the assumption that prostitution "inevitably destroys the emotional life of the worker,"[55] a position she dubiously attributes to Hoigard and Finstad.[56] Chapkis is certainly right to challenge any claim of inevitable destruction, but she promptly goes on to write, "Clearly, performing emotional labor, including sex work, can negatively affect the emotional life of the worker," and she cites Hoigard and Finstad in support,[57] directing the reader to their work "for a disturbing account of the sometimes traumatic consequences of sex work for those in the trade."[58] It is telling, I think, that a self-identified apologist for prostitution who favors decriminalization and is suspicious of exaggerated claims of harm nonetheless accepts as established fact that prostitution is psychologically destructive to some women in the ways Hoigard and Finstad describe. What *proportion* of sex workers are harmed in this way by prostitution? Different scholars make different educated guesses. My claim here is simply that there is sufficient evidence to believe that sex work is *commonly* harmful in these ways. What proportion of sex workers must be harmed in these ways to justify prostitution laws? This is a theoretical question to which I return in chapter 4.

I do not claim that the available evidence establishes with certainty that sex work commonly causes the psychological harms I have identified. It is possible that the psychological damage seemingly caused by sex work results instead from prior psychological conditions, which may have led a person to choose sex work in the first place. None of the evidence I have cited conclusively rules out this possibility. My position here is that the claim that prostitution is commonly psychologically destructive is supported by credible evidence, and is consistent with what we know for sure about prostitution and human nature. This warrants our taking this reason for prostitution laws seriously.

Some may scoff at the evidence that I have presented because it is not based on "real science." It is true that the empirical assumptions that I have made cannot be scientifically demonstrated by controlled experiments or rigorous statistical analysis. Few of us, however, are willing to support only those government policies that can be justified in this way. To take an obvious example, many of us support the criminal law, and we support it only because we believe that it deters murder, assault, and theft. This belief certainly makes sense, but there is no hard scientific evidence for it. There have been no controlled experiments that conclusively demonstrate that the criminal law in modern, economically developed, democratic nations *causes* a significant reduction in these crimes. Are we willing to suspend our support for the criminal law on this basis or to argue that it should be repealed? No.

Laws against murder, assault, and theft might be special because the likely consequences of repealing these laws are so much worse than the likely consequences of repealing other laws. We also support many other laws, however, on the basis of empirical assumptions that cannot be scientifically demonstrated, and we support them even though the probable consequences of repealing these laws are not as serious as a substantial increase in murder, assault, and theft. Consider, for example, campaign finance laws. Many of us support these laws because we believe that unrestricted campaign contributions create a tendency in legislators to vote against the public interest. Although this is certainly plausible, there are no controlled experiments that conclusively demonstrate this. From the scientific point of view, our support for campaign finance laws is based on little more than a reasonable hunch.

Consider, too, laws against statutory rape: laws that prohibit legal adults from having consensual, nonincestuous sexual relations with postpubertal adolescents who are legal minors. Although one might defend these laws on the ground that legal minors cannot give their informed consent to sex with legal adults, informed consent is generally not required unless the relevant conduct poses a significant risk of harm.[59] More to the point, many of us would cease to support laws prohibiting statutory rape if we thought that sexual relationships between legal minors and legal adults were harmless. The scientific evidence, however, that consensual sex between legal minors and legal adults is harmful is sketchy at best.[60] There is anecdotal evidence that these relationships are harmful, to be sure. The scientific evidence, however, that these relationships are harmful is, as far I have been able to ascertain, not much better than the scientific evidence that prostitution is commonly harmful. Do we think that such laws should be repealed on this ground? No.

Many other examples could be given of coercive policies that we accept as justified on the basis of scientifically unproven empirical assumptions. One might try to defend these policies by claiming that none of these policies threatens significant interests, but this is false. Campaign finance laws, for example, limit a person's ability to participate effectively in the political process. Laws prohibiting statutory rape limit the freedom of postpubertal individuals to engage in consensual intimate relationships. Even laws against murder, assault, and theft threaten all of us with the risk of wrongful arrest, conviction, and imprisonment. For this reason, most of us would be making an arbitrary exception if we were we to reject the paternalistic case for prostitution laws on the ground that these laws threaten significant interests and are based on scientifically unproven empirical assumptions.

The principle that there is sufficient reason to accept an empirical proposition as the basis for a coercive government policy only if it has been demonstrated via rigorous scientific methods rules out many government policies that most of us support. For this reason, most of us would reject this principle. Many of us, however, would still accept the following principle: the more important a liberty is or the less grave the harm that is predicted to occur as a consequence of not limiting this liberty, the stronger the epistemic case must be for accepting the propositions that identify this harm and provide the justification for limiting this liberty; the less important a liberty is or the graver the harm at stake in not limiting this liberty, the weaker the epistemic case may be for accepting these propositions (although the case must always be sufficient to justify accepting them). This principle is relevant here because some prostitution laws limit important liberties, and the harm that is predicted to result from not limiting these liberties, although serious, is not the most serious kind of harm. If this principle is valid, the evidence must therefore be quite strong that these harms will increase if these important liberties are not limited.

Perhaps the evidence that I have presented for the proposition that prostitution is commonly harmful is not strong enough to justify the most restrictive prostitution laws. In this book, however, I do not defend the most restrictive policies. I defend only moderately restrictive policies. Consequently, the evidence on which the paternalistic argument is based need not be strong enough to justify certainty about the empirical premises of this argument. It need only be strong enough to warrant acceptance of these assumptions. I believe that it is.

This may be a good place to say something about the relation between my paternalistic argument for prostitution laws and feminist theory. There are different ways to understand what feminist theory is. One way is to see it as a theoretical orientation that pays special attention to the ways in which women have historically been oppressed as a group; of the interests that might have been advanced by this oppression; and of the ways in which this oppression and these interests might continue to distort our perceptions of reality, our factual knowledge, and our moral reasoning. In presenting the evidence that prostitution is commonly harmful to the girls and women who do it, I have drawn heavily on studies by scholars who identify themselves as feminists. I have not, however, self-consciously adopted a feminist orientation in presenting or evaluating this evidence. I have aimed only to maintain a general attitude of unbiased, open-minded inquiry. Perhaps my attitude toward this evidence is insufficiently objective because I do *not* approach this evidence from a feminist point of view. Or perhaps my attitude toward this evidence is insufficiently objective because, unwittingly, I *do* approach it from a feminist point of view. Ultimately what matters is not the attitude of the person who presents the evidence; what matters is how good the evidence is and what conclusions it warrants. If the evidence that prostitution is commonly harmful is less reliable than I think it is, this is certainly a flaw in the paternalistic argument. Because, however, the quality of the evidence is itself likely to be debated, it makes sense to assume for the sake of philosophical inquiry that this evidence is good enough, in order to focus our attention on the philosophical question of whether this argument *would* justify prostitution laws in some form *if* its empirical assumptions were sound.

IV. Different Policies

I have now presented a paternalistic rationale for prostitution laws, but I have not yet said much about the kind of prostitution laws that this rationale might justify. Four different kinds of policy are commonly distinguished in the literature: prohibition, abolition, regulation, and decriminalization. Here I use these terms as follows to refer to different kinds of legal restriction. Although not everyone uses these terms in this way, this is one of the ways in which these terms are commonly used.[61]

Prohibition refers here to any set of policies that categorically criminalizes the sale and purchase of sexual services, or that categorically prohibits behavior closely associated with the sale or purchase of sexual services, such as street solicitation, and that categorically prohibits the operation of a sex business or agency, including acting as a paid agent for sex work.[62] I use the term *impermissive prohibition* to refer to a set of policies that criminalizes the sale and purchase of sexual services as such. I use the term *permissive prohibition* to refer to a set of policies that does not criminalize the sale and purchase of sexual services as such, but that does criminalize closely related activities such as streetwalking and "kerb crawling"—cruising in a car in search of sexual services. Many jurisdictions in the United States adopt some form of impermissive prohibition, because they make the sale and purchase of sexual services misdemeanors as such.[63] A number of U.S. jurisdictions, however, adopt a permissive form of prohibition, because they do not make the sale or purchase of sexual services a misdemeanor, but make only closely related activities misdemeanors, such as street solicitation or working in a brothel. Most U.S. jurisdictions also make the operation of brothels and other sex businesses a felony, although a few brothels are licensed and regulated in rural Nevada. The policy of prohibition is also sometimes referred to as *repression* or *suppression*.

Abolition refers here to any set of policies that does *not* categorically criminalize the *sale* of sexual services as such and does not criminalize closely related activities such as street solicitation, but that does categorically criminalize the *purchase* of sexual services or criminalizes behavior that is commonly used to procure such services, as do the British kerb crawling laws, and that also criminalizes the operation of a sex business (with more than one employee) and working as a paid agent for sex work.[64] I use the term *impermissive abolition* to refer to policies that criminalize the purchase of sexual services as such, as Sweden does, as well as the operation of brothels and other sex agencies. I use the term *permissive abolition* to refer to policies that do not criminalize the purchase of sexual services as such, but that do criminalize closely related activities such as kerb crawling, as well as the operation of brothels and other sex businesses. Because neither the purchase nor the sale of sexual services is criminalized as such in the United Kingdom, and because kerb crawling and brothels are prohibited there, British policy is commonly characterized as *abolitionist*. Given the system of classifications adopted here, however, the British policy is more accurately characterized as a form of permissive prohibition. This is because although Britain does not criminalize the sale of sexual services as such, it does criminalize street solicitation,[65] a common method of selling sexual services, as well as kerb crawling,[66] a common method of procuring them.

Regulation refers here to any set of policies that criminalizes neither the sale nor the purchase of sexual services as such, nor categorically criminalizes any closely related activity, such as street solicitation or kerb crawling, nor the operation of a sex business, but does impose restrictions on the sale, purchase, and operation of a sex business that do not apply to other commercial transactions or businesses, such as age restrictions, zoning restrictions, and health and safety regulations. I use the term *impermissive regulation* to refer to policies that, via criminal or civil penalties, impose higher age restrictions on sex work than are generally imposed for legal consent to sex or to legal employment. I use the term *permissive regulation* to apply to policies that impose no age limits beyond the normal ages for sexual consent and legal employment.[67] Note that although Germany and the Netherlands have relatively permissive policies, both adopt an impermissive form of regulation, as I have just defined it, because the age at which a person can legally sell sex in the Netherlands (eighteen) is higher than the age of sexual consent and legal employment (sixteen), and the age at which a person can legally be employed to work in a German brothel (eighteen) is higher than the general age of legal employment. No modern nation, as far as I know, adopts a policy of permissive regulation. In the past regulation was also referred to as *reglementation* and is now sometimes referred to as *legalization*. Here, though, I use the term *legalization* to refer only to *permissive* regulation or to full decriminalization.

Full decriminalization refers here to any set of policies by which the criminal law treats the sex trade as it treats any other trade; applies the same criminal laws to minors and their employment as it does to other jobs (consistent with general laws regulating age of employment and sexual consent); and imposes no restrictions on the advertisement of sexual services and the operation of sex businesses that it does not impose on businesses in general. No modern nation, as far as I know, adopts a policy of full decriminalization. Full decriminalization is also sometimes referred to as a policy of *normalization* or *laissez-faire*.

To prevent confusion, I should point out that the term *decriminalization* is also sometimes used to refer to the absence of criminal penalties for the *sale* of sexual services, or for closely related activities such as street solicitation. In this sense, any abolitionist policy would be a form of decriminalization. The term *decriminalization* is also sometimes used to refer to the absence of criminal penalties for both the purchase and sale of sexual services and for closely related activities. In this sense, any form of regulation is a form of decriminalization. Sometimes I will use the term *decriminalization* in this way when I speak specifically of the decriminalization of the sale or purchase of sexual services. The term *full decriminalization*, however, I apply only to policies that are less restrictive than permissive regulation.

Note, too, that I use the terms *prohibition, abolition, regulation*, and *full decriminalization* to refer to different systems of legal rules. Although this usage is common in the literature, it is also common to use these terms to refer to different policy *goals* or *aims*. Thus a policy might be characterized as a form of *prohibition* if its *aim* is to repress prostitution on the assumption that it is immoral. A policy might be characterized as a form of *abolition* if its *aim* is to reduce prostitution on the assumption that it is harmful to sex workers. A policy might be characterized as a form of *regulation* if its *aim* is not to reduce prostitution on the assumption that it is immoral or harmful, but only to reduce the associated ills, such as customer violence, ancillary crime, disease, public nuisance, and child sexual exploitation. Here I avoid the motivational use of these terms for the following reason.

Used to refer to motives, any of policies that I have identified would be an abolitionist policy if it were motivated by the aim of reducing the harms caused by doing prostitution. Even full decriminalization might be motivated by this aim if, for example, the harm of prostitution were thought to come solely from the social stigma and this stigma were thought to come from criminalization. If, however, a form of prohibition, regulation, or full decriminalization were characterized as *abolitionist* on these motivational grounds, this would conflict sharply with the way these terms are used in the literature to characterize different degrees of restrictiveness. Some commentators seem to assume that different kinds of restriction correspond to different policy aims or goals, but this assumption is unwarranted. Because my question here is what kind of policy might be justified by the paternalistic argument sketched above, it makes sense to use these terms to refer only to different kinds of legal rules. Used in this way, these terms imply nothing about motive.

As noted above I will use the term *legalization* to refer either to full decriminalization or to permissive regulation. Legalization in this sense is what civil libertarians typically favor when they advocate "the legalization of prostitution" and it is what antilegalization activists typically oppose. If we understand the term *legalization* in this way, then the central claim of this book is that we may justifiably oppose the legalization of prostitution on paternalistic grounds. In other words, at least one of the following policies can be justified by the paternalistic argument compatible with our rights to liberty: impermissive regulation in some form, abolition in some form, or prohibition in some form. Each of these policies has costs, however. So we must now consider what these costs are and whether they might be justified by the paternalistic rationale that I have now presented.

V. The Costs of Prohibition

American critics of prostitution laws typically direct their criticism toward the policy of prohibition. This makes sense because prohibition is the policy adopted everywhere in the United States except a few counties in Nevada. The most common objection to this policy is that it worsens the situations of sex workers. As traditionally enforced, streetwalkers have been fined for plying their trade, and then have been jailed for failing to pay their fines. Because the easiest way to pay the fines is to do more prostitution, some have argued that the system of fines does not effectively deter those who have done sex work from continuing to do it; it functions only to provide an additional incentive to do more of this work, albeit at a lower rate of return.[68] For this reason, some critics have characterized a government that enforces a policy of prohibition as "the biggest pimp of all."[69] Some nations that prohibit prostitution also make it illegal to live off the earnings of a prostitute. The benign purpose of this policy is to deter abuse and exploitation by pimps, but it has the undesirable effect of placing the unemployed live-in boyfriends or girlfriends of prostitutes in legal jeopardy, and these relationships may be the best part of a sex worker's life. Where prostitution is illegal, sex workers are typically also more vulnerable to having their children taken away by child protective services, and a prostitute might also lose her welfare benefits if her work is discovered by her case worker. Where prostitution is illegal, prostitutes are also typically in a poor position to claim health benefits or worker's compensation or retirement benefits, which puts them at a disadvantage relative to other workers. Finally, where prostitution is illegal, prostitutes are typically in a weak position to organize unions, and so to engage in collective bargaining with brothel owners in ways that might improve their working conditions.

Because these objections to prohibition are so common, it is worth pointing out that none of them actually applies to the policy of prohibition itself. If the government prohibits the sale and purchase of sexual services only by making them "administrative violations," and makes neither sale nor purchase a misdemeanor or a felony, then prohibition need not be enforced by fines. If, alternatively, the government makes sale and purchase misdemeanors, it might still not impose on prostitutes any of the other commonly mentioned burdens. Thus it might not criminalize living off the earnings of a prostitute. A prostitute might not be deprived of custody of her child or of her welfare benefits simply on the grounds that she has been convicted of prostitution. A government might provide health and retirement benefits and other forms of public assistance to everyone who needs them, regardless of their employment history. The government might even permit sex workers legally to organize unions and bargain collectively with (illegal) brothel owners. If the penalties for conviction for prostitution are sufficiently light, it might be rational for sex workers to engage in such labor organizing even if prostitution itself is illegal.[70] None of the most common objections to prohibition is therefore a decisive argument against prohibition as such or to prohibition in every possible form.

The most common form of prohibition in the United States, however, does make prostitution as such a misdemeanor, and this policy does make prostitutes worse off. To focus on the central issue, let us assume for the sake of argument that a person who is convicted of prostitution always has the opportunity to avoid a jail sentence, whether for multiple convictions or for refusing to pay fines, by agreeing to and performing conditions of probation, including, for example, court-ordered counseling and community service. Being arrested, charged, and tried for prostitution are nonetheless bad experiences in themselves,[71] and a criminal record for prostitution makes finding other kinds of work more difficult in the future. Even if these things do not actually happen, the risk that they will happen can negatively affect the sex worker. So if prostitution is a misdemeanor or if closely related activities such as street solicitation are misdemeanors, all those who engage in the relevant prohibited activity will be worse off in these ways as a result.

Because any prohibitionist policy of this kind will make prostitutes worse off in some way, some may think it is absurd to suggest that prohibition might nonetheless be justified by a paternalistic argument. Can it be good for a person to be arrested, or fined, or jailed, or to be put at risk for arrest, fines, and jail? A paternalistic defense of prohibition, however, need not assume that any of *these* things is good for someone. It need assume only that this policy has benefits in deterrence that outweigh these costs. Suppose that prohibition is more effective than any other policy in deterring young women from starting this work.[72] Or suppose that this kind of prohibition is more effective than any other policy in getting women who are doing this work to their own detriment to stop. If the penalties are sufficiently mild, these benefits of prohibition might be great enough to justify the various costs of enforcement.

Some may think that it makes no sense to defend prohibition as benefiting prostitutes or would-be prostitutes because it is worse to spend time in jail than it is to do this kind of work, even self-destructively, and because any effective policy of prohibition must involve at least the threat of jail. This objection, however, is confused. To see why, note that it is also worse for a person to be imprisoned for shoplifting than it is for anyone who owns, works for, or shops in a department store to have something stolen from it. It does not follow from this that criminal laws prohibiting shoplifting are unjustifiable. The benefits to individuals of having a legal rule prohibiting shoplifting might still be sufficiently great to justify the resulting risks of arrest and conviction to those who are tempted to break this law. If a law against shoplifting can be justified in this way by its deterrent benefits, then so might a prostitution law. Moreover, prohibition might be justified by its deterrent benefits even if a jail sentence for failing to comply with the terms of probation is itself worse than any specific harm that is caused by breaking this law. So it is not absurd to suggest that prohibition might be justified paternalistically.

As a matter of fact, however, I do not believe that prohibition can be justified by the paternalistic argument. The strongest objection, it seems to me, is that prohibition limits the sexual autonomy of adults by criminalizing a consensual sex act. Discretionary control over one's own sexual activity, over what sexual acts voluntarily to engage in with other willing adults, is central to sexual autonomy, to control over one's sex life, to control over one's body, and so to personal autonomy. Laws that prohibit the sale of sex deprive a person of this kind of discretionary control. It is true that sex workers typically regard the service they provide primarily as work and not as sex. Commercial sex is nonetheless a kind of sex. It involves a person's sexual organs and the sexual use of her body. It expresses and shapes a person's attitudes toward her sexuality and toward her body in a way that nonsexual activities do not. It evokes emotions and other responses that non-commercial sexual activity also evokes, and it affects the character of a person's other intimate relationships. For all these reasons it makes sense to regard the sale of sexual services as a *kind* of sexual act, and on this basis it makes sense to treat the freedom to sell sexual services as a significant component of a person's sexual autonomy. This is presumably why some sex workers regard prostitution laws as an offensive intrusion by the government into their *personal* lives even though they regard their prostitution as work.[73] It is important that adults have the discretion to make personal choices about the kind of sex they engage in with other adults, even if these choices are unwise. So it is objectionable for the government to prohibit a person from using her own body and sexuality for prostitution.

Against this one might argue that prohibition does not restrict anyone's *sexual* autonomy; it restricts only a person's *commercial* autonomy, because prohibition does not prohibit any *kind* of sex act in the way, for example, that sodomy laws do. One might argue along similar lines that laws that prohibit vote selling do not restrict anyone's *political* autonomy, because they do not prohibit people from taking any particular political position; they restrict only their commercial autonomy, in prohibiting them from making a certain sale. Why, then, should we believe that prohibition threatens sexual autonomy, any more than vote selling laws threaten political autonomy?

This analogy between prostitution and vote selling seems convincing on the following assumptions. Suppose that the right to vote is valuable only for the following reasons: (1) it bestows on citizens the valuable status of political equal; (2) it provides important opportunities and incentives for political deliberation; and (3) it enables citizens formally to express their support or opposition to policies and candidates. Because these goods can be achieved without allowing citizens to sell their votes, and some of these goals (particularly the second) are undermined by vote selling, the reasons that warrant a right to vote do not warrant a right to sell one's vote. Suppose, along similar lines, that sexual autonomy is valuable only because discretion over what kinds of sex to engage in is necessary for people to initiate and maintain valuable kinds of healthy intimate relationships. If the freedom to sell sex is not instrumental to initiating and maintaining healthy relationships of this kind, and in fact tends to threaten their formation, then the freedom to sell sex is no more essential to sexual autonomy than vote selling is to political autonomy.

The freedom to sell sex, however, is different from the freedom to sell one's vote. Sexual autonomy is valuable not only as a means to initiate and maintain healthy intimate relationships; it has intrinsic or nonderivative value as well. The decision to have a commercial sexual relationship initiates and expresses a distinctive way of valuing one's own sexuality and one's own body and influences what attitudes one has toward sex and one's body in the future. Commercial sex thus has a distinctive psychological and symbolic meaning *as a sex act*. A commercial sexual relationship is also a distinctive kind of *sexual* relationship. The discretion to engage in consensual sex acts and to have consensual sexual relationships that seem situationally appropriate is intrinsically valuable or valuable "for its own sake."

So it makes sense to claim that prohibition fails to respect sexual autonomy in a way that laws that prohibit vote selling do not threaten political autonomy.

Some might protest that selling one's vote also has distinctive meaning as a political act—as an expression of contempt toward the political process. There are, however, other ways for individuals to express contempt toward the political process that do not threaten to undermine the integrity of the political process in the way that the legality of vote selling would. Moreover, the freedom to express contempt toward the political process in this particular way is not connected to personal autonomy in the same way that the freedom to engage in commercial sex is. The freedom to engage in whatever sexual act seems situationally appropriate is directly related to control of one's body and of one's sex life. The freedom to express contempt toward the political process in whatever way seems appropriate is not.

Despite what I have just said, some will remain unconvinced by this objection of personal autonomy to prohibition, or "privacy," as it is sometimes called. There are, however, other good objections to prohibition as well. Working as a prostitute has benefits, and for some these benefits might outweigh the costs. Prohibition thus criminalizes an occupational choice that might be the best all things considered for some people under some circumstances, even in thriving, postindustrial economies.[74] Prohibition also makes prostitution less safe. If it is illegal to sell sexual services, those who do so are less likely to rely on the police for protection, and less likely to press charges and testify against those who commit crimes against them, for fear of being prosecuted themselves.[75] In this way, prostitution will be safer if the sale of sexual services is decriminalized.[76] Finally, although the burden of criminal liability is not generally a decisive objection to a law that criminalizes a form of harmful conduct, the criminalization of sex work does make the situations of sex workers worse in identifiable ways. For this reason some argue that prostitutes are "doubly victimized" by a policy of prohibition, because prostitution itself is already bad enough.

These objections, taken together, lead me to doubt that prohibition can be justified by the paternalistic argument stated above. The paternalistic function of prostitution laws is to reduce the number of commercial sex transactions and so reduce the harm caused to sex workers by doing prostitution. The primary benefit of this policy to any particular individual is thus to reduce her risk of doing work that harms her. The burdens, however, that an effective policy of prohibition would place on the working prostitute in limiting her sexual autonomy, in criminalizing a kind of work that is advisable for her, in making sex work less safe, and in imposing the various burdens of criminal liability, seem greater and more direct. Whether these objections are decisive against prohibition in every possible form is open to debate. I believe, however, that these objections are sufficiently weighty to warrant the conclusion that laws that make sex work or street solicitation misdemeanors are not paternalistically justifiable. For this reason I do not defend prohibition in this book, or argue that it can be paternalistically justified consistent with taking our rights to liberty seriously.

VI. Abolition or Regulation?

Even if prohibition cannot be justified by the paternalistic rationale for prostitution laws, abolition or regulation in some form might be justified by this argument. Although the paternalistic rationale might seem to favor regulation, for reasons given shortly, regulation is also open to objections, which might seem to favor abolition. After discussing the pros and cons of both policies, I conclude that the paternalistic rationale for prostitution laws might warrant either a permissive form of abolition or a strong form of impermissive regulation.

Many, perhaps most, prostitutes start sex work in adolescence.[77] Perhaps they are encouraged by girlfriends who explain that it is an "easy" way to make money, more than they could make at an entry-level service job. Perhaps they are encouraged by their boyfriends to make money in this way, to buy drugs or other luxuries that they both enjoy, such as a nice car. Perhaps they are encouraged by an older man who flatters them and pays more attention to them than anyone else does, including their parents. Perhaps they are encouraged to start by family members who need the money for rent or grocery bills or to buy alcohol and drugs. Or perhaps a girl needs money to survive because she has run away from home or from an institution. Perhaps she has run away to escape sexual or other kinds of abuse. Perhaps she has been thrown out by her parents or legal guardians because they find her difficult to control. I assume that if prostitution were fully decriminalized, more girls would start selling sexual services for all these reasons and that more harm would result as a consequence.

It is true that girls who begin prostitution as adolescents are likely to have other problems that lead them to make this choice. Perhaps they have been sexually abused by a family member, or abused in some other way or neglected by their parents.[78] Perhaps they have learning disabilities or other difficulties with impulse control or planning. They would have these problems in any case. So it is reasonable to wonder how much harm prostitution laws reduce, given that most of those who choose this work are already troubled in some way. I assume that by getting into the habit of selling sexual services a young person severely compounds whatever problems she has initially and makes them worse and harder to deal with in the future. Many young people with problems find themselves at a crossroads. If they make one turn, they will be all right. If they make another turn, they will carry emotional scars throughout their lives and will lose important opportunities that they can never fully recover. The primary function of prostitution laws, as I see it, is to reduce the number of young people who take this self-destructive turn.

This argument, however, may seem to favor a regulationist policy over an abolitionist one. Abolitionist policies either generally criminalize the purchase of sexual services, as Sweden does, or generally criminalize ancillary activities involved in obtaining such services, as do the British kerb crawling laws. These policies are not limited to the purchase of sexual services from girls or young women. So if the primary purpose of prostitution laws is to reduce the number of young people who do this work, it seems we should favor some form of impermissive regulation that permits adult prostitution above a certain age, as do the policies of Germany and the Netherlands.

There are, however, at least four objections to regulationist policies of this kind. First, the harm of prostitution that I have described does not vanish at any particular age. Although starting prostitution as an adolescent may be particularly destructive of a person's emotional health and development, it does not follow that it is not also destructive for someone in her twenties or thirties.[79] Furthermore, many sex workers start working illegally as adolescents where prostitution is regulated, just as they do where it is prohibited. Their continued work in their twenties and thirties is therefore based on a self-destructive choice that was made in their youth. Assuming that the government should protect young people from harm by reducing their opportunities to make certain ill-advised choices as legal minors, it seems that the government should also protect adults from the same harm by reducing their opportunities to make these same ill-advised choices as legal adults *when they make these ill-advised choices as legal adults only because they made these ill-advised choices as legal minors.* Assuming, then, that there will be more adult prostitution under regulation than under an abolitionist policy,[80] there are good paternalistic reasons for preferring an abolitionist policy.

A second objection to regulation is that even if the only goal were to reduce the amount of sex work done by young people, a legal market in prostitution will inevitably increase underage prostitution.[81] If it is legal to buy sexual services from someone who is eighteen or to hire someone who is eighteen to work in a brothel, it will be easier for younger girls to pretend that they are of legal age and for sex business operators to take advantage of this.[82] Because most customers are perfectly willing to hire girls and young women, underage prostitution will increase as a result.

A third objection to regulation is that a legal market in prostitution will inevitably increase international trafficking in women.[83] By *trafficking* I mean the transportation of women for sex work by force or fraud.[84] If prostitution is legal in a country, it will be easier profitably to employ illegal immigrants as prostitutes, and so easier to employ immigrants who are the victims of deception and coercion. A practical response is to increase enforcement of immigration laws and the regulation of sex businesses. This, however, will not eliminate the problem because illegal immigration cannot be prevented. If there is no penalty for buying sexual services in general, demand will increase and supply will increase to meet this demand. If this demand can profitably be met by sex businesses using illegal workers without bearing too much risk—as is obviously true of many other small businesses—then illegal workers will be employed. Trafficking will then increase proportionately to meet the increased demand for illegal sex workers. It is true that if there are higher penalties for employing a victim of sex trafficking than there are for employing other illegal immigrants, then employing a trafficked woman is more risky. Because, however, the kind of force and fraud involved in trafficking is difficult to prove in court (especially when the victim is a prostitute), and because trafficked women who are not legal residents are often reluctant to press charges and testify for fear of deportation, the risk will not be so much higher than that involved in employing nontrafficked illegal workers and therefore arguably it will not be high enough to deter sex business operators from employing trafficked women and children.[85]

A fourth objection to regulation is that, at least in some forms, it facilitates adult prostitution in a way that seems to express government endorsement of it. A democratic government represents its people. Hence there are reasons for us to want our government not to facilitate private practices that we reasonably regard as harmful and exploitive and not to appear to endorse them. Consider in this connection the legal recognition and enforcement of self-enslavement contracts. Because we may reasonably regard self-enslavement contracts as harmful and exploitative to those enslaved, there is good reason for us to want not to participate in this practice as citizens, even indirectly, via the operation of our contract law. Even if the government should not *prohibit* private self-enslavement contracts, there are good reasons for us to want our governments not to *facilitate* them by recognizing their validity in civil law.[86] Assuming that prostitution is generally harmful in the ways that I have described, there is arguably also good reason for us to want our government not to facilitate it or appear to endorse it. The government, however, will facilitate prostitution and will appear to endorse it if it licenses prostitutes and requires them to undergo health inspections for licensing, as some government agencies do.

Some may take this fourth objection to regulation as an argument for full decriminalization. At least this policy has the virtue of not appearing to express government endorsement of prostitution. Full decriminalization, however, is open to the first three objections to regulation that I just raised, and will almost certainly lead to a general increase in prostitution and so to an increase in the associated harms. If, then, we take these harms seriously enough to think that the government ought to do something to reduce them, and we accept the four objections just made to regulation, we may be led to endorse a policy of abolition instead.

The most restrictive abolitionist policy that I know of is the Swedish policy, which prohibits the purchase of sexual services from sex workers of any age.[87] Because Swedish law does not impose criminal penalties on the sale of sexual services, it does not make sex workers worse off by fining or jailing them; nor does it directly curtail the sexual autonomy of adult sex workers (although it does limit their economic opportunities); nor does it criminalize a choice that might be the best for some people under some circumstances. Swedish law also permits a prostitute to support a boyfriend or girlfriend with her earnings, and to live with another prostitute, provided that the premises are not used primarily or substantially for prostitution. The Swedish policy of abolition is therefore not open to the strongest objections that are commonly directed at the American policy of prohibition. This policy also seems to have reduced prostitution in Sweden.[88]

The Swedish policy nonetheless imposes burdens. The strongest objection, it seems to me, is that this policy criminalizes the purchase of a service that may have genuine psychological benefits for some clients. Some men may lack the confidence to pursue noncommercial sexual relations because they believe they are unattractive to women or inadequate in some other way. Perhaps commercial sex creates only an illusion of intimacy, but this illusion might alleviate painful feelings of loneliness, isolation, and of being unwanted. Some men may also have unusual sexual desires and have difficulty finding nonprofessionals who will do what most excites them in a nonthreatening, nonjudgmental manner. The psychological health of these men may not be ideal, but we should still recognize that they may genuinely benefit from these services.[89]

Debate between abolitionists who favor the Swedish model and regulationists who favor the Dutch model is sometimes shrill. Regulationist critics portray advocates of the Swedish policy as moralistic do-gooders who naively expect that the government can eradicate prostitution once and for all. Abolitionist critics portray advocates of the Dutch policy as corrupt and indifferent government officials who feel no compunction about sacrificing the welfare of women for the twisted recreational amusement of men. One explanation for the shrill tone is that despite the strong emotions on both sides, the justifiability of both positions depends partly on empirical assumptions about which neither side is justified in feeling certain. If underage prostitution and trafficking are substantially reduced by the Swedish policy, compared to what exists under the Dutch policy, as some abolitionists maintain,[90] this is a good objection to the Dutch policy.[91] If this is not the case, however,[92] then some form of impermissive regulation may be the most restrictive policy that can be justified, given the legitimate interests of adults in sexual freedom. When one cannot prove one's assumptions, it is natural to adopt an attitude of moral superiority to those who reject them, which may explain the shrill tone. The quality and tone of this debate would be improved, though, if both sides were to admit that the superiority of their favored policy depends at least partly on empirical assumptions about which no one is justified in feeling certain.

Because I am uncertain of the relevant facts, I am uncertain as to whether the Swedish policy of abolition is justifiable. I believe that it might be justified *if* this policy results in substantially less adolescent prostitution than any feasible alternative or *if* it results in substantially less trafficking, as its defenders maintain. If, on the other hand, sexual services address a genuine psychological need of some clients *and* a well-enforced policy of permissive abolition or impermissive regulation would control adolescent prostitution and trafficking nearly as well, then the Swedish policy, in categorically criminalizing the purchase of sexual services, would seem to involve an unjustifiable restriction of adult sexual freedom. Prostitution may be psychologically harmful to older women as well as to younger ones, but at some point—whether we say this is eighteen, twenty-one, twenty-five, or thirty—it is reasonable for a society to expect its competent adult members to look after their own welfare and so reasonable for individuals to protest government policies that deprive them of valuable opportunities in order to reduce the likelihood that other adults will make self-destructive choices. It is also important to bear in mind that a government with a regulationist policy need not be indifferent to the harms to mature adults of doing sex work. It might still adopt policies that help older women who want to get out of the sex business to do so, by providing government-funded shelters and counseling, for example, or by providing opportunities for adult education.[93] In this way, a regulationist government can recognize that sex work is often harmful and can express appropriate concern for those adults who do this work to their own detriment.

Even if the Swedish policy is unjustifiable, however, some other, more permissive, abolitionist policy might be preferable to regulation. Consider the following alternative policy: neither the sale nor the purchase of sexual services is criminalized as such, but it is a criminal offence (a) to purchase sex from anyone who lacks a valid identification proving that he or she is at least twenty-one, (b) to purchase sex on the street, (c) to operate a brothel or "escort" service, and (d) to work as a paid agent for sex work. This policy would allow those individuals who gain genuine psychological benefits from commercial sex to acquire these services legally, through private newspaper and Internet advertisements, for example, but it might also reduce harmful sex work more than any policy of regulation would.

Many purchases of sex are "opportunistic": they are made on impulse when presented with an opportunity.[94] If it is illegal to purchase sex on the streets, there will be fewer opportunities for legal purchase, and so fewer harmful transactions. Sex businesses, such as brothels and escort agencies, also provide opportunities that make it easier for clients to obtain sexual services. So if these businesses are prohibited, there will be fewer opportunities to purchase these services, and so fewer transactions. Sex businesses also provide opportunities and incentives to do prostitution that would otherwise not exist. Where brothels are legal, it is possible to go to a legal establishment and apply for a job as a prostitute. If hired, one will have a steady flow of customers, which might result in doing more prostitution than one would have done otherwise, thereby increasing the harm. Some sex business owners and managers also put pressure on prostitutes to do more of this work than they otherwise would and to serve customers that they would otherwise refuse.[95] Escort agencies and brothels also make prostitution easier to do, by arranging meetings with clients or by providing a workplace, and they make prostitution seem more appealing by (sometimes bogus) promises of a high income. For all these reasons, it is reasonable to believe that where sex businesses are legal, there will be more prostitution, and so more harm to prostitutes.

A common argument for regulation, and against abolition, is that regulation improves sex worker safety. Where brothels are legal, it is possible for a prostitute to work in a government-regulated business that is generally safer than working on the streets or as a call girl. The risks of working as an independent contractor are also an incentive for a prostitute to work with a pimp, who may abuse and exploit her. From these considerations some conclude that a genuine concern with the welfare of sex workers warrants some form of regulation as opposed to any abolitionist or prohibitionist policy.

One must be wary, though, of placing too much weight on the safety argument for regulation. For one thing, prostitutes are in danger of customer violence in legal brothels as well as elsewhere.[96] The danger of prostitution comes from violent customers; violent customers seek prostitutes in brothels as well as outside of them; and brothel owners do not always do enough to protect their workers. It is also true that many sex workers prefer to work independently as streetwalkers or call girls, despite the greater danger of doing so, even where brothels are legal.[97] They find waiting around in a brothel with nothing to do boring and inefficient, whereas if there is no action on the street they can leave. Some sex workers, too, find the hours or the control of brothel managers oppressive, and owners and managers take a substantial percentage of the fee, thereby making the work much less profitable.[98] For all these reasons a significant percentage of sex workers continue to work independently as streetwalkers or call girls even where brothels are legal and legally regulated. Prostitution therefore remains dangerous even under a policy of regulation, and the need for protection from pimps remains.

It is also important to understand that sex workers do not rely on pimps solely for protection; they rely on them, too, for company, emotional support, and fun. This is evidenced by the fact that some prostitutes who work in legal brothels also have pimps on the outside.[99] Given the complicated emotional dynamics of these relationships,[100] and the kinds of individuals who choose them, it is doubtful that the associated abuse and exploitation would vanish with regulation.

Although regulation is often defended as making prostitution safer, it is possible that over time more prostitutes would actually be at risk of violence under regulation than under an abolitionist policy. It is possible that where brothels are legal more people start to do sex work in legal brothels (for the reasons given above), but that many then leave to do sex work on the street because they become dissatisfied with the working conditions in the brothels (for the reasons given above). It is also possible that where brothels are legal more people start to do sex work in brothels but that many are asked to leave by the management because they are difficult or unprofessional, and that they then turn to sex work on the street or in illegal brothels, which are less safe. In view of these and other empirical possibilities, it is possible that although *some* prostitutes will be safer under a policy of regulation, because they work in well-managed, legal brothels, more prostitutes will be at risk of violence, because there will be more prostitutes doing unsafe sex work outside of well-managed legal brothels than would do this work under an abolitionist policy. If this is true, then a regulationist policy would actually increase the number of persons who are at risk of violence, contrary to what its advocates maintain.

It is also important to bear in mind that the risk of violence is not the only thing that is bad about prostitution. If we take into consideration *all* the negative aspects of prostitution, and we do not give undue weight to the safety benefits of regulation, it is not unreasonable to conclude that a permissive abolitionist policy would promote human welfare better than any regulationist policy would.

A permissive policy of abolition, however, also has costs, which must also be balanced against its benefits in reducing harmful prostitution. If, for example, it is illegal to purchase sexual services on the street, then those who are tempted to do so risk arrest for seeking a certain kind of recreation. The danger of arrest may be part of the fun for some, but the risk of embarrassment and the possible negative consequences for their marriages and jobs are bad things for most customers, and possibly bad for their families too. It is also true that kerb crawling laws, in depressing the number of willing clients, decrease the opportunities for streetwalkers to sell their services, which is a disadvantage for those (if any) for whom this kind of work is an advisable choice. Another objection is that if it is illegal to operate a sex business, or to work as a broker or paid agent, then it is illegal for an experienced prostitute to use her knowledge of the business to operate an agency, and in this way to stop doing this work herself. There are others, too, who lose lucrative business opportunities where it is illegal to operate a sex business.

All these costs can be justified, it seems to me, if a permissive policy of abolition substantially reduces harmful sex work compared to any form of regulation. It is also arguable, though, that, in view of these costs, an impermissive regulationist policy would be better, all things considered. Germany and the Netherlands, in allowing a client or a sex business to hire anyone over seventeen for prostitution, probably do not do enough to protect vulnerable young people. More restrictive forms of impermissive regulation are also possible, though. Consider the following alternative, suggested by Margo St. James's comment about age cited above: the government prohibits purchasing sex from anyone under twenty-five, hiring anyone under twenty-five for work in a sex business, and working as a paid agent for a sex worker under twenty-five, but regulates sex work by adults over twenty-four in order to promote the health and safety of prostitutes and their clients. This strong form of impermissive regulation would presumably do more than the regulationist policies of the Netherlands and Germany to reduce the number of young people who do sex work to their own detriment. Unlike the Swedish law, however, this impermissive form of regulation would allow adults to purchase sexual services from older adults without legal risk and it would allow entrepreneurs to take advantage of the various business opportunities that such a market would create. If the primary goal of prostitution laws is to deter young people from starting this work, this policy is arguably superior to any permissive policy of abolition, because it would arguably advance this goal effectively while imposing fewer costs.

A practical objection to this proposal is that it is not politically feasible. There is a natural tendency to think that once a person has reached a certain age, eighteen or twenty-one, say, she is entitled to all the rights of adulthood. Many are inclined to believe, for example, that if a person may risk her life by joining the armed forces, she ought to be legally permitted to buy alcoholic beverages. Arguments of this kind do not have the intellectual merit that they are commonly thought to have. Thus, contrary to popular belief, the ideal minimum age for military service implies nothing with respect to the ideal minimum age for the legal purchase of alcoholic beverages. Arguments of this kind nonetheless have psychological force, and for this reason it may not be politically feasible to address the problem of underage prostitution by raising the legal age of sex work to twenty-five, because this policy will (incorrectly) seem arbitrary and unfair to too many voters.

If a strong impermissive policy of regulation of this kind is not politically feasible for this reason, this might be a decisive strategic argument to advocate some form of abolition instead. Abolitionist policies, however, might also be politically unfeasible in some countries, because too many voters believe, incorrectly, that it makes no sense to penalize customers and not prostitutes. This might provide a decisive strategic argument to advocate the kind permissive prohibition that one finds in the United Kingdom instead of any abolitionist policy. For the sake of philosophical reflection, however, we should set aside questions of political feasibility and try to identify the range of policies that might be warranted by the relevant considerations, assuming that they are all politically feasible.

Which policy, then, should someone *favor* who accepts the paternalistic rationale for prostitution laws presented in this chapter, assuming that they are all politically feasible? The answer depends on the overall costs and benefits of these policies, which depends on their consequences. Because we do not know what the actual consequences of all these policies would be if effectively implemented, we are in not in a position to know which specific policy is best. This would be a serious weakness in the argument of this book if its aim were to identify the best prostitution policy, all things considered.

This, however, is not its aim. My aim here is to show that prostitution laws in *some* form can be justified by the paternalistic argument compatible with our rights to liberty, provided that its empirical assumptions are sound. What I conclude from this discussion is that either permissive abolition or impermissive regulation in *some* form can be justified by this argument.

2

Government Moralism

I. What's Wrong with It?

Anyone who defends prostitution laws is likely to be challenged at some point to explain what is *wrong* with prostitution. So it is worth pointing out that the argument of the previous chapter does not presuppose that there is anything wrong with prostitution. That is, it does not assume that there is anything intrinsically or categorically wrong with exchanging sex for money. Nor does it presuppose that there is anything intrinsically or categorically wrong with promiscuity, anonymous sex, sex outside of marriage, or recreational or nonprocreative sex. The paternalistic case for prostitution laws does not rest on the prohibitions characteristic of traditional sexual morality. It rests on the view that prostitution commonly harms sex workers and that prostitution laws reduce this harm by reducing the amount of prostitution that is done.

Because so many people seem to believe that exchanging sex for money is morally wrong, the case for prostitution laws might seem to be strengthened by this claim. When pressed to defend it, however, one is hard put to come up with a convincing explanation. How could taking money for providing a service, which is something people permissibly do all the time and for all sorts of reasons, be intrinsically or categorically wrong when this service is sex, given that sex is also something people permissibly do all the time and for all sorts of reasons? In trying to answer this question, we may find ourselves making obscure and puzzling statements about the sacredness or inherent preciousness of sex, which, if nothing else, is sure to put us on the defensive dialectically.[1]

The judgment that exchanging sex for money is wrong is also arguably objectionably moralistic in the following sense: it applies moral categories where they do not belong. The statement that an act or decision is wrong is used in different ways in our culture, but it is most naturally and uncontroversially made about decisions and actions that negatively affect others against their will. When a moral judgment is used to express disapproval of other kinds of acts, it seems to float free of its firmest grounds and so, perhaps, to reflect an unexamined prejudice.

It is also true that when we judge that an act is intrinsically or categorically wrong, we are claiming that this kind of act is wrong under all circumstances. Because we can imagine circumstances in which exchanging sex for money seems morally permissible, the claim that it is intrinsically or categorically wrong seems dogmatic and unimaginative. Imagine a single woman with no children living in a port town who has a sailor boyfriend who gives her money when his ship comes in. Suppose that, although she likes him, she would not continue to have sex with him were it not for the "rent money" he gives her when he is in town, and that they both tacitly understand this. If they treat each other with respect and consideration, it is hard, for me at least, to see what valid moral principle the arrangement violates.

Some antilegalization activists choose instead to take the bait offered by the "What's wrong with it?" question and answer that prostitution is a form of "violence against women."[2] I think there is some truth to this, which is that sex work has negative psychological effects similar to those of other kinds of sexual abuse, such as rape and adult-child incest. Obviously, though, exchanging sex for money *need not* involve violence as this is ordinarily understood, and in fact usually does not. Moreover, there is no reason to suppose that every single exchange of sex for money has the negative psychological effects associated with sexual abuse or that every sex worker is negatively affected in these ways. The claim that prostitution is a form of violence against women, or a form of sexual abuse, therefore fails to provide a convincing explanation of what is *intrinsically* or *categorically* wrong with prostitution, understood simply as the exchange of sex for money.

A stronger response, in my opinion, to the "What's wrong with it?" challenge is to say, "Probably nothing." Or "Probably nothing if you are asking 'What is intrinsically or categorically wrong with exchanging sex for money?'" An opponent of legalizing prostitution can agree that some exchanges of sex for money are morally unobjectionable, like the one imagined above between the woman and her sailor friend. All she needs to claim is that prostitution is *commonly* harmful, and that this is sufficient to justify some laws that function to reduce prostitution.

II. Sexual Freedom

One reason to make clear that prostitution laws do not depend on the premise that prostitution is intrinsically or categorically wrong is that this premise is questionable. Another reason is to make clear that one may consistently support prostitution laws while rejecting the general principle that the government may limit our sexual freedom for moralistic reasons. The notion of a moralistic reason is difficult to define, but, as I am using the term here, moralistic reasons to prohibit prostitution would include the reason that sex outside of marriage is a sin; that promiscuity is a vice; that the majority disapproves of prostitution; that exchanging sex for money is intrinsically wrong, an "intrinsic evil," or wrong independent of its negative impact on anyone. If reasons of this kind were good enough to justify the government in prohibiting prostitution, they might also be good enough to justify the government in limiting our sexual freedom in other ways. Because this seems wrong, it is important to make clear that this is not presupposed or entailed by the paternalistic case for prostitution laws.

In this connection it is worth commenting on Justice Scalia's controversial dissenting opinion in *Lawrence v. Texas* that unless majority disapproval is counted as a "rational basis" for state laws restricting sexual conduct, many forms of sexual regulation are unconstitutional, including "state laws against bigamy, same-sex marriage, adult incest, prostitution, masturbation, adultery, fornication, bestiality, and obscenity."[3] If Scalia were right about this, a defender of prostitution laws would have to claim that majority disapproval is sometimes a sufficient justification for laws that limit our sexual freedom. Scalia, however, makes no attempt to defend his assumption that the only rational basis for each of the laws he mentions is majority disapproval, and it is easy enough to come up with alternative justifications for at least some of them. For instance, one can defend prostitution laws by the argument that prostitution commonly harms sex workers in the ways I have described. If this is a reasonable belief, then reducing this harm would provide a rational basis for prostitution laws. As a consequence, these laws might be constitutional even if majority disapproval alone is *never* a constitutionally sufficient reason for the government to prohibit a form of sexual conduct, contrary to what Scalia supposes.

Does the case for prostitution laws nonetheless imply that the government might justifiably restrict our sexual freedom for other reasons? If other kinds of sexual activity are commonly harmful in the way that prostitution is, then there are similar reasons for policies that reduce these other activities. The belief that prostitution is commonly harmful, however, does not entail that other kinds of sexual behavior are similarly harmful. It does not entail, for example, that homosexuality and nonmarital sex are similarly harmful. So the case for prostitution laws does not entail that the government is justified in adopting policies that reduce homosexual or nonmarital sex.

There is anecdotal evidence, I suppose, that promiscuity is harmful, which is that people often regret earlier promiscuous periods of their lives. In our current culture, however, promiscuity is not stigmatized to the same degree that prostitution is and so does not have the same negative impact on opportunities and important relationships. It is also important to bear in mind that the noncommercially promiscuous person is one who seeks sexual encounters with people he or she sexually desires and enjoys, which creates an important difference between promiscuity and prostitution. Moreover, without the monetary incentive to continue, a person is less likely to continue his or her promiscuous behavior when it starts to become depressing or when it begins to interfere with important relationships. It is true that promiscuous sex is sometimes anonymous, as in a bar or a bathhouse, and has this feature in common with some forms of prostitution. The argument for prostitution laws, however, is not that prostitution involves anonymous sex. The argument is that prostitution is psychologically destructive in the ways described in the previous chapter, and that it results in the loss of important opportunities, and that it has a negative impact on important relationships, without sufficient compensating benefits. Because promiscuity does not typically have the same kind of negative impact on a person's life, the argument for prostitution laws implies nothing with respect to laws aimed at reducing promiscuity.

Even if there were reasons for laws restricting other kinds of sexual conduct similar to the reasons for prostitution laws, the justifiability of prostitution laws would not entail that these other restrictions of our sexual freedom are also justifiable. A coercive policy must be judged not only by the ills it seeks to reduce, but also by the burdens this policy imposes on individuals and by the likelihood that this policy will reduce these ills. Because the burdens imposed by one restriction of our sexual freedom might be greater than the burdens imposed by another restriction, and one restriction might be less likely than another to achieve its desired result, one restriction might be unjustifiable even if the reasons in its favor are just as strong as the reasons in favor of another restriction that is justifiable. So even if promiscuity *were* commonly as harmful as prostitution, the claim that prostitution laws are justifiable would not entail that laws prohibiting promiscuity are justifiable too.

To illustrate, compare the Swedish abolitionist policy with a law that prohibits fornication. It is possible that whereas a law prohibiting the purchase of sexual services does *not* intrude unduly on our freedom to direct our own lives by our own values, a law prohibiting fornication would intrude too much; that whereas a law prohibiting the purchase of sexual services does *not* unduly limit our opportunities for learning or personal growth, a law prohibiting fornication would limit these opportunities too much; that whereas a law prohibiting the purchase of sexual services does *not* license too much police intrusion into our homes, a law prohibiting fornication would license too much police intrusion; and so on. It is also possible that whereas a law prohibiting the purchase of sexual services is likely to reduce prostitution significantly, a law prohibiting fornication is unlikely to reduce promiscuity significantly. For all these reasons, it is important to keep the question of whether prostitution laws are justifiable separate from whether the government is justified in limiting sexual freedom in other ways. Conflating these issues is a rhetorical trick used too often both by civil libertarian critics of prostitution laws and by conservative defenders of homosexual sodomy laws.

III. Degradation

One of the most common objections to prostitution is that it is degrading. Leading liberal theorists, however, have argued that this is an illegitimate reason for the government to restrict sexual conduct. Ronald Dworkin writes, "A community might think that the conduct it outlaws, though not against justice, is demeaning or corrupting or otherwise bad for the life of its author. It might think, for example, that the life of a homosexual is a degrading one, and it might outlaw homosexual relations on that ground. Liberal equality [Dworkin's view] denies the legitimacy of [this] reason for outlawing conduct."[4] A similar position is taken by John Rawls in *A Theory of Justice* in which he writes, "Justice as fairness [his view] requires us to show that modes of conduct interfere with the basic liberties of others or else violate some obligation or natural duty before they can be restricted." Rawls takes this to rule out the proposition that "certain kinds of sexual relationship are degrading and shameful" as a reason that can justify the government in limiting individual liberty.[5] If prostitution laws could be justified only by the proposition that prostitution is degrading, they would therefore seem to violate constraints on reasons that Rawls, Dworkin and other liberal theorists of rights have endorsed.

Although prostitution laws are commonly defended, however, by the proposition that prostitution is degrading, it does not follow that prostitution laws are ruled out by any principle that Rawls or Dworkin endorses. This is because prostitution laws might nonetheless be fully justified by *other* reasons, ones that the principles of Rawls and Dworkin allow. It is certainly not necessary to say that prostitution is "degrading" in order to defend prostitution laws, and in fact I did not say this or explicitly rely on this claim in chapter 1.

This observation, however, might prompt some to wonder what the relation is between my paternalistic argument for prostitution laws and the judgment that prostitution is degrading. If the claim that prostitution is degrading just is the claim that it is harmful in the ways I have described, and prostitution laws cannot be justified other than as reducing this harm, and the fact that a course of conduct is degrading in this way cannot justify the government in restricting it, then the paternalistic defense of prostitution laws that I have offered fails. To this possibility one might respond that Rawls and Dworkin are simply wrong to rule out reasons of degradation. But, as I explain in chapter 5, I think they are right to do so. So I want to explain here why the reasons given for prostitution laws in chapter 1 are consistent with this view.

To say that something is degraded is to say that it is lowered in quality or value. This is what it means, for example, to say that pollution degrades the natural environment, or that a bombing campaign has degraded the enemy's command and control capabilities. This notion of degradation might also apply to a person's life. Thus one might say that drug addiction is degrading in lowering the quality of a person's life. One might believe that drug addiction lowers the quality of a person's life by making it less admirable or praiseworthy. When we say that an act or activity is degrading *to a person*, however, we often mean something quite different than that it lowers the quality of her life in making it less admirable. We often mean that it lowers *her* in some way.

How might a person be lowered by an action or activity? It might (a) reduce this person in rank or formal status, (b) stigmatize her or lower the regard or esteem in which she is generally held, (c) express contempt toward her, (d) humiliate her, (e) destroy or impede the functioning of important capacities of hers, (f) be dishonorable, shameful, or undignified, or (g) be subjectively experienced by her as having one of these qualities.

When used to express a negative evaluation of prostitution the statement that prostitution is degrading seems most often to mean (b), (c), (d), (e), or (g): that prostitution is stigmatizing; that it commonly involves expressions of contempt toward the prostitute; that it is humiliating; that it impairs psychological functioning; or that it is *experienced* by the sex worker as dishonorable, shameful, or undignified. Far less often does the claim that prostitution is degrading mean that prostitution *is* dishonorable or shameful or that it lowers the quality of a person's life by making it less admirable.

Catharine MacKinnon, for example, writes that "the social status of prostituted women remains the lowest and least respected, the most contemptible and degraded."[6] A prostitute observes, "For a woman in a society like ours, being a prostitute is the lowest of the low, it's degrading."[7] Here it is degradation in sense (b) that seems to be meant: that prostitution stigmatizes a person or lowers the regard or esteem in which she is held.

New York Times columnist Bob Herbert, after using the phrase "systematic, institutionalized degradation" to describe the sex industry in Las Vegas, goes on to argue that in the commercial sex trade "females are bought, sold, raped, beaten, shamed, and in many cases, physically and emotionally wrecked."[8] This suggests that by degradation he means (c), (d), and (e), being treated with contempt, humiliated, and psychologically damaged. Hoigard and Finstad portray the life of prostitution as characterized by "degradation, humiliation, and insult."[9] This again suggests (c) and (d): being subject to contempt and humiliation. Dorchen Leidholdt of the

Coalition Against Trafficking in Women and Jessica Neuwirth of Equality Now discuss the "psychological degradation of prostitution," referring to the psychological damage inflicted by it, and so seem to have (e) in mind: the impairment of psychological functioning.[10]

According to Evelina Giobbe, prostitutes report "feelings of degradation, defilement, and dirtiness, sometimes for years after leaving prostitution."[11] Another study reports that adolescent prostitutes "report having felt 'degraded,' 'dirty,' 'bad.'"[12] In this context the claim that prostitution is degrading suggests (g): that prostitution is *experienced* as shameful, dishonorable or undignified.

Because (b), (c), (d), (e), and (g) appear to be what is most commonly meant when opponents of legalization claim that prostitution is degrading, I will refer to these as the "ordinary meanings" of the claim that prostitution is degrading. If, however, the judgment that prostitution is degrading is understood in one of these ways, then it turns out that the paternalistic argument for prostitution laws presented in chapter 1 does rely on the assumption that prostitution is degrading, despite the fact that I did not use this word. The first thing I mentioned in explaining what is bad about prostitution is that it is commonly experienced as being humiliating and abusive and that it commonly results in lasting feelings of shame. In the same paragraph I observed that this work makes it difficult for sex workers to enjoy sex and to form stable, trusting, mutually supportive, and respectful intimate relationships, in which case prostitution impairs psychological functioning. Shortly afterward I pointed out that because this work is stigmatized, it results in the loss of important opportunities and has a negative impact on important relationships.

Because the argument of chapter 1 relies in these ways on the assumption that prostitution is degrading, some might conclude that this argument is ruled out by the principles of Rawls and Dworkin. This conclusion, however, is unwarranted. When Rawls and Dworkin maintain that it is wrong for the government to prohibit an activity for the reason that it is degrading, they are claiming that the fact that an activity is shameful or that it makes a person's life less excellent, perfect, or admirable is not in itself a legitimate reason for the government to prohibit him from doing it, at least not when the activity is protected by a basic liberty and when the person whose liberty is at stake disagrees with this evaluation. In endorsing this principle they are therefore not ruling out the proposition that prostitution is degrading as part of an argument for prostitution laws *when "degrading" has one of the ordinary meanings just identified.*

Nor is it clear why they would want to rule out claims of this kind. Consider what Dworkin says about rape: "Rape is sickeningly, comprehensively contemptuous because it reduces a woman to a physical convenience, a creature whose importance is exhausted by her genital use, someone whose love and sense of self—aspects of personality particularly at stake in sex— have no significance whatever except as vehicles for sadistic degradation."[13]

Suppose that prostitution is degrading in similar ways, as Giobbe maintains.[14] Dworkin evidently thinks this kind of degradation is a bad thing. Why, then, would he think that preventing this kind of degradation is an illegitimate aim of government policy?

To understand why Rawls and Dworkin would *not* want to rule out this kind of reason for government policy, it is helpful to reflect on why they would hold that judgments of degradation are illegitimate reasons when "degrading" means shameful.

One possible explanation is that this principle supports more specific judgments that Rawls and Dworkin make, such as that it would be wrong for the government to prohibit homosexuality for the reason that it is degrading. This specific judgment, however, might be defended without claiming that reasons of degradation or shamefulness are illegitimate *in general*. One might argue instead that this is a bad reason to prohibit homosexuality simply because homosexuality is not in fact degrading in this sense. In making this argument one would rely on a more general and less controversial principle: that the government is not justified in limiting individual liberty by false propositions. Because Rawls and Dworkin and most of their readers presumably agree that homosexuality is not degrading in this sense, this principle suffices to account for their specific judgment on this matter. Why, then, do they go on to assert the more controversial principle?

I believe that Rawls and Dworkin are following John Stuart Mill and H. L. A. Hart in holding that the government is justified in limiting important liberties, such as sexual freedom, only to protect the important interests of individuals.[15] Because they believe that the judgment that an act is degrading in the sense that it is shameful or that it makes a person's life less excellent or admirable fails to identify an interest of sufficient importance to justify the government in limiting an important liberty, they believe that this judgment alone cannot justify the government in limiting sexual freedom, which is an important liberty. If, however, this is their basis for excluding reasons of degradation, this exclusion should not be interpreted to rule out prostitution laws. This is because the case for these laws, although it may presuppose that sex work is degrading in some sense, nonetheless identifies important interests that would be threatened by legalization, interests that are sufficiently important to justify the government in adopting some restrictions.

To this an advocate of legalizing prostitution might now respond that the judgment that prostitution is degrading could not *alone* justify prostitution laws even if "degrading" has one of its ordinary meanings. He might argue that even if an activity is stigmatizing, or expresses contempt, or is humiliating, or is experienced as shameful, these facts alone cannot justify the government in adopting prostitution laws. This position, however, is consistent with the paternalistic argument of chapter 1. In stating this argument I did not give as the *sole* reason for prostitution laws that prostitution is experienced as humiliating, disrespectful, or shameful. I said that *because of* how it is experienced it commonly results in lasting feelings of worthlessness and self-hatred and interferes with a person's ability to have healthy, stable, intimate relationships. Nor did I offer as a justification for prostitution laws the simple fact that it is stigmatized. I said that *because* it is stigmatized it results in the loss of important opportunities and has a negative impact on important relationships. If we understand the degradation of prostitution in any of these ordinary ways, it is therefore not the degradation *alone* that justifies prostitution laws in my view; it is rather the degradation *combined with* the negative *consequences* of being degraded in these ways, consequences that are serious enough to be a legitimate object of government concern.

The judgment that prostitution is degrading might of course also mean that prostitution has all the negative consequences that I identified in chapter 1. If so, then my argument for prostitution laws just *is* that prostitution is commonly degrading. It would be an error, though, to infer from this that prostitution laws are ruled out by any principle that Rawls or Dworkin endorses. Rape is also degrading, and we should not conclude from this that laws against rape are inconsistent with liberal principles. A policy is not ruled out by liberal principles simply because the treatment that it prohibits might properly be described as degrading. It is ruled out by these principles only if it cannot be justified without relying on the premise that the conduct in question is shameful or unadmirable. Because prostitution laws can be justified without relying on this premise, they are compatible with the principles of Rawls and Dworkin identified above.

IV. Morals Legislation

The view that it is wrong for the government to prohibit a form of conduct for the reason that it is degrading might be understood to be an implication of a more general principle, that the government should not "legislate morality." Despite what I have just said about degradation, some might continue to object to prostitution laws on this ground. A facile retort is that the government legislates morality all the time, when it prohibits murder and theft, for example. This response, however, misses the point. As I understand it, the objection to legislating morality is that the government should not prohibit activities by law unless there are good, nonmoralistic reasons to do so. Because laws against murder and theft can be fully justified by nonmoralistic reasons, they do not violate this principle.

The notion of a moralistic reason is difficult to define, but here are examples of moralistic reasons to prohibit murder and theft: murder and theft are sins; the dispositions to murder and steal are vices; most people disapprove of these actions; and these actions are intrinsically wrong, or wrong independent of any negative impact they have on anyone. Because laws against murder and theft can be justified without relying on any of these propositions, the government is not "legislating morality" in the relevant sense when it prohibits them. These laws can be justified by the fact that it is bad for people to lose their lives and property and for their lives and possessions to be less secure, when this is combined with the assumption that these ills are less likely to occur when the government prohibits murder and theft. Because prostitution laws can also be fully justified without relying on moralistic reasons, as I explained above, the government is also not "legislating morality" in the relevant sense when it adopts these laws.

Closely connected, though, to the view that the government should not legislate morality is the view that the government should not adopt and enforce what is sometimes called *morals legislation*. There are different ways to understand what this is, but we might understand it to include any legislation that is adopted for moralistic reasons. A policy is adopted *for* a moralistic reason, in the sense intended here, if this reason is the primary reason for the policy in the minds of its supporters. I have just claimed that prostitution laws *can be justified* without reference to moralistic reasons. In identifying a policy as morals legislation, however, one might be making a claim about its motivation, and not about the available justifications for it. One might be claiming that this policy is or was adopted *for* moralistic reasons in the sense just defined. Prostitution laws might be moralistic in this sense even if they can be justified as reducing harm.

Whether prostitution laws are a form of morals legislation in this sense, however, is not directly relevant to whether they are justifiable. This is because the motives that initially cause a government to adopt a policy or that now cause the government to maintain this policy are not directly relevant to assessing whether or not there are good reasons for the government to have this policy. To see this, suppose that murder laws in Massachusetts were originally adopted on the grounds that a Christian government should seek to carry out and enforce God's will here on earth and that murder is contrary to God's will as revealed in the Bible. Suppose that state governments should not limit individual liberty unless this policy can be fully justified without relying on religious reasons of this kind. Does it follow that murder laws in Massachusetts are now unjustifiable? No. Regardless of how they were originally motivated, these laws are fully justified now because there are perfectly good nonreligious reasons for them.

Sometimes a decision that is defensible on the merits is nonetheless morally objectionable because the process through which this decision was reached was unfair. If, for example, gender is irrelevant to doing a job well and a job applicant is rejected because she is female, then even if she is not the best candidate, her rejection is morally objectionable because the process through which she was rejected was unfair, in counting an irrelevant consideration against her. A legislative process that leads to the adoption of a justifiable government policy might be similarly objectionable if this policy was adopted only because illegitimate considerations were counted in its favor. Some may believe that this is true of morals legislation: if a law is adopted because moralistic reasons are counted in its favor, then the process through which this law was adopted is unfair or illegitimate. If the process through which a policy is adopted is unfair, then, some might conclude, the government is not justified in having this policy.

I reject this view. If the legislative process through which a policy is adopted is unfair, then the process is objectionable. It does not follow that the *policy* is objectionable or that it is wrong for the government to have this policy.[16] Because, however, some readers might believe that any policy that is adopted for moralistic reasons is consequently illegitimate, I want to explain why, if prostitution laws are adopted for the paternalistic reasons identified in chapter 1, they would not be objectionable on this ground.

V. Paternalistic, Not Moralistic

If prostitution is legalized, more people will be harmed by work that they choose to do. This, in essence, is the paternalistic argument for prostitution laws. Some might think that paternalism of this kind is wrong. In the next chapter I explain why I do not think so. If, however, all paternalistic reasons were moralistic reasons, prostitution laws would be moralistic if adopted on the basis of this argument. If moralistic policies were objectionable, prostitution laws adopted on the basis of this argument would then be objectionable too. So I want to explain why paternalistic reasons are not moralistic reasons.

Here are some examples of moralistic reasons to prohibit prostitution: sex outside marriage is a sin; promiscuity is a vice; the majority disapproves of prostitution; and exchanging sex for money is intrinsically or categorically wrong. These reasons differ from paternalistic reasons in two important ways. First, these moralistic reasons do not identify preventing harm to anyone or protecting the important interests of anyone as the rationale for prohibiting prostitution; they identify only the violation of some standard. Nor does their assertion as reasons presuppose that this standard functions to protect anyone's interests or to protect anyone from harm. Paternalistic reasons, in contrast, necessarily identify some way in which a form of conduct is harmful to those who engage in it or some way in which a person who engages in it might be worse off as a result. Second, the reasons I have identified as moralistic all express or presuppose some kind of disapproval that it makes sense to regard as *moral*. Paternalistic reasons, in contrast, do not express moral disapproval. They express the belief that it is *unwise* or *imprudent* or *inadvisable* for someone to engage in the relevant form of conduct, but this judgment does not license and is not typically accompanied by the feelings of resentment or righteous indignation that typically accompany distinctively *moral* disapproval.

Hart implicitly recognized this distinction between moralistic and paternalistic reasons when he took the position that although some forms of paternalism might be justifiable, what he called *legal moralism* is not.[17] Joel Feinberg made this distinction more explicit where he distinguished *legal moralism* from *legal paternalism*.[18] This distinction has also been recognized by philosophically sophisticated writers on prostitution, such as David Richards and Lars Ericsson.[19] It has also been recognized implicitly by some sex workers. Consider here how one prostitute describes her reaction to feminists who oppose prostitution: "When they tell me, 'You shouldn't do it, it's bad for you.' I hear, 'You shouldn't do it, it's bad.' And I hear them saying, 'I'm superior, what a wonderful person I am to speak to you and lift you up, you fallen woman.'"[20] This woman is observing that she has a tendency to hear paternalistic concerns as moralistic ones, and in this way notices the difference between them.

Different explanations might be given of the political significance of the distinction between paternalistic and moralistic reasons, but here is one way to understand it. One might hold that coercive government policies can be justified only as protecting or advancing the important interests of individuals and that none of the moralistic reasons identified above identify important individual interests. Either they fail, as stated, to identify *interests*, or the interests they identify are not sufficiently important to justify coercive government policies. Some paternalistic reasons, however, do identify important individual interests, and so can justify some coercive government policies.

Whether or not this is the best explanation of the significance of the distinction between moralistic and paternalistic reasons, this distinction is sufficiently clear, I think, to appreciate the following point. When I claim that prostitution laws are not moralistic if adopted for the reasons given in chapter 1, I mean that they are not motivated by the kinds of reasons I have identified in this chapter as moralistic. I do not mean that they are not motivated by paternalistic reasons. This position is perfectly coherent, in my view, because the paternalistic reasons that I have identified for prostitution laws are not moralistic ones. Why it makes sense to hold that paternalistic reasons, but not moralistic ones, can justify restrictions on prostitution is a question to which I return in chapter 5. Here my point is simply that there is a difference between these kinds of reasons, and so it makes sense to characterize a prostitution law as paternalistic but not moralistic.

Prostitution laws are commonly criticized, not only as moralistic, but also as *puritanical* or *religious*. So it is worth pointing out that these characterizations are also inaccurate if prostitution laws are motivated by the kinds of paternalistic concerns that I have identified. To judge a policy to be puritanical is to judge that it is motivated by a desire to prevent people from having fun, and, more specifically, to prevent them from experiencing sensual pleasures, on the assumption that having fun or sensual pleasure is bad. The paternalistic argument for prostitution laws does not presuppose that fun or sensual pleasure is bad. It is consistent not only with the belief that recreational sex is good, but also with the belief that the pleasure a person gets from *paid* sex is good. It holds only that the costs of legalizing prostitution outweigh the benefits and that it should therefore not be legalized. To characterize a policy as religious is to judge that it is motivated by a religious belief. The paternalistic argument for prostitution laws that I sketched in chapter 1 is not motivated by and does not rest on any religious belief. It is consistent with atheism. It is consistent with the view that there is no life after death; that there is no Holy Scripture or no scripture that has special metaphysical or spiritual validity; that no organized religion has a special claim to spiritual or political authority; that all the defining claims of the world's great religions are false; and that we would be better off without religion. It is also consistent with the rejection of all these negative claims about religion and so with traditional monotheism.

Some readers might be suspicious of the distinction I have drawn here between paternalistic and moralistic reasons because they suspect that a person's motivation in defending prostitution laws is always implicitly moralistic. There are many risky occupations, and many ways in which people are harmed by their work, and many ways in which people act self-destructively. Why focus on *prostitution* unless one believes that there is something distinctively problematic about *sexual* labor? What reason is there to believe this, other than the belief that in selling sex a person mistreats the precious human capacity for sexual intimacy? Isn't the focus of this book implicitly moralistic despite what I have just said?

I do not think so. The focus of this book can be explained within the context of contemporary liberal theory without assuming that exchanging sex for money is sinful, immoral, or intrinsically wrong. Some have claimed that the liberal theories of Rawls and Dworkin entail that drug and prostitution laws violate our rights.[21] In supporting these laws many people seem to disagree with this. So it makes sense to consider whether or not these liberal theories really have this implication and whether these policies really are unjust. Suppose that Rawls and Dworkin are right that prostitution laws, drug laws, and other laws of this kind cannot be justified by moralistic reasons. It does not follow that these laws are unjustifiable because there are nonmoralistic reasons for them. Are these nonmoralistic reasons good enough, then, to justify these laws within the kind of liberal individualistic framework that both Rawls and Dworkin endorse? Even if prostitution is not immoral, it makes sense to examine this question, simply to know what justice requires.

The topics of drug and prostitution laws have also had a long history in liberal theory. Mill discusses these policies in *On Liberty* and argues that they cannot be justified consistent with his harm principle.[22] These policies are also commonly cited as examples of paternalism and are commonly criticized on this ground. So if one is interested in the general theoretical question of whether paternalism is morally justifiable, it makes sense to examine closely whether drug and prostitution laws in some form can be justified on paternalistic grounds. I have written elsewhere about drug laws.[23] Here I discuss prostitution laws.

Some may remain suspicious. Why focus on prostitution instead of other occupations with which paternalistic interference might be justified? Isn't this because one believes that there is something particularly problematic about *sexual* labor? I think not. The paternalistic argument for prostitution laws presupposes that prostitution is problematic as an occupation, but only because it has the bad consequences identified in chapter 1. Perhaps prostitution is particularly problematic, but if it is, this is only because few, if any, other occupations have the same bad consequences. The judgment that these consequences are bad is not a moralistic judgment. It is not identical to the judgment that prostitution is intrinsically wrong, an "intrinsic evil." Nor is it necessary to make moralistic judgments of this kind in order to recognize these bad consequences or to be concerned with them. Personally, I do not believe that exchanging sex for money is intrinsically or essentially wrong. I believe that prostitution is nonetheless commonly bad for people and that it is therefore a legitimate object of government concern.

VI. Historical Motivation

One reason why prostitution laws are thought to be moralistic is that people believe that our current prostitution laws were originally adopted for moralistic reasons. This belief surrounds prostitution laws with an aura of illegitimacy and fosters the (mis)perception that prostitution laws are inherently moralistic. Given that prostitution laws *might* be motivated by nonmoralistic concerns, it is a mistake in any case to see these laws as *inherently* moralistic, but I believe that the historical claim is also false. American prostitution laws were originally adopted primarily for paternalistic reasons, and not for moralistic ones.

The historical question of motive is obviously complicated by the fact that prostitution laws of one kind or another have existed in America since the early colonial period. Presumably the motives of those who supported these policies have varied at different times and places. Current prostitution policy in the United States, however, is commonly traced back to the early twentieth century. During the late nineteenth century both prostitution and street solicitation were illegal in most cities and towns, but brothels were tolerated by the government in many jurisdictions and much enlightened opinion favored an official policy of regulation. In the early twentieth century, however, both regulation and de facto toleration were decisively repudiated by local, state, and federal governments in favor of an official policy of nontolerance. This policy has continued to the present. So when the original motives of American prostitution policy are discussed, the focus is often on the motives of government officials and antiprostitution activists in the early twentieth century. I will follow this practice and suppose that the "original motives" relevant to characterizing current American policy are the motives of those early-twentieth-century reformers who advocated an official policy of nontolerance as opposed to an official policy of toleration.

Because supporters of a policy often have different motives, it is not clear that it makes sense to identify one motive as *the* motive or even as the *primary* motive of a government policy. I will assume, however, that a law that prohibits a form of conduct is moralistic if and only if the primary reason for this policy in the minds of most of its supporters is that this conduct is inherently shameful, or sinful, or a product of vice, an "intrinsic evil," or wrong independent of its negative effects on anyone. Obviously there is no way of knowing for sure whether or not this is true of the policy of nontolerance that was widely adopted in the United States in the early twentieth century. I believe, however, that the available evidence warrants the opposite conclusion. When we look at what the most influential advocates of this policy had to say in its favor, the paternalistic argument for nontolerance has much greater prominence than any purely moralistic argument.

Jane Addams begins *A New Conscience and an Ancient Evil* (1912) by comparing prostitution to slavery and, partly on the basis of this comparison, she endorses the *abolition* of commercialized vice. She concludes, "As that consciousness of human suffering, which already hangs like a black cloud over thousands of our most sensitive contemporaries, increases in poignancy, it must finally include the women who for so many generations have received neither pity nor consideration [i.e., prostitutes]; as the sense of justice fast widens to encircle all human relations, it must at length reach the women who have so long been judged without a hearing."[24] Addams's use of the words *suffering* and *pity* is revealing, as is her suggestion that a properly enlarged sense of justice must include the welfare of prostitutes.

Maude Miner concludes *Slavery of Prostitution* (1916) in a similar spirit with "A Plea for Emancipation" that includes the following passage:

> If the heart cries of young girls who are suffering the tortures of this dreadful life could be made to ring perpetually in our consciences, we would not tolerate the existence of such a horrible wrong. We would arise with tremendous power and crush the enemy. To free men and women from physical bondage the life-blood of our nation was spent [in the Civil War]. A worse slavery exists in our midst today. Women are held in moral and spiritual bondage which deadens and destroys their highest powers. To free them from vice, we must summon greater enthusiasm, zeal, and courage, than would be required for physical combat.[25]

Miner, like Addams, focuses on the suffering caused by prostitution and likewise suggests that justice requires us to try to eliminate its cause.

The arguments of progressive social reformers do not necessarily provide the best explanation of why the government actually adopts a policy they advocate. Concern for the welfare of prostitutes, however, is also evident in the municipal vice commission reports that did provide the basis for official prostitution reform in the early twentieth century. The influential 1911 report of the Vice Commission of Chicago, for example, refers to "the moral and physical harm which results from vice,"[26] and it includes prostitution among the "practices which are morally and physically debasing and degrading, and which affect the moral and physical welfare of the inhabitants of the city."[27] Furthermore, it speaks of "the sad life of prostitution,"[28] "the ghastly life story of fallen women,"[29] and "the unfortunate women" who do this work.[30]

Because the Chicago Vice Commission characterizes prostitution as *degrading*, some may conclude that its primary reasons for rejecting regulation and official tolerance were moralistic rather than paternalistic. It is clear from the context, however, that the degradation referred to was understood as something that is bad *for* the prostitutes—as something that makes *them* worse off—as opposed to something that it is bad only for society or that mars the world in some way, say by making it less pure.

The primary model of the Chicago Vice Report is thought to be a report on prostitution in New York City that was produced a decade earlier by the Committee of Fifteen. This earlier report had also characterized prostitution as degrading. "Every modern system of regulation avows the purpose of preventing, as far as possible, the degradation of those who are not yet depraved, and the rescue and restoration to honorable life of fallen women who are still susceptible to moral influences."[31] This, too, sounds moralistic, but the statement must be read in context. It was made in order to contrast modern prostitution laws with medieval ones. The difference identified by this passage is that whereas medieval prostitution policy was motivated only by a concern to protect the welfare of persons *other* than the prostitute, modern prostitution policy is motivated by concern to protect the welfare of prostitutes or the welfare of the girls and women who might become prostitutes.

Because the Chicago Commission and the Committee of Fifteen both refer to the *moral* welfare of the inhabitants of the city, some may conclude that their motives were primarily moralistic. The term *moral welfare*, however, was commonly used in contrast to *physical welfare* as we would now use the term *psychological welfare*. Because concern for a person's psychological welfare is no more inherently moralistic than concern for her physical welfare, we should not infer from the use of this term that the aims of either the Chicago Commission or the Committee of Fifteen were primarily moralistic. It is true that a person's moral welfare was generally understood to include more than her pleasure or enjoyment; it was understood to include also the development of the "highest powers" to which Miner refers. This, however, does not make the motives of the policy moralistic as opposed to paternalistic because it is reasonable to believe that the development of our higher powers contributes in some way to our welfare. This was certainly Mill's view in *Utilitarianism*, for example.[32]

Another reason why the original motives of the early-twentieth-century opponents of regulation and official tolerance might be thought to be moralistic is that they often used the terms *vice* and *immorality* as synonyms for prostitution. This might suggest that they wanted to suppress prostitution primarily because it is a vice or a form of sexual immorality. This inference is also unwarranted, however. Euphemistic references to sexual activity were common, and there is no reason to suppose that the use of certain words to refer to a kind of activity identify the primary reasons to be concerned with it. Thus although Miner refers to prostitution as *vice*, it is clear that her primary concern with prostitution is with the suffering that she believes this activity causes, and not with the fact that it is a form of sexual immorality.

The paternalistic interpretation of the motives of the early-twentieth-century reformers is further supported by Walter Lippmann's *A Preface to Politics*, which was written partly in response to the Chicago Vice Commission Report and was sharply critical of it. The Chicago report opens with the following declaration: "Constant and persistent repression of prostitution the immediate method: absolute annihilation the ultimate ideal." Lippmann did not quarrel with this *as an ideal*. He agreed that prostitution is generally bad for those who do it. "The miseries it entails are genuine miseries," he writes, "not points of etiquette or infringements of convention. Vice issues in pain. The world is worse for it."[33] For this reason Lippmann did not criticize the Commission's goal of "absolute annihilation"; rather, he criticized its policy recommendation of "constant and persistent repression." To eliminate prostitution, Lippmann argued, one would have to address the root causes, particularly male sexual desire and inadequate economic opportunities for young women. As a consequence, society would have to reject the norm against extramarital sex (which he thought the Commission uncritically endorsed) and radically alter the distribution of wealth that leaves so many young women with inadequate resources. Because the Commission failed to recognize how radically society would have to change in order to eradicate prostitution, Lippmann argued, its policy recommendations were hopelessly ill-suited to achieving the Commission's ultimate goal.[34] He nonetheless attributes good motives to the Commission. "I do not mean that the members weren't deeply touched by the misery of these thousands of women," he writes. "The Commissioners had a good deal of sympathy for the prostitute's condition."[35]

Looking, then, at what leading opponents of regulation and official toleration said about prostitution at the time, and at what one influential critic said about their motives, I believe we are warranted in concluding that their primary motives were paternalistic, and not moralistic. To be sure, the special significance that prostitution had for Progressive social reformers like Addams and Miner requires further explanation. Many social ills plagued early-twentieth-century American society. So it must be explained why prostitution was commonly characterized as "*the* social evil." One plausible explanation is that prostitution provided a symbolic focal point for anxieties many Americans felt about major changes in American society, including the movement of many young people from family farms into cities, a more aggressively competitive market economy, and the influx of European Catholics into what had been a largely Protestant nation. As one historian, however, who endorses this explanation points out, it "does not invalidate the humanitarian concerns of the antiregulationists."[36] So it does not follow from this explanation that civic opposition to a policy of toleration was motivated primarily by moralistic reasons and not paternalistic ones.

Another historian of early-twentieth-century American prostitution does characterize the goals of the reformers as *moralistic*,[37] which seems to contradict the interpretation defended here. She also, however, characterizes prostitution as *degrading* in her own narrative voice, in a way that suggests that she believes that being degraded in this way is bad for the person degraded.[38] She also knows from the relevant primary sources that many supporters of prostitution were paternalistically concerned with prostitution precisely because of the degradation they believed it involved. Why, then, does she think that the motives of those who supported these laws were moralistic? I suspect that she thinks this only because she fails to draw the distinction I have made here between moralistic and paternalistic reasons and so believes that prostitution policy was moralistic precisely in virtue of being paternalistic. Had she carefully distinguished paternalistic reasons from moralistic ones, I do not believe she would have characterized the goals of the reformers as moralistic.

VII. Current Motives

The original motivation for most American prostitution laws, I have just argued, was primarily paternalistic, not moralistic. A critic of prostitution laws, however, might reasonably point out that it is not the *original* motives that matter to the evaluation of current policy, but *current* motives. The reason we still have prostitution laws, he might think, is the majority's belief that prostitution is immoral. If so, then our current prostitution laws are moralistic.

Is there any good reason, though, to believe this? In a compendious discussion of prostitution laws in twentieth-century America, John Decker identifies ten distinct motives for American prostitution laws.[39] The first is "protection of conventional morality," which is a kind of moralistic motive. The second is "a humanistic concern for the prostitute," which is a paternalistic motive. Decker goes on to claim, "The protection of the conventional morality is the primary motive for controlling prostitution." If so, then American prostitution policy is moralistic. Decker, however, offers no evidence for this claim. Moreover, he interprets the judgment that prostitution is degrading as providing a "humanitarian" or paternalistic reason,[40] and he must have known from reading the relevant sources that this is one of the most commonly given explanations of what is bad about prostitution. Why, then, does he claim that the "protection of conventional morality" is the *primary* motive? It is tempting to suggest that he holds this, not because there is any evidence for it, but because it supports his own civil libertarian opposition to prostitution laws. If this *were* the primary motive for prostitution laws, they would be easier to discredit and so more amenable to repeal.

A less cynical explanation of Decker's conclusion is the understandable belief that only moralistic motives could explain the American policy of *prohibition*. Perhaps a policy of *abolition* could be justified by paternalistic considerations, but how on earth could a policy of *prohibition* be justified in this way? How could anyone believe that punishing prostitutes for sex work can be justified as advancing *their* interests? Assuming that no one could reasonably believe this, it makes sense to infer that the best explanation of the American policy of prohibition is a moralistic desire to punish sin or vice or, perhaps, to protect a moral code that holds that prostitution is wrong.

Although understandable, this line of reasoning is flawed. For the reasons given in chapter 1,[41] it is not difficult to see how someone might support a policy of prohibition on paternalistic grounds. One might believe that prohibition provides the most effective deterrent to girls who are considering doing this work and who will be harmed by it. Or one might believe that prohibition is in the best interest of young women who have already decided to do this work to their own detriment. Suppose, to illustrate, that prohibition provides a legal basis for forcing young prostitutes into a program of rehabilitation. Because a program of coercive rehabilitation might benefit young people by giving them an incentive to stop doing this work and by helping them to find alternatives, it might be to their benefit. I do not endorse this argument, but it is an error to assume that no one could sincerely advance it.[42]

A recent discussion of the available polling data concludes that "most Americans see prostitution as immoral" and also that there is "no majority support for relaxation of prostitution laws."[43] Although this might appear to warrant the conclusion that current policy is motivated primarily by moralistic reasons, it does not. To see why, imagine that polling data were to reveal that most Americans see murder as immoral and that there is no majority support for the relaxation of murder laws. Would this warrant us in concluding that the *primary* motive for murder laws is moralistic, as opposed to the nonmoralistic motive of wanting to protect people's rights or wanting to protect them from harm? No, because it is reasonable to believe that most Americans think that murder is immoral *because* it is harmful or violates individuals' rights. Suppose, then, that most Americans believe that prostitution is immoral because they believe it is self-destructive or because they believe it commonly involves abuse and exploitation by pimps and customers. If so, the judgment that prostitution is immoral would not constitute a moralistic reason against legalizing it, because this judgment would itself be based on nonmoralistic grounds. Because the data do not indicate that a majority of Americans believe that prostitution is immoral only *because* they think it is sinful or an "intrinsic evil," there is no reason to conclude that their *primary* motives in supporting prostitution laws are moralistic.[44]

Is there any reason, though, to believe that American prostitution laws are *not* moralistic? One reason is given by the history told in the previous section. If this history is sound, then the original motives of our current policy were primarily paternalistic, and not moralistic. Another reason is that the motives for prostitution laws in other modern Western countries do not appear to be moralistic. Consider the 1998 Swedish law prohibiting the purchase of sexual services. The legislative history makes clear that its goal is to reduce prostitution on the assumption that sex work is harmful to sex workers, a form of "violence against women."[45] The Canadian Court of Appeal for Ontario has characterized the grounds for Canadian prostitution laws in a similar way: "The reason Parliament wants to eradicate prostitution is because it is harmful, a form of violence against women, related to men's historical dominance over women."[46]

For the reasons given above, I do not believe that the motives that explain a government's policy are generally relevant to whether or not the government is justified in having this policy. Nor do I defend the American policy of prohibition. Why, then, have I spent any time examining the motivation of American prostitution laws? The answer is that I want the reader to consider the paternalistic argument for prostitution laws in the best light. It seems to me that when people believe that a policy is moralistically motivated, it is harder for them to consider the good reasons for that policy fairly and impartially. So I have sought to rebut the common presumption that American prostitution laws are moralistic in order to facilitate open-minded evaluation of the paternalistic case for prostitution laws.

3

The Permissibility of Paternalism

The paternalistic argument for prostitution laws is that sex work is harmful to those who do it; that this harm would increase if prostitution were fully decriminalized; and that the goal of reducing this harm can justify the negative consequences of at least some prostitution laws. In chapter 1 I identified some ways in which prostitution is commonly harmful to those who do it and I considered different government policies that might be justified as reducing this harm. In this chapter I turn to the philosophical question of whether paternalistic arguments are the right *kind* of justification for laws that limit individual liberty.

Paternalistic policies are thought by some to be inherently wrong or illegitimate, a thought commonly expressed by the claim that it is not the government's business to protect us against ourselves. I reject this view. I believe that it is the government's business to make us better off than we would be without the government, and so to protect our interests and promote our welfare in ways that are consistent with fairness and respect for our rights. Because, in my view, some paternalistic policies protect our interests and promote our welfare within these constraints, it is the government's business to protect our interests and promote our welfare in these ways.

Some government paternalism is wrong. It is wrong for the government to prohibit a form of worship for the benefit of a person's immortal soul. It does not follow that all paternalism is wrong. When there is good reason for someone to prefer her situation with a law that limits her liberty in some way, and this reason has greater weight than anyone's reasons to want this law not to be in place, including her own, then this reason can justify the government in adopting this law. Because, in my view, this claim about reasons is true of some paternalistic prostitution laws, some paternalistic prostitution laws are morally justifiable.

It may be helpful to point out that in defending the justifiability of some forms of paternalism I am assuming an objective conception of individual interests. According to an objective conception, a person has an interest in something if and only if there is good reason for her to want it. What makes this conception objective is that there can be good reason for a person to want something that she does not actually want, and also good reason for her to want something even if she does not believe that there is any good reason for her to want it. According to a subjective conception of interests, in contrast, a person has an interest in something if and only if she *actually* wants it (or would want it if she had the relevant empirical information), regardless of whether there is any good reason for her to want it. In defending the permissibility of some kinds of paternalism I assume that an objective conception of individual interests is correct. In assuming this I believe that I am accepting what is now the dominant view in contemporary moral philosophy.

Opponents of paternalism commonly argue that one cannot consistently support one paternalistic policy without holding that some other more objectionable paternalistic policy is also justifiable. If paternalistic motorcycle helmet laws are justifiable, the antipaternalist contends, then paternalistic laws prohibiting mountain climbing must be justifiable too. This reasoning is fallacious. A paternalistic policy is justified only if the reasons for it outweigh the reasons against it. Because this might be true of one paternalistic policy and not true of any other, support for one paternalistic policy does not commit one to holding that any other paternalistic policy is justifiable. Nonetheless, many seem to be convinced by this argument against paternalism. So in this chapter I explain at length how one may consistently defend paternalistic prostitution laws without committing oneself to more objectionable forms of paternalism.

I start by endorsing a principle of liberty that rules out some of the paternalistic policies that defenders of individual liberty have found most objectionable. I then argue that although this principle rules out many objectionable forms of paternalism, it allows paternalistic prostitution laws in some form. Because one may consistently endorse this principle of liberty while supporting paternalistic prostitution laws, it is possible to defend paternalistic prostitution laws while taking a principled stand against other kinds of paternalism. After stating this principle of liberty, I address the general objection that paternalism violates personal autonomy and I address John Stuart Mill's well-known arguments against paternalism. I then address some specific objections to paternalistic prostitution laws that have been raised in the contemporary philosophical literature by Lars Ericsson, Martha Nussbaum, and David Richards. I conclude with further discussion of the antipaternalist slogan that it is not the government's business to protect us against ourselves.

I. Impermissible Paternalism

Although I defend paternalistic prostitution laws in some form, I accept the following general principle of antipaternalism: if (a) a person has achieved at least that degree of ability at prudential reasoning that we normally expect from a fully mature adult in our society, and if (b) a government policy limits the liberties or opportunities of this person in a way that he or she opposes, and if (c) the liberties or opportunities it limits are important ones for this person to have, and if (d) this person's wish to do what the policy prohibits or aims to discourage does not result from psychosis, acute emotional distress, or ignorance of grave demonstrable consequences, then the government may not adopt this policy unless this policy can be fully justified without counting any benefit to this person in its favor.

This principle does not provide a complete theory of liberty, because it permits laws that limit important liberties such as freedom of expression and freedom of worship provided that they can be justified as benefiting *others*. A complete theory of liberty must also identify constraints on the *non*paternalistic reasons that can justify the government in limiting a person's liberty. The principle of liberty just stated, however, does rule out some policies that liberal theorists have criticized as paternalistic. So it makes sense to regard this principle as *a* principle of antipaternalism. I will refer to it as *my* principle of antipaternalism, because there are other principles of antipaternalism, notably those of John Stuart Mill and Joel Feinberg.[1]

Consider a law that prohibits a form of worship on the ground that a person is better off when he rightly relates himself to God and this form of worship is not the right way to relate to God. Freedom of worship is an important liberty. So if the decision to worship in this way does not result from psychosis, acute emotional distress, or ignorance of grave demonstrable consequences, then, according to my principle of antipaternalism, a law that prohibits a mature person from worshipping in this way cannot be justified as benefiting him, if he opposes this law. If this law cannot be fully justified by other considerations, this policy is therefore ruled out by my principle of antipaternalism.

Consider a law that prohibits homosexual sodomy on the ground that a person is better off when he has only the right kinds of sexual relationship and homosexual relationships are not the right kind. Sexual freedom is an important liberty. So if the decision to have homosexual relationships does not result from psychosis, acute emotional distress, or ignorance of grave demonstrable consequences, then, according to my principle of antipaternalism, a law that prohibits a mature person from engaging in homosexual relations cannot be justified as benefiting him, if he opposes this law. If this law cannot be fully justified by other considerations, this policy is therefore ruled out by my principle of antipaternalism.

Although my principle of antipaternalism rules out some kinds of paternalism, it permits other kinds. Specifically, it permits some paternalistic prostitution laws. Neither abolitionist nor regulationist prostitution policies deprive their intended beneficiaries of liberties or opportunities that are important in the relevant sense. So neither policy is ruled out by this principle.

A liberty or opportunity is important in the sense referred to by my principle of antipaternalism only if at least one of the following conditions is met. First, this liberty or opportunity is necessary for a person to have adequate control over her own life or to have an adequate opportunity to shape the contours of her life according to her own judgment about what the best kind of life is for her to have. Second, this liberty or opportunity is necessary for informed deliberation about what is good or right or provides someone with a necessary incentive to deliberate about what is best and so plays a significant role in the development of this person's capacity for practical reasoning. Third, this liberty or opportunity functions to symbolize a person's status as an equal citizen or full member of society. Fourth, this liberty or opportunity is necessary for someone freely to engage in an activity that she needs to engage in to have a happy or successful life (as judged by some "objective list" of substantive goods).

To illustrate these four dimensions of importance, consider the freedom of an adult to marry the willing partner of her choice. This freedom is important, first, because control over one's marital status and over whom one marries is crucial to having control over one's life, to being able to determine the kind of life one has. Second, the opportunity to decide whether to marry and whom to marry motivates people to think about the kind of life they wish to lead and the kind of person they wish to be and so functions to develop the capacity for practical reasoning. Third, marital freedom symbolizes the status of adulthood and so full membership in our society. Finally, this freedom is important for some people because they would be very unhappy if prohibited from marrying the willing partner of his or her choice.

Given this understanding of importance, a paternalistic policy of *prohibition* might violate my principle of antipaternalism because the freedom to sell sexual services is arguably an important component of having adequate control over one's own life. Having the legal freedom to regulate one's own sex life by one's own values is an important element of having control over the kind of life one leads. In prohibiting a person from selling sex, the policy of prohibition prohibits one way in which a person might order her sex life by her own values and so diminishes the control she has over her sex life. As enforced against adult women who oppose this policy and who are aware of the potential negative consequences, the policy of prohibition is therefore arguably impermissible unless it can be fully justified as benefiting others—

those who are less mentally and emotionally mature, for example, or who want the government to adopt this policy.

Although a paternalistic policy of prohibition might violate my principle of antipaternalism on these grounds, a paternalistic policy of abolition or regulation would not. Consider the Swedish policy of abolition, which criminalizes the purchase, but not the sale, of sexual services. This policy does not prohibit anyone from selling sexual services. So it does not limit anyone's sexual autonomy in this way. It reduces opportunities to sell sexual services (on the assumption that it is effective), but these opportunities are not important in the relevant sense for the intended beneficiaries of this policy to have. Although the absence of legal penalties for the sale of sexual services is arguably essential to having adequate control of one's own body and sexuality, having *fewer opportunities* to sell sexual services is not essential in the same way. Nor does the lack of these opportunities prevent a person from shaping her life in accordance with her own judgment about what kind of life is best for her. Even under a policy of prohibition, a person might embrace the identity of sex worker and the attitudes toward her own body and toward sex that this involves and may publicly express and defend this identity to others, provided that these laws are not rigorously enforced. (See the discussion of Annie Sprinkle below.)

The lost opportunities for sex work are also not necessary for a person to develop her capacity for practical reasoning. Reading about sexual activities, watching films or television shows, reflecting on this information, and discussing it with others are generally sufficient to enable a person to reason about whether it would be good for her to engage in them. If a person needs to experiment with sex work in order to see what it is like and so whether it would be good for her to do, an abolitionist policy permits her to do this legally. In addition, having more opportunities for sex work is not symbolic of adulthood or equal citizenship in our society. Finally, these opportunities are not necessary for the intended beneficiaries of this policy to have a happy or successful life. The *intended beneficiaries* are those who would make choices in the absence of this policy that leave them *worse off* and that they would not make with this policy in place. The welfare of the intended beneficiaries is thus promoted and not reduced by their not having the opportunities to sell sexual services that they lose as a result of this abolitionist policy. So these opportunities are not important in the fourth way either.

Critics of prostitution laws commonly emphasize the value of the opportunities lost by pointing out that sex work provides important economic opportunities for poor women. These critics, however, tend to exaggerate the extent to which sex work is the "only option" within economically developed countries; the extent to which sex work leaves a person better off financially in these countries; and also the proportion of prostitutes in these countries who come from poor families. Some scholars argue that the majority of sex workers in economically developed countries such as Sweden, Great Britain, and the United States come from middle-class families.² Although sex work pays more than other entry-level occupations in the service industries of these countries, it does not typically leave a person in a better financial position than other forms of service work.³ Finally, in economically developed countries, there are plenty of alternatives to sex work. If sex work were the only means of providing food, shelter, and decent clothing to oneself or one's family, then the opportunities to do this work would be important. This may be true in some economically undeveloped countries or in some developed countries with depressed and stagnant economies. It is not the case, however, in thriving advanced postindustrial economies with large middle classes.

If the opportunities the intended beneficiaries of an abolitionist or impermissive regulationist policy lose as a result are not important for them to have in the relevant sense, then this policy does not violate my principle of antipaternalism, even if this policy cannot be justified other than as benefiting them. These opportunities may deprive *others* of opportunities that are important for them to have, particularly clients and sex workers for whom sex work is an advisable choice. So a complete defense of an abolitionist policy must argue that the loss of opportunities to these other persons can also be justified by the paternalistic argument. The limited claim here is that because the opportunities that the intended beneficiaries lose as a result of abolitionist policies and impermissive regulationist policies are not important *for them* to have—at least not in thriving postindustrial economies—these policies do not violate my principle of antipaternalism in economically advanced nations, and are therefore not objectionable in being *paternalistic*, though they might still be objectionable on other grounds.

II. Autonomy

Intelligent reflection on the permissibility of government paternalism must balance the following considerations. Our ability to reason soundly about what is best for us develops gradually, and it does not fully mature in most of us until well into adulthood. As a consequence, it is not unusual for persons who are older and wiser to have a better idea of what is good or bad for a young person than he or she does herself. Moreover, even as adults, our reasoning about what is best for us is imperfect. Sometimes we do not have all the information necessary to make a prudent decision, and sometimes we fail to give due weight to relevant considerations of which we are aware. This is true not only when we are mentally ill or emotionally distressed. Even when we are calm and mentally healthy, we make errors about what is best for us. On the other hand, it is very important that each of us exercises control over our own lives as adults, that we are able to shape the contours of our lives according to our own values, that we are able to experiment with different pursuits to see what brings us happiness, and that we are able to express our values to others by the kind of life we lead. This kind of control is important partly because we are more likely if we have it to discover what gives us satisfaction and enjoyment; but it is also intrinsically or nonderivatively valuable. It is good "for its own sake" that we live our own lives in our own ways and that our lives reflect our own beliefs about what is good and worth pursuing.

The principle of antipaternalism that I endorse seems valid to me because I believe it balances these considerations in the right way. In allowing paternalistic interference with the freedom of those who are immature, gravely uninformed, or mentally impaired, it gives due weight to the fact that our reasoning about what is best for us is often imperfect, and to the fact that acting on flawed judgments can be very bad for us. On the other hand, in prohibiting paternalistic interference with important liberties of those who are mature, well-informed, and mentally sound, and in prohibiting this even when the exercise of these liberties will, as a matter of fact, leave a person significantly worse off, this principle gives due weight to the importance of having control over our own lives as adults. It recognizes that our welfare or well-being is not the only value relevant to government policy, but that personal autonomy or control over one's own life is important too.

Not everyone, however, will agree that my principle of antipaternalism reflects the proper balance of these considerations. They might allow that a paternalistic policy is morally permissible *if* this policy can be fully justified as benefiting persons for whom at least one of the following is true: (1) they have not achieved that degree of ability at prudential reasoning that we normally expect from a fully mature adult in our society, (2) they want the government to adopt this policy, or (3) they choose to act in the relevant way only because they are ignorant of grave demonstrable consequences. My principle of antipaternalism, however, permits paternalistic interference even when one of these three conditions is not met. If the opportunities lost by the intended beneficiaries of a prostitution law are not *important* for them to have, then this policy does not violate this principle, and so is not objectionably paternalistic, although it may be objectionable on other grounds. For this reason, some will think that my principle of antipaternalism is too permissive.

To facilitate the following discussion, I now introduce the distinction, common in philosophical discussions, between *hard* and *soft* paternalism. *Hard paternalism*, as I will use the term here, refers to any policy of which the following is true: it limits a person's liberty or opportunities against his will, and this limitation cannot be justified unless its benefits to him are counted in its favor. An example would be a motorcycle helmet law that requires every motorcyclist to wear a helmet that can be justified only as benefiting informed adult motorcyclists who do not want to wear a helmet. *Soft paternalism*, in contrast, refers to any policy of which the following is true: it limits a person's liberty or opportunities in ways that cannot be justified unless its benefits to him are counted in its favor, but it does not limit his liberty or opportunities against his will or in any way that he opposes. An example would be a seat belt law that is justified as benefiting motorists who want this law because they believe that they should always wear a seat belt but that they will be adequately motivated to do so only with this law in place. Because the principle of antipaternalism that I endorse permits hard paternalistic interference with liberties and opportunities that are not important in the relevant sense, some will think it is too permissive. So I should explain why I believe that the hard paternalistic policies that this principle allows might be morally justifiable.

A common objection to hard paternalistic policies is that they violate, or limit, or interfere with, our autonomy. *Autonomy* has different meanings, but in discussions of paternalism, the central meaning seems to be personal control, personal authority, or personal discretion over what to believe and how to act. If so, the autonomy objection to hard paternalistic policies is that they deprive us of control over how to act and how to lead our own lives.

This, however, cannot be the whole story because most legal prohibitions deprive us of some degree of control, and we think that many of them are justifiable nonetheless. Speed limits, for example, deprive us of discretion over how fast to drive, and so of control over how fast we travel, and so of some control over our bodies, and so of some control over our lives. We nonetheless believe that speed limits are justified by their benefits in reducing our risk of being seriously injured. Furthermore, we believe that speed limits are justified even as enforced against the will of some—truckers, for example—who do not want these laws. The mere fact that a law limits a person's autonomy against his will does not therefore suffice to show that it is morally impermissible. Consequently, the mere fact that a hard paternalistic policy limits a person's autonomy against his will cannot alone explain why it is morally impermissible. If hard paternalism is always impermissible, there must be another reason why.

Antipaternalists seem to believe that a due respect for personal autonomy requires the government to permit mature adults to do as they think best unless their decisions negatively impact others. If so, the government would disrespect a person's autonomy if it were to engage in hard paternalism, but not if it were to limit a person's autonomy against his will for the benefit of others. Why should anyone believe, though, that paternalistic limitations of personal autonomy are inherently more disrespectful of autonomy than nonpaternalistic limitations? A due respect for personal autonomy requires the government to secure, if possible, liberties and opportunities that are necessary for individuals to exercise adequate control over their lives, that are necessary to deliberate well about what is good and right, and that function to symbolize equal and full membership in the adult community. The government must therefore recognize and seek to protect to the greatest feasible extent liberties and opportunities that are important in three of the four ways listed above. A due respect for personal autonomy does not, however, require the government to recognize and protect to the same degree liberties and opportunities that are not important in these ways. Because, then, not all hard paternalistic policies deprive people of liberties or opportunities that are important in these ways, it is puzzling that anyone should think that they all disrespect personal autonomy.

A government policy disrespects a person's autonomy, in my view, only if this person has a valid complaint against the substance of this policy or against the process through which it was adopted. Assuming for the sake of argument that a policy is adopted through a defensible political process, this policy disrespects a person's autonomy only if he or she has a valid complaint against its substance. A person has a valid complaint against the substance of a government policy only if the reasons there are for her to prefer her situation without this policy in place outweigh the reasons there are for anyone to prefer his or her situation with this policy in place. I believe that this is true whenever the conditions (a)–(d) of my principle of antipaternalism are satisfied. When one of these conditions is not satisfied, however, the reasons for someone to prefer her situation with a policy in place might outweigh the reasons there are for her to prefer her situation without this policy *even if this policy limits her liberty or opportunities in ways that she opposes.* If they do, this person has no valid complaint against this policy. If she has no valid complaint against this policy, it does not disrespect her autonomy.

To elaborate, there is a reason for the government *not* to limit a liberty or opportunity if there is good reason for a person to prefer her situation when this liberty or opportunity is not limited. On the other hand, there is a reason for the government to *limit* a liberty or opportunity if there is good reason for a person to prefer her situation when this liberty or opportunity *is* limited by the government. Reasons for a person to prefer her situation when the government does not limit her liberty do not always have greater weight than the reasons for a person to prefer her situation when the government does limit her liberty. There is no general priority of liberty. Liberty is an important value, but it is not the only one. So although the reasons for people to prefer their situations when they are legally free to do something often do outweigh their reasons to prefer their situations when they are not legally free to do this thing, this is not always the case. Sometimes paternalistic reasons for the government to limit a liberty outweigh all the reasons against limiting it. In this case, paternalistic interference is justifiable and so respects a person's autonomy.

The paternalistic argument for prostitution laws is that prostitution causes lasting harm to those who do it and that these policies reduce this harm by reducing prostitution. If so, there is good reason for some people to prefer their situations with these policies in place: those who would do more of this work to their lasting detriment in the absence of these policies. Individuals also have reasons to value their autonomy, or their ability to control and shape their own lives according to their own values, and so to prefer their situations when the government does not limit their liberty or opportunities in ways that make this more difficult to do. In some cases these reasons of autonomy outweigh a person's reasons of welfare to prefer her situation when her liberty or opportunities are limited. This is the case when the liberties or opportunities are important in the relevant sense, even when having these liberties or opportunities makes it more likely that she will be significantly injured in some way. This is not always the case, however, when the liberty or opportunities that a person loses as a result of this policy are not important for her to have in any of the relevant senses, and when there are significant reasons for her to prefer her situation without them. If the empirical assumptions of the paternalistic rationale for prostitution laws are sound, then there are good reasons for some women to prefer their situations without the opportunities they lose as a result of abolitionist and impermissive regulationist policies. These opportunities are not important in the relevant sense for the intended beneficiaries of these policies to have. Consequently, the reasons for some of the intended beneficiaries of these policies to prefer their situations with these policies in place outweigh their reasons of autonomy to prefer their situation without them. These beneficiaries therefore do not have a valid complaint against these policies, and the kind of paternalism that these policies involve does not disrespect their autonomy.

Some may object that all this talk about the *weight* of reasons misses the point. Perhaps it is true, they might say, that paternalistic reasons are not always *outweighed* by whatever reasons there are for a person to value liberty. They are nonetheless invalid. They are invalid, not in being outweighed by the value of autonomy, but in being *blocked*, *silenced*, or *canceled* by it. A due respect for autonomy, some may think, entails a categorical exclusion of paternalistic reasons. This is why paternalism is always wrong.

This position is coherent, as far as I can tell, but I find it implausible. Furthermore, I find it implausible for the same reason that I find implausible other categorical exclusions of reasons that most of us would dismiss out of hand. Consider, for example, the extreme libertarian position that reasons of fairness, equality, and human welfare for the government to provide everyone, via redistributive taxation, with an adequate education and with adequate health care are *silenced* by the value of personal autonomy, and so have *no moral weight at all* as reasons for redistributive taxation. Or consider the extreme anarchist position that the reasons of safety and security for the government to prohibit murder, assault, and theft are *silenced* by the value of personal autonomy, and so have *no moral weight at all* as reasons for the criminal law. As far as I can tell, these positions are also coherent, but they are extremely implausible. They are implausible because they give undue priority to the value of freedom from government interference and do not give nearly enough moral weight to other important values. The position that paternalistic reasons are categorically excluded because silenced by the value of autonomy strikes me as implausible in the same way.

One might argue that there is an important difference between the extreme anarchist and extreme libertarian positions that I have just considered and the extreme antipaternalist position that holds that all paternalistic reasons are silenced by autonomy. Because a person's autonomy is reduced by being murdered, assaulted, and stolen from, the government must prevent this kind of wrongdoing if it is to protect autonomy. And because a person must have adequate education and health care in order to be fully autonomous, the redistributive taxation necessary to provide everyone with adequate education and health care is also necessary to promote autonomy. No argument of this kind, one might think, can be given to explain why paternalistic reasons are legitimate. This, however, is false. People cannot exercise autonomy unless they are alive and have a functioning brain. So paternalistic policies that prohibit suicide and riding a motorcycle without a helmet are likewise necessary to promote autonomy. Once one allows that autonomy is sometimes protected or promoted by limiting individual liberty, there is no reason to suppose that it can be protected or promoted only on nonpaternalistic grounds, and never on paternalistic ones.[4]

An antipaternalist might now suggest that respect for autonomy requires the government to follow principles that afford *maximum* autonomy. Because, he might suppose, a person's autonomy is reduced by his being wronged, the government must prevent wrongdoing if it is to maximize autonomy. Any limitation of liberty, however, beyond what is necessary to prevent wrongdoing, results in a loss of autonomy, and is therefore incompatible with a due respect for autonomy. This on its own does not rule out paternalism because it is arguable that a person wrongs himself when he acts self-destructively. If, however, the *volenti non fit iniuria* maxim is valid—to one who consents no wrong is done—it seems to follow that paternalism disrespects autonomy.

This particular explanation, however, of why paternalism is wrong rules out criminal penalties that many of us think are perfectly justifiable. Consider the New York law prohibiting bakeries from employing bakers for more than sixty hours a week that was struck down by the U.S. Supreme Court in the notorious *Lochner v. New York* decision.[5] The purpose of this law was to protect bakers' health on the assumption that working longer hours in a bakery is unhealthy. An adult, however, works in a bakery voluntarily unless he works there as the direct result of threats of physical harm from another person or as a result of ignorance of the nature of his act. Assuming, then, that the New York bakers were not threatened with violence and knew what they were doing, they were not *wronged* by the bakery owners in working more than sixty hours a week—not if the volenti maxim is valid. Consequently, if criminal penalties can be justified only as preventing wrongdoing, and the volenti maxim is valid, New York was not justified in adopting this policy. Many of us believe to the contrary, that it was justified in adopting it.

To this one might respond that the bakery owners *did* wrong the bakers in employing them for more than sixty hours a week, even though the bakers consented. If so, however, then the volenti maxim is not valid and cannot explain what is wrong with paternalism. Furthermore, if it is possible for one person to wrong another by engaging in an exchange to which they both consent, then prostitution laws might be defended on the same grounds. One might argue that sex workers are wronged by their customers and by the third-party entrepreneurs who facilitate this work even though the sex workers consent to do it. Finally, if it is possible to wrong another person by engaging in a transaction to which both consent, it is puzzling why we should assume that a person cannot wrong himself. Why not suppose instead that I can wrong myself by voluntarily engaging in harmful or reckless behavior, and that paternalism is therefore justified as preventing this kind of wrongdoing?

Rather than insisting, though, that a person can be wronged by her own voluntary actions or by exchanges to which she consents, it seems better to defend both the New York bakers' law and prostitution laws by rejecting the premise that a due respect for individual autonomy permits only criminal penalties that can be justified as preventing wrongdoing. Criminal penalties can also be justified as protecting individuals' interests provided that three conditions are met: (1) these interests are important, (2) the penalties are necessary to protect these interests and are proportional in gravity to the harm they seek to deter, and (3) these interests are not outweighed by any autonomy interests that this policy threatens. Assuming that the New York bakers' hours law met these conditions, this policy was therefore compatible with a due respect for individual autonomy. If a prostitution law also meets these conditions, then the paternalism it involves is likewise compatible with a due respect for autonomy.

Some may conclude that I simply do not understand what respect for autonomy involves. My example of the New York bakers' law might be unconvincing to them not because they think that this law was consistent with respect for autonomy, but because they think this law was obviously inconsistent with respect for autonomy. I think the New York law did not disrespect the bakers' autonomy, but others may disagree. How should we proceed in the face of this kind of philosophical disagreement?

In the face of irresolvable philosophical disagreement, it is tempting to try to place the burden of proof on those we disagree with, but this temptation should be resisted. There are two different ways to understand the idea that someone bears the burden of proof in a philosophical argument, and neither of them is sound. First, one might hold that if a person cannot prove that his philosophical position is correct, and this position seems incorrect to us, then we are justified in rejecting it. Second, one might hold that if a person cannot prove to us that his philosophical position is correct, then *he* is not justified in accepting it. Both claims are false. What justifies us in holding a philosophical position is (a) that the reasons in its favor seem to us to outweigh the reasons against it; (b) that this judgment about reasons is consistent with the other judgments about reasons that we make; and (c) that this judgment about reasons remains stable under our critical scrutiny. Even if someone else cannot prove that a position is true, and even if this position seems false to us, we might not be justified in rejecting this position because we might not have thought enough about this position or because our rejection of it is inconsistent with other things we believe. So the first claim regarding the burden of proof is incorrect. And because a person might be justified in this way in holding a philosophical position even if he cannot prove that it is true, the second claim is also incorrect.

From this conception of philosophical justification it follows that one person might be justified in believing that paternalism is consistent with respect for autonomy, whereas another is justified in believing that it is not. I recognize this possibility and because I believe that the antipaternalist position is internally coherent, I do not aim to demonstrate that no one is justified in holding it. My aim is less ambitious than this. It is to explain how someone might be justified in holding the contrary position, that paternalism is permissible and consistent with due respect for autonomy. I explain this by stating the judgments about reasons that support this position and by showing how this judgment about reasons is consistent with other judgments that others and I make about the value of personal autonomy and the importance of individual liberty.

III. Defining Paternalism

I have just explained why I do not believe that all hard paternalism disrespects personal autonomy. I have not yet defined paternalism, however, or explained precisely the way in which prostitution laws are, or might be, paternalistic. I have avoided this because I have yet to find an entirely satisfactory definition.[6]

According to one possible definition, a government policy is paternalistic if and only if it violates a valid principle of antipaternalism. To illustrate, suppose that the following principle of antipaternalism is valid, which Mill appears to have endorsed: the government may not limit a person's liberty against his will unless this policy can be justified as preventing harm to others.[7] If this principle of antipaternalism is valid, then, according to this definition of paternalism, a policy is paternalistic if and only if this policy limits a person's liberty against his will and it cannot be justified as preventing harm to others.

It would be odd, however, to characterize as paternalistic every policy that satisfies this definition. This because the term *paternalism* is commonly used to refer only to policies that are *motivated* by paternalistic concern,[8] and this definition makes no reference to motive. To illustrate, imagine a general twenty-five mph speed limit on the interstate highways. Suppose a legislature adopts this policy because its members mistakenly believe that this policy is justified by the good of protecting each driver from the safety risks posed by other drivers. Suppose that this policy cannot in fact be justified in this way because its benefits in traffic safety are decisively outweighed by its enormous costs in efficiency and convenience. Suppose, then, that Jones opposes this policy. It follows that this policy limits Jones's liberty to drive faster against his will and it cannot be justified as preventing harm to others. This policy is therefore paternalistic according to the above definition. Because, however, the legislature does not adopt this policy to protect drivers against themselves but only to protect them from other drivers, it seems inaccurate to characterize this policy as paternalistic, because none of the legislators is paternalistically motivated.

From this one might conclude that a policy should be characterized as *paternalistic* if and only if it is motivated by paternalistic concern. This motivational definition of paternalism also has odd consequences, though. Imagine that the government prohibits drunken driving solely in order to prevent drunk drivers from harming themselves, but that this policy can in fact be fully justified as protecting other persons from being harmed by drunk drivers. Is this policy therefore paternalistic? The *motives* of those who support it are paternalistic, but why is the *policy* paternalistic, given that the system of rules that constitute this policy can be fully justified by nonpaternalistic reasons?

These puzzles may lead one to favor a hybrid characterization of paternalism that combines claims about motive and justification. Here is one example of this kind of approach: a government policy is paternalistic toward S if and only if (a) this policy limits S's choices by deterring S from choosing to perform an action or by making it more difficult for S to perform it; (b) S prefers S's own situation when S's choices are not limited in this way; (c) the government has this policy only because those in the relevant political process believe or once believed that this policy will benefit S in some way; and (d) this policy cannot be fully justified without counting its benefits to S in its favor. According to this definition, a policy is paternalistic only if it is motivated by paternalistic concern, but it is not paternalistic if it can be fully justified by nonpaternalistic reasons. In this way, this account avoids both of the odd consequences just identified.

Not everyone, however, will be satisfied with this particular definition. For one thing, it seems the government might act paternalistically in *creating* options or by *increasing* choices, and not only by *limiting* them. Imagine that the government makes free psychotherapy available to gay people to help them change their sexual orientation, and that it does this with the aim of helping them to lead happier, more satisfying lives, and that this policy cannot be justified in any other way. Some might think that if the intended beneficiaries do not want this policy, then it is objectionably paternalistic even if it does not, strictly speaking, *limit* anyone's choices. Others might think that a policy could be paternalistic toward a person even if he or she wants it. Imagine someone who wants the government to make his marital decisions for him because he thinks he is unlikely on his own to choose a suitable mate. This policy is arguably paternalistic, even though this person wants the government to adopt it, in virtue of the parental role that the government would thereby play in guiding this person's life.

These two objections might be addressed by reformulating the definition of paternalism. It is doubtful, though, that any definition of paternalism will match *all* of our intuitions because we have different and conflicting intuitions about what policies are paternalistic. For this reason I will not attempt to define paternalism in a way that satisfies everyone. Instead, I will offer a definition that clarifies how I use the term in the following discussion. As I use the term, a *paternalistic policy* is one that satisfies the following description: the strongest reasons in its favor are paternalistic, and it cannot be justified by nonpaternalistic reasons. A *paternalistic reason* for a policy is any reason for a policy that satisfies the following description: the policy limits a person's liberty or opportunities in some way, and this reason identifies some way in which this person is benefited by this limitation.

This definition of paternalism will strike some as inadequate because it makes no reference to motive. This, however, is not a decisive objection to my using the term *paternalistic* in this way here. For reasons given in the previous chapter, the motives that cause the government to adopt a policy are not generally relevant to assessing whether the government is justified in having this policy. What is relevant is whether the strongest reasons in its favor can actually justify it. It is possible that the strongest reasons against legalizing prostitution are paternalistic in the sense just defined. It is also possible that none of the nonpaternalistic arguments can justify abolitionist or impermissive regulationist policies. If so, then these policies are paternalistic in the sense just identified. Because some may believe that polices that are paternalistic in this sense are wrong, it is important to explain why this is not true if one wishes to defend these policies on these grounds.

Although I freely use the terms *paternalism* and *paternalistic*, they are admittedly problematic. One reason is that it is difficult to find a definition that matches everyone's intuitions. Another reason is that the terms have negative connotations. The notion that the relationship between a citizen and his government is properly modeled on the relationship between a child and his parents is offensive to many of us, as is the suggestion that it is appropriate for the government and other adults to treat us as though we were children, not to mention the suggestion that the father is the proper seat of parental authority within the family. When a person criticizes a policy as paternalistic he takes advantage of all these negative connotations. I suspect that these terms were invented for rhetorical purposes by those who wanted to discredit certain government policies that they opposed. These are all good reasons to avoid these terms. Nonetheless, they are commonly used within political philosophy and have an accepted, if vague, meaning. They are used to refer to certain kinds of government policy, in order to raise theoretical questions about individual liberty and the kinds of reasons that can justify the government in limiting it. Because this book seeks to address these questions, it makes sense to continue to use these terms here.

Because *paternalism* and *paternalistic* have such negative connotations, some may assume that it is necessary to show that prostitution laws are *not* paternalistic in order to defend them. If this were the case, then a great deal would depend on how paternalism is defined. To defend prostitution laws, one would have to fight over definitions and argue that according to the "best" definition, prostitution laws are not paternalistic. This battle is best avoided. What matters is not whether prostitution laws are paternalistic according to some definition. What matters is whether prostitution laws are justifiable as benefiting those who would otherwise be harmed by doing prostitution. In defining *paternalistic policies* above, I have identified a way in which prostitution laws are (or might be) paternalistic. My claim is that being paternalistic in this way is not in itself a decisive objection to a policy. If we agree to use *paternalism* and *paternalistic* simply as descriptive terms that pick out certain kinds of justifications or policies, we need not be misled by the negative connotations into thinking that every argument or policy to which these terms properly apply is morally objectionable.

Note, too, that when I stated my principle of antipaternalism above, and claimed that some prostitution laws are permitted this principle, I was not offering a *definition* of paternalism. I was not arguing that, according to this definition, prostitution laws are not paternalistic. Rather, I was identifying a principle of liberty, which I endorse, that rules out certain policies that might be paternalistic according to the definition just given, but that does not rule out all such policies. If a policy is permitted by this principle, then, although it might be paternalistic, it is not *objectionably* paternalistic if the strongest reasons in its favor can justify it.

IV. Mill's Principle

Mill famously asserts in *On Liberty* that "the only purpose for which power can be rightfully exercised over any member of a civilized community, against his will, is to prevent harm to others. His own good, either physical or moral, is not a sufficient warrant."[9] Although Mill characterizes this as "one very simple principle,"[10] at least three separate claims are implicit in it. First, that society is never justified in limiting a person's liberty against his will unless this is necessary to prevent someone from being *harmed*. Second, that society is never justified in limiting a person's liberty against his will by the fact that this will prevent *him* from being harmed. Third, that society is *sometimes* justified in limiting a person's liberty against his will by the fact that this will prevent *others* from being harmed. In the next section I consider Mill's main arguments for this principle, in order to see whether they provide good reason to think that paternalistic prostitution laws are unjustifiable. First, though, I want to question whether every paternalistic prostitution law is ruled out by Mill's principle. Because Mill's principle of liberty is commonly taken to be a principle of antipaternalism, it may seem obvious that paternalistic prostitution laws are ruled out by it. This is not so obvious, however, when we examine the details of Mill's principle, the details of my paternalistic argument, and the details of different kinds of prostitution law.

Mill's principle of liberty entails that the government is never justified in limiting a person's "liberty of action" against her will by the fact that this policy will protect her from harm.[11] Neither abolitionist nor regulationist policies, however, directly limit the *liberty of action* of would-be prostitutes, because they do not prohibit anyone from performing sex work or impose any penalties for doing so. These policies directly limit the liberty of action only of clients and third parties with a business interest in facilitating sex work. It does so not for *their* own good, but for the good of those who would be harmed by doing this work. So Mill's principle arguably permits these policies.

Perhaps this conclusion rests on an overly narrow construal of *liberty*. Assuming that abolitionist and impermissive regulationist policies will function as intended, they will reduce the opportunities of women to perform sex work, and so restrict their liberty in this sense. One might think the government "exercises power over" a person it if reduces her opportunities against her will. If so, and this policy cannot be justified as benefiting others, it arguably violates Mill's principle of liberty even if it does not directly prohibit her from doing anything.

It remains the case that prostitution laws violate Mill's principle only if they limit the opportunities of would-be sex workers *against their will*. This might not be the case. Most girls probably do not have a clear opinion as to whether or not prostitution should be legal when they start to do it. Moreover, some prostitutes believe that it ought to be illegal to purchase sexual services precisely because they believe that prostitution is bad for the women who do it.[12] To be sure, other prostitutes believe that prostitution should be fully decriminalized. It does not follow, though, that abolitionist or impermissive regulationist policies violate Mill's principle because these policies might be fully justified as benefiting not those who believe it ought to be fully decriminalized, but only as benefiting *others* who do not think so.[13]

Perhaps a comment is in order about why it seems necessary to include the "against their will" qualification in the first place. Consider the New York law, struck down in *Lochner*, prohibiting bakers from working more than sixty hours a week in a bakery. The purpose of this law was to protect bakers' health on the assumption that working longer hours in a bakery is unhealthy. The bakers could have refused to work longer hours, but they would then have risked being fired. This legislation was therefore necessary to protect the bakers' health while protecting their jobs. Assuming that it was adopted for this reason, it was adopted for the good of New York bakers. Clearly, though, this policy reduced the bakers' opportunities to work longer hours. If it is wrong, then, for the government to adopt policies that reduce a person's opportunities for his own good, this legislation was wrong. Few of us believe it was. Assuming, though, that the New York law was desired by the bakers it was intended to benefit, this policy is permitted by Mill's principle because this principle rules out only policies that are adopted for a person's benefit *against his will*.

Some policies, however, that limit a person's liberty for his own good against his will *are* compatible with Mill's principle. This is because, right after first stating this principle, Mill makes clear that it is "meant to apply only to human beings in the maturity of their faculties."[14] If a prostitution law could be fully justified as benefiting girls and young women who have not yet achieved this degree of maturity, this policy would therefore be consistent with Mill's principle even if it limits their liberty against their will.

Some might think that Mill's maturity qualification implies only that his principle of liberty does not apply to legal minors. Interpreted in this way, it would not permit prostitution laws that could be justified only as protecting girls and women above the legal age of sexual consent and of legal employment.[15] This, however, is not the only possible interpretation. The maturity qualification might be interpreted instead to mean that Mill's principle applies only to those who are *actually* in the maturity of their faculties: only to those who have developed a reliable capacity to reason soundly about what is best for them. This interpretation is supported by what Mill goes on to say about "those backward states of society in which the race may itself be considered in its nonage."[16] Although there are legal adults in such states of society, Mill makes clear that his principle is not to be applied to them. Why? Presumably because despite their biological maturity they have not achieved enough practical wisdom to be immune from justifiable paternalism.

A more demanding interpretation of maturity is supported, too, by reflection on the considerations that warrant the maturity exception in the first place. Why should children and other legal minors not be as free from paternalistic interference as legal adults? The only plausible answer is that children and other legal minors have not developed a reliable capacity to reason soundly about what is best for them. Because we do not automatically gain prudential wisdom on any particular birthday—sixteen, eighteen, or twenty-one—there is no reason to suppose that any of these ages should mark a sharp cutoff point as to when paternalistic interference ceases to be morally justifiable. Moreover, when the activities at issue are as psychologically and socially complex as sex is, it is doubtful that most of us achieve the relevant degree of maturity until well into our twenties, if then. Once we understand the normative basis of Mill's maturity qualification, it is thus arguable that some prostitution laws are compatible with Mill's principle even if they can be justified only as protecting women above the legal age of sexual consent and even if they provide this protection *against their will*.

These observations reveal that paternalistic abolitionist and regulationist policies are ruled out by Mill's principle of antipaternalism only on some assumptions that might be questioned: (1) that these policies limit the *liberty* in the relevant sense of those they are intended to benefit, (2) that these policies restrict their liberty against their will, and (3) that those these policies are intended to benefit are in the maturity of their faculties. If any of these assumptions is false, these policies do not violate Mill's principle, even if they cannot be justified by any nonpaternalistic argument.

The fundamental normative question, though, is not whether prostitution laws are compatible with Mill's principle; it is whether they are morally justifiable. Perhaps an abolitionist or strong regulationist policy can be forced to fit within the parameters set by Mill's principle. It might still involve an objectionable form of paternalism, because Mill's principle might be too permissive. On the other hand, even if a prostitution law violates Mill's principle, the paternalism it involves might be permissible, because Mill's principle might be too restrictive. The fundamental question here is whether the kind of paternalism that prostitution laws involve is morally objectionable. I now explain why I do not think Mill gave any good reason to think so.

V. Mill's Arguments

Mill apparently believed that his principle of antipaternalism could be grounded on the principle of utility he endorsed in *Utilitarianism*.[17] Many have puzzled since about how any general principle of antipaternalism could be warranted by the principle of utility. A utilitarian legislator should, it seems, always evaluate whether or not to support a coercive law by considering whether happiness will be promoted most effectively by the presence of this law or by its absence. If happiness will be promoted most effectively by a coercive policy, a utilitarian legislator should support it; if happiness will be most effectively promoted by the absence of this policy, he should oppose it. Understood in this way, the principle of utility contains no bias against paternalism. If a person's happiness will be increased by a law that limits his liberty against his will, this fact should be counted in favor of this law, just as the fact should be counted in its favor that this law will increase the happiness of others. Mill's principle of antipaternalism, which directs legislators not to count in favor of a law the proposition that this law will make a person better off when this law limits this person's liberty against his will, thus appears to be inconsistent with the principle of utility when employed as a principle of legislative deliberation.

A solution to this puzzle is suggested by what Mill himself calls the strongest argument for his principle: "The strongest of all arguments against the interference of the public with purely personal conduct is that, when it does interfere, the odds are that it interferes wrongly and in the wrong place."[18] Because those in government know less about an individual's situation than he himself does and because those in government care less about an individual's welfare than he himself does, those in government are less likely than he is to have true beliefs about what is best for him.[19] When a law limits a person's liberty against his will, a legislator is therefore unlikely to be correct in believing that this law makes this person better off, and is therefore not warranted in supporting it for this reason. Mill's principle of antipaternalism is thus warranted by utilitarianism, when taken as a principle of legislative deliberation, because no legislator should count in favor of a law a proposition about a person's welfare that this legislator is not justified in believing.

The obvious weakness in this argument is that a legislator might in fact be justified in believing that a person will be benefited by a law that limits his liberty against his will. To illustrate, consider the paternalistic argument for the Swedish policy of abolition. Suppose that the intended beneficiaries of this policy include girls and young women who are not yet in the maturity of their faculties or those who, although in the maturity of their faculties, do not actually oppose this policy. Suppose, though, that this policy can be fully justified via utilitarian reasoning only by also counting in its favor benefits to some women who are in the maturity of their faculties and who oppose this policy. It seems that a legislator might be justified in believing that these women are also benefited by this policy by the following course of reflection: There is good reason, provided by the kind of research that Hoigard and Finstad present,[20] to believe that sex work harms young women who are not yet in the full maturity of their faculties. There is no reason to believe that sex work ceases to be harmful the moment a person attains the relevant degree of maturity. Nor is there any reason to conclude from the fact that someone opposes an abolitionist policy that she is not actually harmed in similar ways by prostitution. After all, a person might oppose this policy for all sorts of bad reasons, reasons that do not reflect a sound assessment of the negative impact of prostitution on her own welfare. Assuming, then, that a legislator is justified in believing that abolitionist policies benefit young women who are not yet in the maturity of their faculties or who do not oppose this policy, it seems that a legislator might likewise be justified in believing that it also benefits some women who are in the maturity of their faculties and who do oppose it. Because this kind of reasoning might be perfectly sound, Mill's "strongest argument" does not seem very strong.

Mill's strongest argument, however, is not his only one. Immediately after declaring that his defense of liberty will appeal only to considerations of utility, Mill adds, "but it must be utility in the largest sense, grounded on the permanent interests of man as a progressive being."[21] Mill is not explicit about which interests these are, but it is reasonable to surmise from what he writes in *Utilitarianism* and elsewhere in *On Liberty* that he means our interests in fully developing and exercising our *higher faculties*—our capacities for theoretical and practical reasoning, our capacities for friendship, artistic creation and aesthetic appreciation, spiritual understanding and growth—and so in the social conditions necessary for full human development.[22] These interests will not be optimally promoted or protected over time, Mill suggests, unless society observes his principle of antipaternalism.

Mill evidently feared that popular majorities will legislate their moral prejudices unless they observe this principle, and that the legislation of moral prejudices will stifle human individuality.[23] In Mill's view, individuality—or uniqueness in personality or way of life—is both a constitutive part of and a necessary means to full human development.[24] Without developing individuality, Mill thought, individuals would not fully develop as human beings because the potential for individuality is a distinctive human capacity, one that distinguishes us from other animals. Mill also believed that the full development and exercise of our higher human capacities for reasoning, aesthetic discrimination, and spiritual experience, among others, requires the development of individuality, because we will not develop and exercise these capacities fully unless we do so in the ways best suited to our particular talents and temperaments.[25] We will not develop our talents for music fully, for example, unless we listen to and play the kinds of music we most enjoy. If paternalistic policies stifle human individuality, they thereby threaten the conditions for full human development.

Mill's concern with human development does not, however, provide a convincing basis for opposing all paternalistic prostitution laws. The paternalistic argument for these laws presented in chapter 1 implies that they *promote* human development by deterring a kind of work that hinders it. If so, prostitution laws arguably result in a *net gain* for human development.

Some might argue that prostitution laws undermine human development because they extinguish a valuable kind of individuality. It is doubtful, though, that either abolitionist or impermissive regulationist policies would have this effect. Let us grant for the sake of argument that some sex work develops and expresses a certain kind of individuality, and that this kind of individuality would be stifled if all sex work were effectively repressed. Complete repression is impossible in a free society. The most that prostitution laws can do is to significantly reduce the amount of prostitution. Would this reduction in prostitution constitute a significant threat to human individuality and so to human development? To appreciate just how unlikely this is, consider Annie Sprinkle, an American sex worker who operates a Web page advocating a "sex-positive" attitude toward sex work.[26] Although sex work is prohibited in most of the United States, Annie Sprinkle publicly defends sex work as a legitimate career choice and is apparently able to find willing clients. In this way she develops her individuality, by inventing, maintaining, and expressing an unconventional persona on the Internet. If the kind of individuality that Annie Sprinkle exemplifies is possible where prostitution is *prohibited*, it will not be extinguished by abolitionist or regulationist policies.

Some might respond that any form of paternalism necessarily stunts a person's development by "taking his power of choice away from him." No coercive policy, however, can literally take a person's power of choice away from him unless it destroys his mental capacities. Some might argue that paternalistic policies are nonetheless objectionable in expressing the insulting view that adults are like children. Soft paternalistic policies, however, do not express this view, and hard paternalistic policies do not necessarily express it either. Both kinds of policy necessarily express only the unobjectionable view that our prudential reasoning is imperfect. And even if every paternalistic policy did express the insulting message to some adults that they are like children, this expression alone would not undermine anyone's development. If the government were to take charge of a person's life in the same way a parent takes care of a child, his development might be undermined, because this might weaken his motivation to direct his own life, either by making it less important to his own welfare to do so or by leading him to believe that he is not competent to direct his own life in this way. No government, however, takes charge of a person's life in this way simply by enacting an abolitionist or regulationist policy on prostitution, however insulting these policies might appear to be.

Some might now argue that observance of Mill's principle is nonetheless necessary to secure the social conditions necessary for human development, because without a general recognition of a principle prohibiting all forms of paternalism these social conditions will be precarious. This, however, is also doubtful. Securing the social conditions necessary for individuality and so for full human development might require general observance of a principle that prohibits all paternalistic interference in *certain areas of conduct*, such as the expression of ideas, religious practice, and noncommercial sexual activity. It is perfectly possible, though, to frame a principle of antipaternalism that rules out paternalistic interference in these areas but permits paternalism in other areas. Imagine, for example, a principle that prohibits paternalism in all areas except traffic safety, drug use, and worker health and safety. Such a principle would presumably protect "the permanent interests of man as a progressive being" *at least* as well as a principle that prohibits *all* forms of paternalism. Consequently, there is no reason to believe that general observance of a principle that prohibits *all* forms of paternalism is necessary to secure the social conditions necessary for human development.

Some might respond that a principle prohibiting all forms of paternalism is nonetheless necessary because there is no principled basis on which to draw distinctions between different kinds of paternalism. Mill himself suggests this where he writes, "The people of all southern Europe look upon a married clergy as not only irreligious, but unchaste, indecent, gross, disgusting. What do Protestants think of these perfectly sincere feelings, and of the attempt to enforce them against non-Catholics? Yet, if mankind are justified in interfering with each other's liberty in things which do not concern the interests of others, on what principle is it possible consistently to exclude these cases?"[27] Evidently it did not occur to Mill that one might exclude these cases on the grounds that freedom of worship and marital choice are especially important liberties. Nor evidently did it occur to him that one might exclude these cases on the grounds that mere prejudice fails to constitute a good reason for a coercive government policy, whether or not the policy seems paternalistic. In any case, this argument against paternalism is unconvincing.

To see why, apply the same form of reasoning to *non*paternalistic government policies. Imagine an anarchist arguing with Mill as follows: "You hold that the government may sometimes interfere with a person's liberty against his will in order to protect *others* from harm. There is, however, no principled basis on which to distinguish permissible harm-to-others-preventing policies from impermissible ones. Assuming, then, that *some* harm-to-others-preventing policies are impermissible—that it is impermissible, for example, to prohibit everyone from driving to prevent people from being injured by others—the government must observe a general principle prohibiting *all* harm-to-others-preventing policies including laws against murder, theft, and assault." This argument is unpersuasive because it rests on two wholly unwarranted assumptions: first, that if there is a good harm-to-others argument for *one* policy that limits a person's liberty against his will, there is a harm-to-others argument that is at least as good for *every* policy that limits a person's liberty against his will; and second, that if there is no decisive objection to *one* policy that limits a person's liberty against his will, there is no decisive objection to *any* policy that does so. In reality, harm-to-others arguments have different weight where different liberties are concerned, and individuals have objections of different weight to different policies that limit their liberty in different ways. Because this is equally true of harm-to-self arguments, it is no more difficult to defend the permissibility of some paternalistic policies without committing oneself to the permissibility of all.

VI. Other Paternalistic Policies

Even if it is possible to make principled distinctions between permissible and impermissible paternalism, the following remains true: if one kind of paternalism is permissible, then not all paternalism is impermissible; if not all paternalism is impermissible, then it is likely that more than one paternalistic policy is justifiable. If a number of paternalistic policies are justifiable, then the permissibility of paternalism might seem to entail that the government would be justified in adopting all of them. This raises the Millian concern that individuality will be stifled if the government adopts *all* the paternalistic policies that it would be justified in adopting if paternalism were permissible.

The permissibility of paternalism, however, does not entail that the government would be justified in adopting all the policies that could be justified if paternalism is permissible. This is because the cumulative negative impact of adopting n paternalistic policies might make adopting the nth paternalistic policy unjustifiable even though the government would be justified in adopting this paternalistic policy on its own. If the cumulative negative impact on individuality, human development, or personal autonomy is sufficiently great when the government adopts *all* the policies that might be justified if paternalism is permissible, the government would therefore not be justified in adopting all of these paternalistic policies, even if paternalism is permissible.

It is also possible to address this concern less abstractly. Suppose that prostitution laws are justified as reducing the number of young people who choose to do this work to their lasting detriment or as reducing the amount of prostitution that is done by those who choose to do it. Prostitution is not the only activity that can cause lasting harm to young people. Driving while intoxicated or riding a motorcycle without a helmet can result in death, permanent brain damage, and paralysis. Boxing or football can also result in death and brain damage. Heavy drug use can result in fatal overdoses, and can also interfere with a person's education and emotional development, closing opportunities that it will be difficult to ever fully recover. Other sexually oriented activities, such as nude or topless "dancing" or acting in sexually explicit films, can also have lasting negative consequences. Suppose, for the sake of argument, that *all* of the following policies could be justified by a paternalistic argument if paternalism is permissible: laws that prohibit persons under twenty-one or twenty-five from riding a motorcycle without a helmet; laws that prohibit young people from engaging in dangerous organized sports that allow intentional violent blows to the head without requiring protective headgear; laws that prohibit the possession of large quantities of illegal drugs such as heroin, cocaine, and methamphetamine, and the sale of such drugs to persons under twenty-one or twenty-five; laws that prohibit businesses from hiring persons under twenty-one or twenty-five as nude or topless dancers; laws that prohibit the hiring of persons under twenty-one or twenty-five to model for sexually explicit photographs or to act in sexually explicit films. Imagine that all these policies were adopted. Would human individuality and human development be stifled? Would we cease to be autonomous? Would liberty be dead? No. Even taken together, these policies do not pose a significant threat to our liberty, to our autonomy, or to our individuality. So this kind of objection to the permissibility of paternalistic prostitution laws is also unconvincing.

Although I just assumed for the sake of argument that a number of paternalistic policies can be justified if paternalism is permissible, it is important to recognize that the paternalistic argument for prostitution laws does not *entail* that *any* of these other policies is justifiable. The paternalistic argument for a prostitution law entails (loosely speaking) that another paternalistic policy is justifiable only if (a) this other policy reduces harm that is at least as serious and to at least the same degree as this prostitution law does, and (b) this other law imposes no greater burden on anyone and has no more costs than this prostitution law does. Any policy that is more burdensome or more costly than this prostitution law might be unjustifiable even if this prostitution law is justifiable. Any law that is less effective in reducing harm might be unjustifiable even if this prostitution law is justifiable. And if the harm that is reduced by this other law is less serious or less objectionable than the harms reduced by this prostitution law, then this other law might be unjustifiable even if this prostitution law is justifiable. Because at least one of these things might be true of all the other paternalistic policies that I just mentioned, the paternalistic argument for prostitution laws does not *entail* that any of these other paternalistic policies is justifiable.

To illustrate, consider paternalistic measures that restrict nude modeling, nude dancing, or acting in sexually explicit films. There are important differences between prostitution and these other sexually oriented activities. Nude modeling does not generally require any sexual contact with other people. Nude or topless dancing, although it may require more physical contact than nude modeling does, requires significantly less physical contact than prostitution does. Furthermore, physical boundaries such as a stage create distance between dancers and patrons, and club managers, who do not want to be arrested for operating a brothel, often monitor the degree of intimate contact, keeping it within legal bounds. Nude and topless dancing are also not stigmatized to the same degree that prostitution is, as evidenced by the fact that dancers typically insist that they are *not* engaged in prostitution. Acting in sexually explicit films is different from both prostitution and nude dancing in typically involving contact with fewer people. The actors typically perform with only a relatively small group of partners whom they know and feel comfortable with. Some female actors work only with other female actors. Finally, there are reasons of freedom of expression against laws that restrict the production and distribution of films and stage performances of a sexual nature that are absent as reason against laws restricting the hiring of people for sexual services. Given all these differences, one may not legitimately infer from the paternalistic argument for prostitution laws that laws restricting nude dancing or acting in sexually explicit films can also be justified.

This is not to deny that nude modeling, nude dancing, and acting in sexually explicit films can have lasting bad consequences or that some of these bad consequences are similar to those of prostitution. Others' knowledge that a person has done this work can limit her opportunities going forward; it can cause problems for important relationships; it can cause embarrassment. Although acting in sexually explicit films may not be stigmatized to the same degree that prostitution is, it is also more public, and so poses a kind of threat to a person's public image and so to a person's future opportunities that prostitution usually does not. These are all good reasons to be concerned with the choice of these kinds of work by young people who are not yet in a position properly to appreciate how this work might have a lasting negative affect on their lives. Furthermore, it seems that the government could impose age restrictions on these activities without significantly threatening any important interests in freedom of expression. On these grounds I suspect the government would be justified in raising the age of legal consent to at least twenty-one, and perhaps even to twenty-five, and so in criminalizing the production or distribution of sexually explicit films or the staging of sexually oriented shows with younger performers.

It is nonetheless important to recognize that this position is not *entailed* by the paternalistic argument for prostitution laws. So one might also consistently accept the paternalistic argument for prostitution laws and yet reject these other paternalistic restrictions as unjustified.[28]

Paternalistic arguments are sometimes dismissed with the comment "but any law could be defended in that way." The thought seems to be that because many laws that limit our liberty are unjustifiable, but any law that limits our liberty could be defended as reducing our risk of harm, this is not a good argument for any law. The premise, however, that any law that limits our liberty could be defended as reducing our risk of harm is either false or irrelevant, depending on how it is interpreted. Everyone will agree that some laws that limit our liberty are unjustifiable, from which it follows that not all laws that limit our liberty can be justified, from which it follows that not all laws that limit our liberty can be justified as reducing our risk of harm. So if *defended* means *justified*, it is false that any law that limits our liberty could be defended as reducing our risk of harm. If, on the other hand, the claim that any law that limits our liberty could be defended in this way means only that it is possible for someone to *say* in defense of any law that limits our liberty, including all those that are unjustifiable, "This law is justified as reducing our risk of harm"; this is true, but it does not show that this *kind* of justification is illegitimate. It is also possible to *say* in defense of any law, including all those that are unjustifiable, "This law is necessary to protect our rights" or "This law is necessary to protect us from being harmed by others." It does not follow that *no* law can be justified as protecting our rights or as protecting us from harm.

Along similar lines, it is sometimes objected that if prostitution laws can be justified by the sorts of paternalistic considerations that I have identified, then many other paternalistic policies can be justified, too, including some that we would regard as outrageous. It is sometimes suggested, for example, that if prostitution laws are justified by the sorts of paternalistic considerations that I have identified, then so are laws prohibiting homosexual sodomy. This is multiply confused. Suppose, for a moment, that the justifiability of laws prohibiting prostitution entails that laws prohibiting homosexual sodomy are also justifiable. Even if this is true, the paternalistic argument that I have given for prostitution laws does not entail that the government is justified in *prohibiting* homosexual sodomy because it does not entail that the government is justified in *prohibiting* prostitution. In my view, the paternalistic argument for prostitution laws warrants only laws that reduce prostitution but do not prohibit it. If so, then the most that this paternalistic argument could entail with respect to homosexual sodomy is that laws are justified that reduce homosexual sodomy without prohibiting it. The suggestion that any such law might be justified will also strike many of us as outrageous. Anyone, however, who attacks the paternalistic argument for prostitution laws on this ground, and does so in good faith, must believe that homosexual sodomy has the same sort of negative impact on a person's life that prostitution seems to have, and if homosexual sodomy commonly *does* have this sort of negative impact, then the suggestion that the government ought to adopt policies that reduce it (without prohibiting it) is not outrageous. These laws are outrageous only on the assumption that homosexual sodomy is harmless. If we assume that homosexual sodomy is harmless, as many of us believe, then the paternalistic argument for prostitution laws does not imply that laws that reduce homosexual sodomy are warranted. And even if homosexual sodomy *were* commonly as harmful as prostitution commonly is, the paternalistic argument for prostitution laws would not entail that laws that reduce homosexual sodomy are warranted, because these laws might impose greater burdens on gay people than prostitution laws impose on anyone. Finally, the case for gay rights rests partly on the belief that gay relationships are similar in value to heterosexual relationships in developing and exercising our human capacities for love and friendship. The paternalistic argument for prostitution laws, in contrast, rests partly on the claim that this work damages these capacities. Assuming that this is true, there is no analogy to be drawn between prostitution laws and laws prohibiting homosexual sodomy.

In short, the justifiability of a paternalistic prostitution law does not entail that any other paternalistic policy is justified because the facts that would justify these other paternalistic policies are different from the facts that justify paternalistic prostitution laws. Some readers might now challenge me to state my theory of justifiable paternalism, to state a set of necessary and sufficient conditions that could be used to evaluate whether any paternalistic policy is justifiable when applied to the relevant set of facts. I doubt that it is possible to state an informative theory of this kind. A paternalistic policy is justified if and only if (a) it reduces harm and (b) this reduction in harm is sufficiently beneficial to justify whatever burdens this policy imposes. This principle identifies necessary and sufficient conditions for justifiable paternalism, but it is uninformative, because it contains no criterion of *sufficiently beneficial* that could be applied to any set of facts in a way that would settle whether the policy is justified. Because there are different kinds of harm, different kinds of benefit, and different kinds of burdens, and because there is no simple model for how to weigh these factors against each other in every case, we are unlikely to find an informative general theory of justifiable paternalism. This does not mean that we cannot reason intelligently about whether a particular paternalistic policy is justifiable. We can do this by considering the specific facts relevant to this policy and by doing our best to reach a defensible judgment of how these considerations are properly balanced against each other in this specific case. This is what I try to do here with respect to prostitution laws.

VII. Ericsson's and Nussbaum's Objections

One kind of objection to paternalistic prostitution laws is that paternalism is wrong in general. I have now explained why I believe this is false. Another kind of objection is that, although some forms of paternalism might be permissible, the specific paternalistic considerations that can be plausibly offered in favor of prostitution laws are not weighty enough to justify them. Lars Ericsson, Martha Nussbaum, and David Richards have all made this objection in one way or another and I now say something in response to them.

Ericsson considers the paternalistic reasons for prostitution laws and concludes that they "carry no weight."[29] Ericsson does not assume that paternalism in general is illegitimate. His claim is that even if some forms of paternalism are permissible, this particular policy is not justifiable on paternalistic grounds. His argument is this: The fact that a job is hazardous or risky is not generally a good reason to prohibit people from doing it. So the fact that prostitution is hazardous or risky is not a good reason to prohibit people from doing it.

Ericsson does not deny that prostitution is hazardous or risky. To the contrary, he writes, "It is a well-established fact that the occupational hazards connected with prostitution constitute a serious problem. The prostitute runs the risk of being hurt, physically as well as mentally. On the physical side there is always the risk of getting infected by some venereal disease... and then there is the risk of assault and battery from customers with sadistic tendencies. On the mental side we encounter such phenomena as depression and neurosis, compulsive behavior, self-degrading and self-destructive impulses, etc."[30] Given this characterization of the negative effects of prostitution, it is surprising that Ericsson concludes that the paternalistic reasons for prostitution laws carry *no* weight. What he should have said, it seems, is that although these reasons carry *some* weight, they do not carry *enough* weight to justify prohibiting prostitution. Mining is at least as risky as prostitution, he suggests, and yet we do not think this justifies prohibiting it.

Note that Ericsson does not limit his argument to the policy of *prohibition*. He considers whether there is any reason to think that prostitution is "undesirable" in a way that would justify society in trying "to prevent people from becoming prostitutes and to try to 'rehabilitate' those who already are."[31] He thinks not. If a job like mining is socially valuable, this is a good reason for the government to try to make it less risky and hazardous, but not to discourage it. Likewise, he thinks, with prostitution, because, although risky and hazardous, it, too, is socially valuable.

There are, however, at least three important differences between mining and prostitution. First, if mining were generally prohibited, or if the sale and purchase of ore and coal were generally prohibited, this would have a huge negative impact on our economy and on our standard of living. Prohibiting the sale and purchase of sex does not have anything like this kind of pervasive negative impact. Second, mining does not have the kind of negative impact on a person's self-esteem, social standing, opportunities, and ability to have healthy intimate relationships that prostitution seems to have. Third, although the physical risks of mining can be substantially reduced by proper safety precautions, the nonphysical risks of prostitution cannot be similarly reduced. They would not be substantially reduced, for example, by legalizing and regulating brothel prostitution, because those who work in legal brothels would still suffer the negative psychological effects of this work and would still lose valuable social and economic opportunities as a result of it. Assuming, then, that mining is far more important to our material quality of life than prostitution is and that prostitution is commonly harmful in the ways identified by antiprostitution activists, the mining analogy is not apt.

Ericsson in fact recognizes that prostitution differs from mining because he recognizes that "depressions and neuroses" and "self-degrading and self-destructive tendencies" are common among prostitutes,[32] and he does not suggest or give any reason to believe that they are common among miners. He does not accept this difference as being decisive, however, because he believes that "the principal cause of these psychological and social 'dysfunctions' is the social anathema attached to their way of life."[33] Ericsson provides no evidence for this empirical claim, and in chapter 1 I suggested that the stigma of prostitution results from the unpleasant nature of this work rather than the other way around. But even if the negative consequences of sex work were caused primarily by the stigma, this would be less relevant to the paternalistic case for prostitution laws than Ericsson seems to suppose. If you are a legislator deciding what prostitution policy to support, and you believe that prostitution is damaging because of the way in which it is stigmatized, and there is little you can do to remove this stigma, but you can reduce the number of women who would suffer the consequences of prostitution by voting for a policy that reduces the number who do it, then, even if the negative consequences of prostitution are caused by the stigma, it might make sense for you to support this policy. Whether or not this makes sense depends on the degree to which the stigma is caused or maintained by this policy and so on how likely the stigma is to vanish without it. Ericsson's mining analogy is apt only on the twin assumptions that the harms of engaging in prostitution are caused primarily by the stigma and that the stigma is caused primarily by official policies that aim to discourage it. Because he gives no evidence for either of these questionable empirical claims, the analogy is unconvincing.

Ericsson concludes his discussion of the paternalistic argument for prostitution laws by writing, "The paternalistic charge rests on two assumptions neither of which is valid. First, it rests on the assumption that society's scorn for whoredom is justified. Second, it rests on the assumption that the hooker is not doing a socially valuable job. From these assumptions together with the fact that harlotry is known to be a hazardous profession the paternalist leaps to the conclusion that prostitution is undesirable and that society should intervene against it for the prostitute's own good."[34] The paternalistic case for prostitution laws, however, does not rest on either assumption that Ericsson questions here. The paternalistic case for prostitution laws rests on the assumption that prostitution is commonly bad for the people who do it, but this does not presuppose that an attitude of *scorn* toward prostitutes is justified. Nor does the paternalistic argument for prostitution laws rest on the assumption that prostitution has no value. The paternalistic argument is perfectly consistent with the proposition that prostitution provides a genuine psychological benefit to clients. The argument assumes only that these benefits do not warrant legalization, given the harms that prostitution inflicts on those who do it.

It is commonly assumed that the paternalistic argument for prostitution laws must go like this:

1. The government should prohibit all risky or self-destructive conduct.
2. Prostitution is risky and self-destructive.
3. Therefore, the government should prohibit prostitution.

This argument is not sound, as Ericsson would be quick to point out, because there are many risky and many self-destructive activities that the government should not prohibit.

This, however, is not the paternalistic argument for prostitution laws that I have presented here. My argument is more like this one:

1. If an activity is risky or self-destructive, the government might be justified in adopting policies that reduce it.
2. Prostitution is commonly self-destructive.
3. Therefore, the government might be justified in adopting policies that reduce it.
4. Whether the government is justified in adopting a particular policy in order to reduce prostitution depends on the details of this particular policy, its costs and benefits.

Ericsson suggests that there is a kind of inconsistency in accepting the paternalistic argument for prostitution laws and not accepting a paternalistic argument for analogous restrictions on mining. There is no inconsistency, though, if the paternalistic argument for prostitution laws is the second one, and not the first.

Nussbaum questions the paternalistic case for prostitution laws in a different way.[35] She does not claim that paternalistic support for prostitution laws is inconsistent with our other policy positions. Instead, she considers a number of specific arguments that have been given for prostitution laws, some of which have a paternalistic dimension, and concludes that none of them is sufficient to justify these laws. These arguments are that prostitution involves health risks and risks of violence; that the prostitute has no autonomy because her activities are controlled by others; that prostitution involves the invasion of the sex worker's bodily space; that prostitution makes it harder for people to form relationships of intimacy and commitment; that the prostitute alienates her sexuality on the market and turns her sexual organs and acts into commodities; that the prostitute's activity is shaped by, and in turn perpetuates, male dominance of women; and that prostitution is a trade that people do not enter by choice, and so the agreements that people make to sell sexual services are illegitimate.[36] Nussbaum argues that none of these arguments can justify the "criminalization" of prostitution.[37]

Nussbaum is not explicit, however, about what she means by *criminalization*. If her claim is that these arguments cannot justify substantial criminal penalties for the *sale* of sexual services, then those who favor abolitionist or impermissive regulationist policies can agree with her. They can also agree with her if her claim is that none of these arguments *alone* justifies the kind of criminal penalties that abolitionist and impermissive regulationist policies involve. If, however, she means that none of these arguments can justify the kind of criminal penalties that abolitionist or impermissive regulationist policies involve *when these arguments are combined with each other or combined with other arguments*, then obviously opponents of legalization must disagree with her. Does Nussbaum give any reason to think they are wrong?

Although she considers seven different arguments for prostitution laws, Nussbaum does not actually consider the argument that leading antilegalization activists give, which is that sex work is harmful in *all* the ways identified in chapter 1. Because this argument had recently been stated by a number of feminist scholars when Nussbaum wrote her essay in the mid-1990s,[38] it is curious that she does not address it more directly. The closest she comes to considering it is when she rejects the argument that "the criminalization of prostitution would facilitate the formation of love relationships on the part of the women who were (or would have been) prostitutes."[39] She finds this argument "implausible" because, she says, "it is hard to see how reinforcing the stigma against prostitutes, or preventing some poor women from taking one of the few employment options they might have, would be likely to improve their human relations."[40] This, however, is not an accurate characterization of the antilegalization argument.

Antilegalization activists maintain that sex work interferes with a person's ability to have healthy intimate relationships and that prostitution laws, by reducing opportunities for sex work, reduce the likelihood that a person will do this work to their lasting detriment. These policies no doubt reinforce the stigma against prostitutes and reduce their employment opportunities as well. The argument against legalization, however, is not that *these negative consequences by themselves* improve anyone's human relations, as Nussbaum seems to suggest. The argument is that these negative consequences are justified by the positive consequences of reducing the psychological damage and other harms done by sex work. It is not "hard to see" how repeated sexual encounters with men one dislikes, who treat one with indifference or contempt, encounters that normally involve feigning sexual interest in exchange for money, would give rise to beliefs, emotions, and other attitudes that would make it difficult to have healthy intimate relationships afterward. Nor is it hard to see how prostitution laws might depress demand for prostitutes and therefore reduce the number of women who do this work to their own detriment. Nor, I think, would Nussbaum find these things hard to see if she were to reflect on an antilegalization argument like the one presented by Hoigard and Finstad in *Backstreets*.

Neither Ericsson nor Nussbaum argues that paternalistic policies are impermissible in general. They question the paternalistic arguments in favor of prostitution laws specifically. Because, however, they do not effectively challenge the factual assumptions of the antilegalization case, they do not present an effective challenge to the kind of paternalism that abolitionist or impermissive regulationist policies might involve. If the factual assumptions of the antilegalization argument are false, then obviously they cannot justify these policies. If, however, these assumptions are true and we are justified in believing them, they seem to provide good paternalistic grounds for legal restrictions of some kind.

VIII. Richards's Argument

Like Ericsson and Nussbaum, David Richards does not hold that paternalism is always impermissible, but he argues that paternalistic justifications must meet a certain general standard, and that the paternalistic justifications for prostitution laws fail to meet this standard.[41] According to Richards, paternalistic interference is justifiable only when the choices it aims to prevent are "irrational."[42] Because, he maintains, the choice to engage in sex work is not irrational, paternalistic arguments cannot justify prostitution laws.[43]

In denying that sex work is irrational, Richards in places seems to mean only that it is not necessarily or always irrational.[44] For reasons given in chapter 1, I agree with this. Sex work might be advisable for some people under some circumstances, and so rational in this sense. This, however, does not undermine the paternalistic case for prostitution laws. The paternalistic case is undermined only if prostitution laws cannot be justified other than as benefiting those for whom sex work is advisable. If prostitution laws can be justified as benefiting those for whom prostitution is *not* advisable—and Richards does not deny that there are such people—paternalistic considerations might justify this policy even if sex work is not *always* irrational.

Richards, however, has another reason to reject the paternalistic argument for prostitution laws: that even if sex work is an inadvisable choice for many, this is not the right kind of irrationality required to bring paternalistic considerations into play.[45] "Only those acts are irrational that frustrate the agent's own system of ends, whatever those ends are. Second, within the class of irrationalities so defined, paternalistic considerations would properly come into play only if the irrationality were severe and systematic (due to undeveloped or impaired capacities, or lack of opportunity to exercise such capacities) and a serious, permanent impairment of interests were in prospect."[46] Because, Richards contends, sex work is not irrational in this sense, paternalistic interference cannot be justified by the proposition that it is unwise or inadvisable.

Against this, one might point out that most of us endorse as ends feeling good about ourselves, having healthy, stable, intimate relationships, being well-regarded by others in society, and having valuable social and economic opportunities. Because most of us endorse these ends, we might reasonably assume that most girls or young women who begin prostitution endorse them too. Prostitution, however, seems to interfere with the achievement of these ends. Those who study prostitution argue that it commonly results in lasting feelings of worthlessness, shame, and self-hatred; that it commonly interferes with the ability to have healthy stable intimate relationships; and that it commonly leads to one's being regarded negatively by others in society, and therefore to the loss of valuable opportunities. If so, then sex work presumably does "frustrate the agent's own system of ends" and so is irrational in this sense.

Richards maintains to the contrary that "there is no evidence that prostitution itself is necessarily an unpleasant experience."[47] If by *necessarily* he means "always unpleasant for everyone who does it," he is probably right. This, however, is irrelevant to the paternalistic case for prostitution laws. If it is an unpleasant experience for *some*, and its unpleasantness has a lasting negative impact on the quality of their lives, then it frustrates their end of personal happiness, and so is irrational for them in this sense. Richards maintains, too, that "there is no evidence that prostitution itself...disables [sex workers] from engaging in other loving relationships."[48] If by *disables* he means "permanently and irreversibly destroys the capacity to engage in loving relationships," then, again, he is probably right. He is wrong, though, if he means that there is no evidence that prostitution has a negative impact on the ability of individuals to have healthy relationships. There is evidence that it does.

In Richards's view, however, it is not enough for justifiable paternalistic interference with an activity that this activity frustrates an agent's own ends. According to Richards, paternalistic interference with a choice is justified only if the irrationality involved is "severe and systematic." Richards is not explicit about what he means by this, but the parenthetical remark that follows suggests that an irrationality is severe and systematic in the relevant sense "when it is due to undeveloped or impaired capacities, or lack of opportunity to exercise such capacities." Richards is surely right that the choice to do sex work does not always result from capacities that are undeveloped or impaired, but he is just as surely wrong to suggest that it never does. Many sex workers start when they are quite young, well before their deliberative capacities have fully developed.

Suppose, though, for the sake of argument, that prostitution laws can be fully justified only as deterring some legal adults from self-destructive sex work. Would the paternalistic justification therefore fail Richards's test? Not necessarily. Some activities interfere with the development and reliable exercise of the capacity for prudential reasoning. This is true, for example, of heavy drinking and drug use. It is arguably also true of sex work. When a person chooses to do this work unwisely as a young person, it can have a lasting negative impact on her ability to choose wisely as an adult. This is because doing this work can lead a person to form deluded and self-destructive patterns of thought as a result. This is not to say that anyone who chooses to do this work must have a defective capacity for prudential reasoning. Sex work might be an advisable choice for some. The suggestion is only that doing this work can warp a person's thinking and thus impair her capacity to think clearly about whether or not she should continue to do it. To this we might add that many sex workers have been victims of child sexual abuse,[49] including child prostitution, and this experience might well affect their ability as adults to make sound judgments about what kinds of sexual conduct are beneficial for them. Suppose, then, that a prostitution law can be fully justified only if its benefits to some legal adults are counted in its favor. If these adults are just the ones who started prostitution self-destructively as young persons or as a result of child sexual abuse, then the irrationality of their choice to do sex work might in fact be "severe and systematic" in Richards's sense.[50]

According to Richards, however, it is not enough that a choice result from an irrationality that is severe and systematic. Paternalistic interference with an irrational choice is permissible, in his view, only if "a serious, permanent impairment of interests were in prospect." Richards does not believe that sex work threatens the serious impairment of any important interest, but he is wrong about this if the empirical assumptions of the argument of chapter 1 are sound. Among our important interests are feeling contented with ourselves and enjoying our lives; achieving our worthy aims and goals; and leading a life that on the whole is a good one for us to have lived, one that does not give us too much reason for regret. In virtue of these interests we also have important interests in having certain opportunities. Antiprostitution activists maintain that sex work seriously impairs these interests. If so, sex work seriously impairs the important interests of some sex workers.

Richards might grant this, and still deny that the impairment of these important interests is *permanent* in his sense. There is a sense in which every injury to an interest is permanent, which is that once the interest is injured in this way, it is permanently the case that it has been injured in this way. Furthermore, if prostitution as a young adult makes it more difficult for a person for the rest of her life to be happy or to achieve her worthwhile aims, then prostitution results in the permanent impairment of interests in this sense too. Richards, however, might respond that an activity permanently impairs an interest in *his* sense only if it makes it impossible for a person to have some good in the future. Death, for example, permanently impairs a person's interest in future happiness, because one cannot be happy when one is dead. Prostitution presumably does not result in the permanent impairment of interests in this sense. So if this is the correct interpretation of Richards's requirement, then paternalistic prostitution laws arguably fail to meet it.

At this point, however, we must ask whether there is good reason to agree with Richards that paternalistic interference is justifiable only when it satisfies this extraordinarily stringent test. Richards suggests that this test is warranted by the kind of contractualist reasoning that Rawls employs, but I think he is wrong about this. Parties in Rawls's original position might agree to Richards's irrationality requirement on *some* interpretation, but they would not agree to it on the very stringent interpretation that is necessary to exclude paternalistic prostitution laws.

IX. Contractualism

Rawls maintains that parties in the hypothetical choice situation he calls the "original position" would agree to allow some forms of paternalism. He writes, "It is also rational for [the parties in the original position] to protect themselves against their own irrational inclinations by consenting to a scheme of penalties that may give them sufficient motive to avoid foolish actions and by accepting certain impositions designed to undo the unfortunate consequences of their imprudent behavior. For these cases the parties adopt principles stipulating when others are authorized to act in their behalf and to override their present wishes if necessary; and this they do recognizing that sometimes their capacity to act rationally for their good may fail, or be lacking altogether."[51]

One might think that if the parties in the original position consent to give the government the authority to adopt policies for their benefit, the only kind of paternalism they are allowing is soft paternalism, because, after all, they are agreeing to allow it. Whether a paternalistic policy is hard or soft, however, depends upon whether it goes against the wishes of the person whose liberty this policy limits. Because a policy might go against a person's wishes even if this person's representative in the original position agrees to give the government the authority to adopt this policy, choice by parties in the original position does not function to render all the paternalistic policies they permit soft. To the contrary, Rawls is arguing that parties in the original position would agree to allow some kinds of *hard* paternalism.

Some may now object that my earlier characterization of the distinction between hard and soft paternalism was simplistic. A policy limits a person's liberty *against his will* in the relevant sense, they might say, only if two conditions are satisfied. First, it is not the case that this person has given prior authorization to the government to limit his liberty in this way. Second, this person would choose to do what is prohibited if he knew all the relevant causal facts known by those around him. Ulysses gave permission to his men not to untie him from the mast as they sailed past the Sirens. So when his men refused to untie him they were not limiting his liberty against his will in the relevant sense. If you knock from my hand a glass of lethal poison that I am about to drink because I think it is water, you have not acted against my will because I would not have intended to drink this liquid had I known what you know, namely, that drinking it will kill me. Some might believe that once we accept this more nuanced understanding of what is involved in going against a person's will, we see that the only kind of paternalism licensed by parties in the original position is soft paternalism. If so, Rawls's contractualism fails to support my contention that some forms of hard paternalism are permissible.

The prior authorization, however, that parties in the original position give is not analogous to the prior authorization that Ulysses gave to his men. This is because the hypothetical agreement of parties in the original position does not constitute any act of authorization on the part of any actual person. The soundness of the argument from the original position therefore does not entail that anyone has given anyone else prior authorization to limit his liberty, in the way that Ulysses did. Nor is the choice by parties in the original position similar to what one would choose if one knew all the relevant causal facts known by those around one. The parties in the original position are situated behind a veil of ignorance that prevents them from knowing the specifics of their situation.[52] So they choose principles on the basis of very general interests that everyone is supposed to have.[53] Because, as Rawls suggests, it is rational for parties in the original position to protect these interests by agreeing to authorize others "to act in their behalf and to override their present wishes if necessary," and this kind of interference might prevent someone from doing what he would choose even if he knew all the relevant causal facts, the parties in the original position agree to allow some forms of hard paternalism.

Consider, to illustrate, why parties in the original position would agree to allow the police to intervene in suicide attempts by adults who do not want the police to intervene. Death typically represents a grave threat to a person's most important interests; people typically decide to commit suicide only when they are extremely depressed; people are prone to make unwise self-destructive choices when extremely depressed; and a person might recover from his depression and begin to enjoy life again if given the chance. Because these facts might apply to a person's decision to kill himself even when this person opposes police interference and even when his decision to kill himself does not result from immaturity or ignorance of the relevant causal facts, it seems that parties in the original position would reject a principle that prohibits *all* forms of hard paternalistic interference. They would want to allow *some* hard paternalistic interference with suicide attempts, if only to put those they represent in a position to think through their decision more carefully and, hopefully, to get effective medication or counseling.

Paternalistic interference with an irrational choice is permissible in Richards's view only if the irrationality involved is "severe and systematic." By this, Richards seems to mean that it is produced by deliberative capacities that are far less developed than those of the average adult—of the sort that we find in young children—or only when it is produced by capacities that are impaired by brain damage, psychosis, or the heavy use of strong psychotropic drugs. Parties in Rawls's original position, however, would not agree to Richards's irrationality requirement on this interpretation. Suppose an adult wishes to kill himself as the result of acute depression. If this person's capacities for prudential reasoning are fully developed and he is not suffering from any psychotic delusions, then the irrationality involved in his wanting to kill himself is not severe and systematic in Richards's sense—the sense necessary to exclude paternalistic prostitution laws. It seems, however, that parties in the original position would permit the government to interfere with suicide attempts by persons like this one. So, it seems, parties in the original position would reject a principle that permits paternalistic interference *only* with choices that result from irrationalities that are severe and systematic in the sense just described.

Would parties in the original position nonetheless allow paternalistic interference only with choices that *permanently* impair interests in the way that suicide does? It is difficult to see why. If a choice will threaten an important interest, and a policy that limits a liberty will deter this choice, and the interest in having the freedom to make this choice has less weight than the interest this choice threatens, because this liberty is not important in the ways described above in section I, then it seems that there would be sufficient reason for parties in the original position to allow the government to adopt this policy. Suppose, then, that sex work injures important interests in the way that antilegalization activists maintain and that the interest in having more opportunities to sell sexual services and the interest in buying sexual services are not important in the four ways identified above for the intended beneficiaries of these policies to have. On these assumptions, the reasons for parties in the original position to permit the government to adopt policies that discourage prostitution seem to outweigh their reasons to prohibit this, even if these policies go against the wishes of those the policies are intended to benefit. Assuming, then, that the empirical assumptions of the argument of chapter 1 are sound, Richards's irrationality requirement is not warranted by Rawls's contractualism on the impermissive interpretation necessary to rule out paternalistic prostitution laws.

This result is confirmed, I think, by T. M. Scanlon's version of contractualism. According to this view, a government action or policy is wrong if and only if it violates a principle that no one could reasonably reject.[54]

Suppose an adult will act to her own detriment unless the government adopts some policy that can be justified only as benefiting her, but that she now opposes this policy. Suppose that her choice to engage in this conduct is not based on ignorance or insanity. If she will be harmed in the absence of this policy, and her interests in not being harmed in this way have greater weight than anyone's interests in having the freedom to do what the policy prohibits, including her own, then she may reasonably reject any principle that prohibits this policy. How can a person reasonably reject this principle if she herself opposes the policy that it prohibits? One answer is that a person is not only her present self. She is also her future self. In this case, her future self may reasonably reject this principle, because the interests of her future self in not being harmed by this choice of her present self have, by hypothesis, greater weight than anyone's interests in having the freedom to engage in the relevant activity, including her own. Consequently, no one may reasonably reject a principle that permits the government to adopt this policy for this person's own good against her will, and this form of hard paternalism is morally permissible.

Richards maintains that paternalistic interference is justified only with choices that are irrational. He then seeks to show that the decision to do sex work is not irrational in the relevant sense. In response I have suggested that sex work is irrational in the relevant sense for *some* of those who do it, which is all that is needed to support *some* degree of paternalistic interference. Richards questions the intellectual integrity of anyone who claims that sex work is irrational, writing that "it is as if the extant moralistic condemnation of prostitution inexorably shaped the reading of the facts so as to confirm that the putatively immoral conduct was personally irrational as well."[55] In view of Richards's apparent obliviousness to the relevant empirical evidence—evidence that Ericsson, who also opposes prostitution laws, accepts without question—it seems more accurate to say that Richards has been blinded by his own sexual libertarian ideology to the ways in which sex work is harmful. In any case, we can agree that there is a strong interpretation of Richards's irrationality requirement that would make paternalistic prostitution laws very difficult to justify even if prostitution is commonly harmful in all the ways identified in chapter 1. As I have now explained, however, this strong irrationality requirement is not warranted by the kind of contractualism that Richards apparently endorses.

Rawls's and Scanlon's versions of contractualism are not the only ones, and there are other versions that would rule out hard paternalism, including whatever hard paternalism prostitution laws might involve. Hard paternalism is ruled out, for example, by a libertarian version of contractualism according to which the government is permitted to adopt a policy only if every adult member of that society would freely consent to give the government the authority to adopt this kind of policy if rational and informed. Because adult sex workers, clients, and businessmen in the sex industry who oppose prostitution laws would not, if rational and informed, freely consent to give the government the authority to limit their opportunities to sell or buy sexual services, the government would not be permitted to adopt prostitution laws for the protection of others if this version of contractualism is sound.[56] This libertarian version of contractualism, however, fails to provide a plausible criterion of legitimate government authority because many policies that someone would not freely consent to if rational and informed are nonetheless morally permissible. A committed segregationist, for example, would not if rational and informed freely consent to give the government the authority to adopt antidiscrimination laws, but such policies are nonetheless morally permissible. In view of counterexamples like these, the ideal of unanimous agreement provides a plausible criterion of legitimate government authority only if interpreted by the kind of ideal contractualism presented by Rawls and Scanlon. As we have just seen, however, their versions of contractualism provide little reason to believe that hard paternalism is always wrong.

X. The Government's Business

If asked to explain what is wrong with paternalism, few would say that it is wrong because parties in the original position would reject it or because it is prohibited by a principle no one could reasonably reject. Not many more would say that it is wrong because it stunts individuality or because it disrespects personal autonomy. Most people would say that it is simply not the government's business to protect us from ourselves; it is the government's business only to protect us from others. Before concluding this chapter, I should therefore say more about why I find this objection to paternalism unconvincing.

It is the government's business, in my view, to adopt any policy that there is sufficient reason for it to adopt. Because, in my view, there is sufficient reason for the government to adopt some paternalistic policies, it is the proper function of government to protect people against themselves in these ways. Some may think that what policies there is sufficient reason for the government to adopt depends on what the proper function or purpose of government is, and they might think that the only proper function or purpose of the government is to protect people against each other. I reject this view. In my view the function of government is to protect our rights and to make us better off than we would otherwise be in ways that are compatible with our rights and with treating each of us fairly. Because, in my view, some paternalistic policies make people better off than they would otherwise be and they make them better off without violating anyone's rights and without treating anyone unfairly, it is the business of the government to adopt these policies.

Some may believe, to the contrary, that paternalism *does* violate our rights. Mill seems to have believed something like this. For the reasons given above, however, I do not think that Mill gives us any good reason to agree with him. Nor, for the reasons just given, do the contractualist views of Rawls and Scanlon provide any reason to think that paternalism always violates our rights. Some may think that paternalism violates our rights precisely because it is not the government's business to protect us against ourselves, but I find this argument no more persuasive than the argument against sodomy that procreation is the only legitimate function of sex. Just as it is hard for me to see why procreation is the only legitimate function of sex, it is hard for me to see why protection of an individual from harm by others is the only legitimate function of government. I will say more in the next chapter about why I do not think paternalism violates our rights. Before concluding this chapter, though, I will briefly discuss two lines of argument that seem to lead some to think that it is not the government's business to protect us against ourselves, in order to explain why I find both of these arguments against paternalism unconvincing.

One reason to think that it is not the government's business to protect us against ourselves is that the government is properly concerned only with the *public sphere*. Assuming that self-regarding conduct lies wholly within the *private sphere*, it follows that it is not the business of government to protect us against ourselves. The assumption, however, that it is wrong for the government to limit liberty in the private sphere requires substantial qualification before it can be accepted, and, once it is duly qualified, it no longer implies that paternalism is always wrong.

Suppose we understand the private sphere to include certain kinds of places (like the home) or certain kinds of relationships (like the relationship of family members) or certain kinds of activities (like sexual activity). Then it is plainly false to say that it is wrong for the government to interfere in the private sphere, because it is plainly permissible for the government to prohibit parents from having sexual relations with their children in their homes. Suppose, then, that we understand the private sphere to include just that part of a person's conduct that has no affect on anyone but himself. Although it may then be true that it is wrong for the government to interfere in the private sphere, this no longer rules out paternalism. This is because most of the conduct with which paternalistic interference might be justified *does* affect others in some way. For example, the decision to drive a motorcycle without a helmet affects other drivers by making it more likely that in an accident they will kill someone or by raising their insurance costs. Indeed, very little conduct falls within the private sphere in *this* sense because most of our conduct affects others to *some* degree. So although the principle of privacy might be valid on this interpretation, it does not imply that all forms of paternalism are wrong.

The principle that it is wrong for the government to interfere in the private sphere is best understood, I think, not as a general premise from which conclusions about the permissibility of specific forms of government interference can be drawn, but rather as an abbreviation of more specific principles that are valid on independent grounds. Thus when we say that it is wrong for the government to interfere in the private sphere, what we often mean is just that it is wrong for the government to prohibit consenting adults from engaging in noncommercial sexual relations with each other in nonpublic areas. If this principle is valid, however, it is not *because* it is always wrong for the government to interfere in the private sphere or to interfere with personal activities that take place in nonpublic places. It is rather because the burdens that *this particular kind* of interference imposes on individuals are greater than any burden someone would bear if the government were never to interfere in this way. If this is correct, then the principle of privacy does not warrant the general conclusion that paternalism is always wrong. On this account, the principle of privacy is valid only to the extent that specific principles of privacy are valid, and the validity of these specific principles of privacy is based on valid judgments about the relative weight of burdens. If, as I believe, a proper weighing of burdens sometimes warrants government paternalism—in the ways indicated above in my discussions of autonomy and contractualism—this way of defending the principle of privacy does not warrant the conclusion that paternalism is always wrong.

Another reason why someone might think that it is not the government's business to protect us against ourselves is that it is the government's business to do only what we, the people, have actually given it the authority to do. Because we, the people, have never actually given the government the authority to protect us against ourselves, it is not the business of government to do so. This argument, however, rests on two questionable assumptions.

The first is that we, the people, have never given the government the authority to protect us against ourselves. Perhaps those who ratified the U.S. Constitution did not give the *federal* government the authority to protect people against themselves; perhaps they gave the federal government the authority only to regulate commerce, make treaties, provide for the common defense, and so on. The federal government, however, is not our only government. We also have state governments, and state supreme courts have historically interpreted state constitutions to give state governments the authority to protect people against themselves, which is some evidence that this authority was actually granted to the states by the people.

The second questionable assumption is that the government is entitled to perform a function only if we, the people, have actually given it the authority to do so at some point in our history via some discrete political act, such as ratifying or amending the Constitution. Our government now has many functions that we, the people, never formally gave it in this way, including the function of making monetary policy through a national bank, providing retirement and medical benefits through a system of income taxation, and discouraging racial discrimination in places of public accommodation, private housing, and employment. If these functions are legitimate, as they seem to be, then it is the government's business to exercise some forms of authority that we, the people, have never actually given it. So even if we, the people, never gave the government the authority to protect us against ourselves, it might still be the business of the government to do so.

Finally, even if it is the business of government to do only what we, the people, have actually given it the authority to do, this fails to explain why paternalism is wrong *in principle* because we, the people, might now give the government this authority, in which case it would now be government's business, according to this theory, to protect us against ourselves.

4

Individual Rights

If abolitionist and regulationist policies can be justified by the argument of chapter 1, they are not objectionably paternalistic or objectionably moralistic. This is the argument so far. These policies, however, might still violate someone's rights, and if they do, they are morally impermissible. I have now argued, in effect, that abolitionist and regulationist policies do not violate the rights of their intended beneficiaries in being paternalistic or moralistic toward them. These laws, however, might still violate the rights of *others*: clients, for example, or sex workers for whom sex work is an advisable choice. In this chapter I argue that if the empirical premises of the paternalistic argument are sound, *some* restrictions on sexual commerce violate *no one's* rights.

The term *right* is sometimes used to refer to valid moral principles of a certain kind. It is also sometimes used to refer to *basic* or *fundamental* liberties. The primary question here is whether prostitution laws violate someone's rights in the first, valid moral principle sense. I will begin, however, by considering whether prostitution laws violate anyone's rights in the second, basic liberty sense in order to set this issue aside.

I. Basic Liberty

We commonly refer to basic liberties such as freedom of political speech and religious liberty as *rights*. In doing so, we convey the belief that these liberties have a special moral importance or a special status in our constitutional law. Sexual freedom is now regarded by many as a basic liberty, and the freedoms to buy and sell sexual services are arguably included in sexual freedom. So prostitution laws might violate our rights in the basic liberty sense.

Against this conclusion, one might argue that the freedom to buy and sell labor is not generally treated as a basic liberty. The U.S. Supreme Court and most political philosophers do not count as basic adults' freedom to buy and sell labor to perform certain kinds of dangerous or harmful tasks, to buy and sell labor above a certain number of hours a day or week, or to buy and sell child labor. Moreover, government policies that limit our opportunities to make or accumulate money are not ordinarily treated as threatening basic liberties. Zoning and environmental protection laws limit opportunities to make money, and taxation limits the opportunities of individuals to accumulate money, but these laws are not generally seen as threatening basic liberties.

Because there are considerations for and against treating the freedoms to sell and buy sexual services as basic, it makes sense to look to a theory of basic liberty to decide the matter. There are different theories, however, and they have different implications for prostitution laws.

On a historical theory, a liberty is basic just in case it has been treated as basic by our legal and political institutions over time: our political and legal institutions have recognized that the government may not limit this liberty in the absence of very strong or "compelling" reasons. Freedom of political speech, for example, has been treated as basic in this way, because the Supreme Court has consistently held that only the strongest reasons can justify prohibiting the expression of a political opinion. Neither the freedom to sell nor the freedom to buy sexual services has been treated in this way.[1] So neither is a basic liberty according to the historical theory.

A glaring defect in the historical theory is that a system of political institutions might not treat a liberty as basic even though it *ought* to do so. The Supreme Court did not treat the freedom to marry persons of other races as a basic liberty until 1967,[2] and it ought to have done so earlier. For this reason no plausible theory of basic liberty can tie basic liberties so closely to past legal practices. It must identify an adequate evaluative basis for distinguishing between basic and nonbasic liberties, one that plausibly identifies all and only those liberties that *ought* to be regarded as basic.

One kind of normative theory is the democratic theory, according to which a liberty is basic just in case it is "essential to democracy." Freedom of political speech is basic, according to this theory, because fair political procedures are essential to democracy and without freedom of political speech the political process would not be fair to all the participants. This is because without freedom of political speech, citizens would not have an adequate opportunity to voice their political opinions and thereby influence the outcome of the political process. Not all the liberties we regard as basic, however, are essential to fair political procedures. Laws that discourage certain forms of religious or sexual practice, for example, might emerge from fair procedures, and might be compatible with maintaining these procedures over time. To capture the ordinary notion of basic liberty, we must therefore go beyond what is required for fair political procedures. We must identify other important values or interests relevant to assessing the justice of basic social institutions and hold that basic liberties are those that play a crucial role in advancing these values or protecting these important interests.

One theory of this type is the "two moral powers" theory of John Rawls. According to this theory, basic liberties are those that must be recognized and protected in order to secure the social conditions necessary for the adequate development and full and informed exercise of two moral powers: a capacity for a conception of justice and a capacity to form, revise, and rationally pursue a conception of the good life.[3] At least two different interpretations of this theory are possible, however, and they have different implications for prostitution laws.

On one interpretation, a person must be free to live the life he believes is best for him, provided that this life does not involve assault, theft, fraud, or breach of contract, if he is fully to develop and exercise his two moral powers. If someone believes that buying or selling sexual services is part of the best life for him, the liberty to do so is therefore basic. On this interpretation, however, too many liberties are basic. Consider the kind of freedom of association that includes the freedom of restaurant owners to refuse to serve members of racial minorities. If some restaurant owner believes that operating a restaurant that does not serve racial minorities is part of the best life for him, this kind of freedom of association is a basic liberty, according to this interpretation. Not only does this seem wrong in itself, but if this liberty is basic, then Rawls's principle of the priority of liberty entails that this liberty may not be limited to promote equality of opportunity,[4] which also seems wrong.

On another interpretation, the full development and exercise of the two moral powers requires only an adequate opportunity to deliberate about what is right and good and to guide one's actions by one's own judgment about what is best *in whatever circumstances one finds oneself*. Because the freedom to refuse to serve racial minorities is not necessary to deliberate soundly about what is right and good, this liberty is not basic, according to this interpretation. Neither, then, is the freedom to sell or buy sexual services. The problem with this interpretation is that it seems to imply that only freedoms of thought, expression, and discussion are basic, because only these freedoms are necessary for individuals to *deliberate* about what is right and good and to guide their actions by their own judgments about what is best *in whatever circumstances they find themselves*—circumstances that may include, among other things, laws prohibiting certain kinds of religious and sexual conduct. So on this interpretation, freedom of worship and reproductive and sexual freedoms are not basic. This seems wrong in itself and is also clearly inconsistent with Rawls's own view.

Without further elaboration, the two moral powers theory therefore seems to identify either too many liberties as basic or too few, depending on how we interpret the idea of the social conditions necessary for the adequate development and full and informed exercise of the two moral powers. This difficulty may have a satisfactory solution. Until we know what it is, however, we cannot rely on this theory to settle the issue of whether the freedom to sell or buy sexual services is basic.

These difficulties may lead us to doubt that we will ever find a satisfactory general theory of basic liberty.[5] We may begin to doubt that any theory will clearly identify all and only those liberties that ought to be treated as basic by reference to a short list of important political values, such as fair political procedures or the social conditions necessary for the full development and exercise of our moral powers. We may begin to suspect that different basic liberties—such as freedom of political speech, worship, movement, marriage, and sex—are important for fundamentally different reasons. If we accept this pluralistic view, then we must examine the specific interests advanced by the freedoms to buy and sell sexual services in order to assess whether these liberties should be counted as basic.

In the previous chapter I identified four ways in which a liberty might be important. There my specific aim was to explain why prostitution laws, although perhaps paternalistic, are not objectionably so. One might, however, also use this account of importance to illuminate the notion of a basic liberty. One might say that a necessary condition of a liberty being basic is that at least one of the following conditions is satisfied: (a) this liberty is necessary for someone to have adequate control over her own life; (b) this liberty is a necessary social condition for people to deliberate fully about what is right and good; (c) this liberty functions to symbolize someone's status as an equal citizen or full member of society; (d) this liberty is necessary for someone freely to engage in an activity that she needs to engage in to have a happy or successful life (as judged by some "objective list" of substantive goods).

If a liberty satisfies none of these conditions, it makes sense to deny that it is basic. Take, for example, the freedom of entrepreneurs to sell the sexual services of others. One need not sell the sexual labor of *others* in order to have adequate control of one's *own* sexuality, body, or life. Having this freedom is not necessary for full deliberation about what is right and good. This freedom is not symbolic of full membership in our society or of equal citizenship. And no one needs to sell the sexual services of others in order to have a happy or successful life as this is ordinarily understood. So if satisfying one of these conditions is necessary for a liberty to be basic, it makes sense to deny that the freedom of entrepreneurs to sell the sexual services of others is a basic liberty.

We cannot reach the same conclusion so quickly, however, about the freedom to sell one's *own* sexual services or about the freedom to buy them. This is because these freedoms arguably do satisfy at least one of the conditions just mentioned. Thus it is arguable that a person does not have adequate control over her own body and so her own life unless she has the freedom to sell sexual services, and it is arguable that people with uncommon psychological needs need to buy sexual services in order to be happy.

Not everyone, though, will be willing to conclude from these considerations that the freedom to sell and buy sexual services are basic liberties. Even if one takes seriously the autonomy interests of sex workers, one might think that there is a moral limit to what one is entitled to do with one's own body, and that the freedom to sell sex falls beyond this limit. Even if one takes seriously the welfare interests of customers, one might think that a person who needs to buy sexual services to feel happy is abnormal. Whether a liberty is properly counted as basic, one might think, depends on the role it plays in protecting the important interests of normal, psychologically healthy people.

We seem to be back where we started: reasons can be given for and against treating the freedom to sell and buy sexual services as basic. How should we proceed? I suggest that we set the issue aside. Not only is it difficult to decide whether these liberties should be counted as basic, deciding this would not alone settle the question of whether prostitution laws violate anyone's rights. Few, if any, rights are absolute. Even freedom of political speech might be justifiably limited in order to prevent the certain and imminent catastrophic destruction of human life. So a basic liberty is not necessarily violated whenever it is limited. A right (in the basic liberty sense) is *violated* only when it is limited by the government *for insufficient reason*. Consequently, even if the freedom to sell and buy sexual services were basic liberties, these rights would not be violated by prostitution laws if there were sufficient reason for them. The central moral issue is therefore not whether the freedom to sell and buy sexual services *are* rights (in the basic liberty sense), but whether there is sufficient reason for laws that restrict these liberties.

II. Individualism and the Burdens Principle

Sometimes we use the term *right* to refer to basic or fundamental liberties. Other times we use the term more generally to refer to moral limits to how others, including the government, may permissibly treat us in bringing about states of affairs that are otherwise desirable. There are moral limits, we think, to what the government may do to us in advancing the interests of a dynastic family, a ruling class, a dominant racial group, "the national interest," and even the welfare of society as a whole. These limits we call *rights*. Historically this idea gained currency as a way of objecting to certain kinds of domination and oppression, such as absolute monarchy and slavery. More recently the idea of rights has gained theoretical significance as an explanation of what is wrong with act utilitarianism, according to which we should always act so as to maximize happiness in the aggregate. Sometimes it is wrong to act in this way. It was wrong for the Roman government to force slaves to fight to the death as gladiators even if this spectacle maximized happiness in the aggregate by entertaining the Roman masses and fostering political stability. To explain what was wrong with this, we might say that this policy violated the slaves' rights.

Understood in this way, rights against the government rest partly on a general form of moral reasoning that I call *individualism*. According to individualism, we must evaluate government policies partly by making one-to-one comparisons of the burdens that individuals bear as the result of these policies. Individualism forbids us from evaluating government policies solely by considering their net aggregated benefit, or net benefit summed over individuals. If a policy would impose a burden on someone that is much greater than any burden anyone would bear under an alternative policy, then individualism entails that this policy is wrong, even if this policy would maximize welfare in the aggregate. Thus it would be wrong for the government to establish and maintain a system of slavery even if this system would maximize social welfare in the aggregate, because this system would impose a burden on the individual slave that is much worse than the worst burden anyone would bear in the absence of this system.

Individualism is an essential component of some of the most influential contemporary theories of political rights. It is essential to Rawls's view, for instance, that the government should observe principles that would be chosen by rational individuals in an original position of equality behind a "veil of ignorance."[6] This is because, according to Rawls, not knowing "behind the veil" what specific situation he or she is in, each individual will reject any principle that places a substantial burden on someone unless someone would bear a substantial burden when this principle is not observed. Individualism is also essential to Dworkin's view that the government must treat each person with equal concern and respect.[7] This is because Dworkin commonly reasons as though the government treats a person with equal concern and respect in adopting a policy that burdens her substantially only if someone would be substantially burdened in the absence of this policy.[8] Individualism is also essential to Scanlon's view that the government should observe principles of conduct that no one could reasonably reject.[9] This is because, according to Scanlon, a person can reasonably reject a principle of government conduct if the government's observance of this principle places a burden on her that is substantially greater than the worst burden anyone would bear, were the government not to observe this principle.[10]

Individualism identifies a general method of reasoning about whether or not a government policy violates a person's moral rights. It does not, however, tell us what rights *are*. Rights, in my view, are valid moral principles that state that certain actions are prohibited unless certain reasons for them are present. Rights *against the government*, then, are valid moral principles that state that certain government policies or actions are impermissible unless there are certain reasons for them. The right against arbitrary arrest, for example, is a valid moral principle that forbids the government from arresting a person unless there is good reason to believe that he has broken a valid law.

One way in which specific principles of this kind are valid is that they are warranted by individualism. The specific form of individualism that I endorse as a basis for our rights to liberty is given by what I call the *burdens principle*. This principle holds that it is wrong for the government to prohibit a form of conduct if this policy imposes a burden on someone that is *substantially greater* than the worst burden anyone would bear in the absence of this policy. The relative weight of burdens is to be assessed by the relative weight of personal reasons, or reasons for individuals to prefer their own situations under various policy alternatives.[11] If there is a reason for me to prefer my situation under a policy, p, and this reason has much greater weight than any reason there is for you to prefer your situation under another policy, q, then I bear a burden under policy p that is substantially greater than any burden you bear under policy q.

Specific rights to liberty are grounded on the burdens principle in the following way. Suppose that, in the absence of some coercive policy, someone will bear a burden, b, that is at least as bad as the worst burden this policy imposes on anyone. Suppose, too, that the worst burden this policy imposes on someone is substantially worse than any burden *other than b* that someone will bear in the absence of this policy. Then the specific principle is valid that the government may not limit individual liberty in this way unless this is necessary to protect individuals from bearing burden b. The specific principle is valid, for instance, that the government may not limit the public expression of a political opinion unless it is certain that someone will be gravely injured as a direct result. This is because any government interference with political expression that does not satisfy this condition would impose a burden on someone that is substantially worse than any *other* burden someone would bear in the absence of this form of interference.

One might propose instead that a policy violates a person's rights if it imposes a burden on someone that is simply greater—even *slightly* greater— than the worst burden anyone would bear in its absence. Why, then, do I hold that the relevant burden must be *substantially* greater to constitute a rights violation? The answer is that any plausible theory of individual rights must leave adequate room for aggregative considerations. Suppose that a few drivers are burdened by a highway speed limit, but that this policy reduces the risk to a great many people of dying in a car accident. Suppose that the burden on the few is slightly greater than the burden on the many because it involves the certainty of some loss—the loss of a faraway job, for example, because one cannot commute to this job unless one drives very fast—whereas the burden on the many involves only a small risk of loss, albeit a much greater loss than the few must suffer. Under these conditions I do not think that the government would necessarily violate the rights of the few in adopting this policy to reduce the total amount of harm.

It is admittedly unclear why a theory of rights should allow room for aggregative considerations if individualism in some form is valid as a general constraint on government policy. Perhaps this position is intellectually unstable. Perhaps our moral reasoning should either be thoroughly individualistic or thoroughly aggregative. If forced to choose between these unattractive alternatives, I would choose a thoroughgoing individualism and deny that the numbers count. I would then reject the burdens principle as I have stated it, and say instead that a person's rights are violated by any government policy that imposes a burden on her that is greater than the worst burden anyone would bear in the absence of this policy, and that if the burdens on both sides are equal it does not matter which policy the government adopts. I cannot, however, bring myself to believe that aggregative considerations have so little moral weight. So I settle for a hybrid view on which the burdens principle as stated is the correct individualistic test for whether a person's rights are violated by a policy that limits his liberty, acknowledging that I do not understand how aggregative and individualistic considerations fit together on the most fundamental level.

The central claim of this book is that paternalistic prostitution laws in some form are compatible in principle with liberalism. Liberalism, as I understand it, is committed to the thought that individuals have rights that the government must respect. Rights against the government are understood here to be valid moral principles of the kind just identified and can be justified in two ways. First, they can be grounded on the kind of individualistic moral reasoning of which the burdens principle is an example. Second, they can be grounded on valid generalizations about reasons for government action that identify certain kinds of reasons as too weak to justify the government in adopting certain policies. My primary aim in this chapter is to show that paternalistic prostitution laws in some form are consistent with those rights that can be grounded on the burdens principle. Because paternalistic prostitution laws are consistent with these rights only if certain judgments about the relative weight of burdens are sound, and because people can reasonably disagree about the relative weight of burdens, I will not attempt to *prove* that paternalistic prostitution laws in some form are compatible with our rights. I will attempt to show only that this conclusion is supported by a reasonable judgment about the relative weight of burdens, and that it therefore makes sense for someone to support these laws while claiming to take individual rights to liberty seriously.

III. The Rights of Sex Workers

Prohibiting a person from selling sexual services deprives her of a kind of control over her body and her sexuality. It deprives her of the legal freedom to treat her sexuality as a service or as a commodity, and so prevents her from freely ordering her own sex life by her own values. This is an important objection to the policy of prohibition and the beginning of an argument that this policy violates the rights of sex workers.

The thought that prohibition violates the sexual autonomy of sex workers is sometimes greeted with derision by critics of prostitution, who suggest that there is *no* sense in which a person genuinely exercises autonomy when she engages in prostitution. Women perform this work, they contend, only as a result of external coercion, mental illness, or an internal compulsion, such as drug addiction. Anyone who defends prostitution as an exercise of personal autonomy, they suggest, is motivated only to protect male sexual access to women or to subordinate women as a group.

The claim, however, that no one freely chooses to do sex work is clearly contradicted by the available evidence.[12] It is true that some people engage in prostitution only as the result of external coercion. It is also true that many are led to it by substance abuse and other mental health problems. It remains the case that *some* women who are not drug addicts freely choose to do this work because they prefer it to their other employment options. They can make more money at prostitution than at other jobs. They like the flexible hours and being their own boss. Although sometimes unpleasant, they do not find this work unbearable. In considering whether a prostitution law violates the rights of sex workers, one must consider the rights of every sex worker whose freedom this policy limits. One may not consider only the rights of those who are compelled in some way to do this work. One must also consider the rights of those who freely choose to do it or would freely choose to do it in the absence of legal penalties.

Even so, the claim that prohibition limits sexual autonomy may be greeted with skepticism. Why not suppose instead that prohibition limits only a person's *commercial* autonomy or freedom of contract? To claim that a policy limits a person's *sexual* autonomy seems to identify a stronger objection to it than the claim that it limits her commercial autonomy. Many laws limit a person's commercial autonomy, including laws that prohibit the sale of weapons and dangerous drugs and laws that prohibit racial discrimination in places of public accommodation. We do not think these policies are morally objectionable on this ground. So the claim that prohibition limits a person's sexual autonomy may seem to smuggle in a stronger objection to it than is warranted by the facts. Why, then, do I suppose that prohibition limits sexual autonomy?

The short answer is that prostitution involves sex. It involves a person's sexual organs and the sexual use of her body. It expresses a person's attitudes toward her sexuality and her body; it expresses the way she values her sexuality and her body. It seems to have a formative influence on a person's sexual identity, her attitudes toward sex and toward her body, and it seems to affect the quality of her intimate relationships. Commercial sex also sometimes evokes emotions and feelings that noncommercial sexual interactions evoke. Because sex work is related to a person's sexuality in all these ways, it makes sense to regard the decision to do or not to do it as a part of a person's sexual autonomy, as a component of having complete control over one's sex life.

The freedom to sell services is an important component of personal autonomy in other areas as well. Consider the freedom to accept pay for serving as a legislative representative or for serving as the government's chief executive officer, or the freedom to accept pay for political consulting or political advertising. These freedoms are important components of political liberty; they are important to having control of one's political life. Or consider the freedom to accept pay for performing religious ceremonies and functions, such as the liturgy and confession. These freedoms are important components of religious liberty; they are important to having control of one's religious life. Or consider the freedom to accept pay for performing in a play or movie or for performing music. These freedoms are important components of artistic freedom; they are important to having control over one's life as an artist. If the government were to prohibit the sale of these political, religious, or artistic services, most of us would see this as an outrageous infringement of our political, religious, and artistic liberties, and not only of our commercial liberty. And we would protest these policies, not only as threatening important interests of the buyers, but as threatening important interests of the sellers as well.

The sale of sexual services is admittedly different from the sale of political, religious, and artistic services. There are important political, religious, and artistic goods that are gained by having the legal freedom to accept pay for political, religious, and artistic services. It is certainly questionable that a person gains important sexual goods by having the legal freedom to accept pay for sexual services. To the contrary, it seems that prostitution can damage a person's capacity to enjoy sex and damage a person's capacities for love and friendship. The value of sexual autonomy, however, is not exhausted by the sexual goods that it promotes; it has nonderivative value as well. Personal control over the sexual use of one's own body has intrinsic value. The discretion to engage in consensual sex acts and to have consensual sexual relationships that seem situationally appropriate is valuable for its own sake.

Some may remain skeptical. Few of us believe that laws that prohibit the sale of recreational drugs threaten the personal autonomy of the *seller*. Why, then, should we believe that laws that prohibit the sale of *sex* do? The answer is that control over one's body and over one's sexuality is more central to control over oneself and over one one's own life than the freedom to sell products generally is.

Laws that prohibit prostitution are in fact more similar to laws that prohibit the *use* of drugs than they are to laws that prohibit the *sale* of drugs. Those who believe that drug laws are wrong believe this partly because they think it is important for people to have the legal opportunity to experiment with eye-opening or mood-altering experiences, provided that these experiences are not too dangerous to themselves or others. Laws that prohibit the use of recreational drugs seem to intrude too far into a person's space, and to remove important forms of legal discretion and control over the kinds of experience one has. On this basis, it makes sense to hold that laws that prohibit drug use violate personal autonomy. Judging by reports from those who have done sex work, prostitution is also a strange experience. It is not only a sexual experience, it is an *unusual* sexual experience, one that reveals aspects of others and of oneself that most sexual experiences do not. In this way, prostitution can be similar to certain drug experiences. It can be like a strange journey, one that reveals things about human reality that one would otherwise not know, at least not in the same way. Many of the experiences that sex workers have are negative, even traumatic, and can have a lasting negative impact on their lives. This is a good reason for laws that reduce prostitution. Laws that *prohibit* prostitution, however, prohibit people from having certain unusual experiences, sexual experiences that are uniquely characteristic of a certain way of life, a life that might be chosen by a person who is unusually adventurous, experimental, or unconventional. In this way, laws that criminalize prostitution are like laws that criminalize drug use. The *sale* of drugs is not eye opening in the way that drug *use* is. So laws that prohibit the sale of drugs do not infringe on personal autonomy in the way that laws that prohibit drug use do. They also do not prohibit a way of life that is strange and revealing in the way that prostitution is. One might argue, to the contrary, that the experience of being a drug dealer is also strange and revealing. If so, however, this is a function of the fact that selling drugs is illegal. If the manufacture and sale of recreational drugs were legal, then the experience of selling them would be no stranger and no more revealing of human nature than being a sales representative for a pharmaceutical or alcoholic beverage company. In presenting the argument for prostitution laws in chapter 1, I assumed that what is bad about prostitution is not entirely a function of its illegality. In explaining here why it makes sense to see prohibition as threatening sexual autonomy, I assume that what is unusual about the experience of doing sex work is likewise not entirely a function of its illegality. Imagine what doing this work would be like, even legally. Wouldn't the experience of selling sex be disturbing and strangely revealing even if prostitution were completely decriminalized? Wouldn't the decision to sell sex still have a greater impact on one's self-conception, one's sexual identity, the quality of one's intimate relationships, and one's experience of humanity than would the decision to sell other products and services? I think it would, and that this is a reason to regard prostitution as an exercise of sexual autonomy.

Because some may remain unconvinced, I should make clear that the central thesis of this book does not depend on the claim that prohibition infringes sexual autonomy. My central thesis is that paternalistic prostitution laws in some form can be justified compatible with the fundamental principles of liberalism. If prostitution is not an exercise of sexual autonomy, this thesis is easier to defend. The contrary belief, however, that prostitution is an exercise of sexual autonomy is also reasonable. So it makes sense to assume here for the sake of argument that it is correct. My goal is to show that paternalistic prostitution laws in some form are compatible with our rights to liberty and so with liberalism. If this position could be defended only by denying that prohibition threatens sexual autonomy, this would weaken the case, because this defense might then be faulted for failing to take seriously what some regard as the most serious objection to prostitution laws. If, on the other hand, prostitution laws in some form can be defended while acknowledging that prohibition threatens important interests in sexual autonomy, then the claim that *other* prostitution laws are nonetheless compatible with liberalism will be more convincing.

In chapter 1 I identified three main objections to the policy of prohibition: (1) it restricts the sexual autonomy of sex workers and would-be sex workers; (2) it prohibits an occupation that is an advisable choice for some; and (3) it makes sex work less safe for those who choose to do it. Even if all these objections are sound, it does not directly follow that prohibition violates anyone's rights. Selling sexual services is commonly bad for people. So it can be in a person's interest to be deterred from doing this work by government policies. Suppose that prohibition does a far better job than any feasible policy of abolition or regulation of deterring self-destructive sex work, and so significantly reduces a person's risk of harm, compared to what she would face under any more permissive policy. This policy would still be burdensome in limiting individuals' sexual autonomy. One might reasonably deny, however, that this policy violates anyone's *rights* because one might reasonably deny that the burdens imposed by prohibition are *substantially worse* than the increased risk of self-destructive conduct under any more permissive policy.

Perhaps it seems obvious that prohibition violates the rights of prostitutes. Enforcing a policy of prohibition must involve at least the threat of jail—if only to enforce fines and terms of probation—and being jailed for prostitution is worse for a person than doing sex work, even self-destructively. This observation, however, is not decisive.

As I pointed out in chapter 1, laws that prohibit shoplifting are justifiable even though it is worse to be imprisoned than to have something stolen from a store that one owns, works at, or shops at. This judgment can be reconciled with the burdens principle in the following way. We assume that there are good reasons to want to live in an environment where shoplifting is prohibited, grounded perhaps on the fact that if shoplifting is permitted, this will substantially reduce the availability of retail goods over time. We then assume that these reasons to want to live in an environment where shoplifting is prohibited are not decisively outweighed by the reasons there are for individuals to want the legal freedom to take whatever they want from a store without paying. Being imprisoned is bad, to be sure, but because one can avoid prison by not taking things from stores without paying for them, and one's reasons to want the freedom to take whatever one wants without paying do not (generally) have great weight, these reasons do not decisively outweigh the reasons there are for people to prefer their situations when shoplifting is prohibited.

The policy of prohibiting prostitution might be reconciled with the burdens principle in a similar way. One starts from the assumption that there are good reasons for individuals to prefer their situations when they are at a lower risk of doing self-destructive sex work. One then argues that the reasons for individuals to want the legal freedom to do this work are not very weighty. Even though prohibition involves the threat of jail, individuals can avoid jail either by choosing not to do this work or by meeting the conditions of probation. Because, by hypothesis, the reasons to want the legal freedom to do this work are not very weighty, the choice between not doing this work, meeting the conditions of probation, or risking jail is not very burdensome. It is not a choice that individuals have weighty reasons to want to avoid. So prohibition does not violate the burdens principle.

In fact, however, there are weighty reasons for individuals to want the legal freedom to do this kind of work. Individuals have weighty reasons to want legal control over their own sexuality, including the legal discretion to do sex work. They also have significant reasons for wanting the legal freedom to do work that is advisable for them to do. The government thus imposes a substantial burden on individuals for whom sex work is an advisable choice when it prohibits sex work. This policy might nonetheless be reconciled with the burdens principle if the reasons for individuals to want the government to adopt this policy were very weighty. However, as I pointed out in chapter 1, the primary benefit of prostitution laws to any particular individual is to reduce her risk of doing work that harms her. Prohibition might reduce this risk substantially if the penalties for doing sex work are harsh. If the penalties are harsh, however, then this policy would arguably violate the burdens principle because the reasons for a person to want to exercise her sexual autonomy and to do work that is (otherwise) advisable for her without risking harsh penalties arguably have substantially greater weight than anyone's reasons to want to be at a lower risk of being harmed by sex work that she chooses to do. If, on the other hand, the penalties for doing sex work are mild—if, for example, it is easy to avoid jail and prison by agreeing to government-funded counseling and community service—then a policy of prohibition is unlikely to reduce a woman's risk of choosing self-destructive sex work much more than a well-enforced policy of abolition or regulation would. If prohibition does little more than abolition or regulation, then the reasons for women for whom sex work is an advisable choice to want their sexual autonomy not to be curtailed in this way would seem to have substantially greater weight than the reasons for anyone to prefer her situation under a policy of prohibition. On these assumptions, it makes sense to hold that prohibition violates the rights of sex workers for whom sex work is an advisable choice.

Abolitionist and regulationist policies, however, do not prohibit anyone from selling sexual services. So they do not violate the rights of sex workers and would-be sex workers on these grounds. Do they violate their rights on other grounds? Both policies reduce a person's opportunities to make money via sex work, assuming they are effective, but many government policies reduce our opportunities to make money, and we do not think they violate our rights on this ground alone. Consider, for example, laws that prohibit highway billboards in order to preserve the natural beauty of our roadways. These laws reduce the opportunities of those who own land along the highways to make money, but we do not conclude from this that they violate anyone's rights to liberty. Money is good; the more of it the better. At least in developed postindustrial economies, however, our interests in having more opportunities to make money do not seem so weighty that they always trump competing interests that might be protected by governmental regulation, including interests in health and safety and environmental quality. Because the interests that prostitution laws protect seem to me to be at least as weighty as the interests that some permissible zoning and environmental regulations protect, neither abolitionist nor regulationist policies seem to me to violate the rights of sex workers solely on the ground that these policies reduce their opportunities to make money.

IV. The Rights of Customers

Neither abolitionist nor regulationist policies violate the rights of sex workers, I have just argued. Impermissive abolitionist policies, however, limit the sexual freedom of clients by prohibiting them from buying sexual services, and so arguably violate their rights on this ground.

Some men purchase sexual services for company, to alleviate loneliness and stress.[13] Perhaps they feel that they are unattractive to women and so have a hard time pursuing noncommercial sexual relations. Perhaps they need the kind of physical closeness and seeming physical acceptance that paid sex provides in order to relieve their sense of isolation or of being unwanted. Perhaps their existence is painful to them without this experience of physical intimacy. Other men may find sex within committed relationships stressful. They may truly enjoy sex and get the psychological relief that it provides only in interactions that are psychologically simple and unburdened. Other men may have unusual sexual tastes, and find it difficult to meet nonprofessionals who will do the things that most excite them. They may, for example, enjoy being hurt and humiliated, and find that only prostitutes provide this experience in a nonjudgmental and unthreatening way. The psychological health of these men may not be ideal, but if these individuals are genuinely benefited by sexual services, we must give some weight to their interests in having the legal freedom to purchase them.

If paying for sex were a form of violence against women, as some antilegalization activists contend, it might make sense to dismiss the interests of customers as having little or no weight. Paying for sex, however, is not a form of violence in the ordinary sense. The sale of sexual services is ordinarily consensual, and the transaction ordinarily involves no physical harm or specific threats of harm. Paying for sex may sometimes be psychologically sadistic—if, for example, the customer enjoys the fact that the sex worker feels humiliated by the transaction and does not enjoy it. There is, however, no reason to believe that paid sex is *always* sadistic in this way. Some clients may also be perverted in that they enjoy paid sex only because they are indifferent to or deluded about the psychological states of the person with whom they are having sex. It is doubtful, though, that paid sex is *always* perverted in this way, and even if it were, it is unclear why this fact alone should cancel the interests customers have in obtaining whatever psychological benefit paid sex provides them.

Concerns about the moralistic nature of prostitution laws are commonly based, I think, on the perception that these laws are paternalistic toward sex workers and would-be sex workers. For this reason, I argued in chapter 2 that the paternalistic nature of these laws does not make them objectionably moralistic. There is, however, another way in which these laws might be moralistic. If political support for prostitution laws is based on indifference to the interests of customers and this indifference is based on a moral judgment that fails to warrant giving these interests so little weight, political support for prostitution laws is objectionably moralistic on this ground.

Perhaps paid sex does not play the sort of positive role in anyone's life that I have just imagined. Perhaps the kind of sex that people experience with prostitutes is almost always unsatisfying. Although these encounters may be exciting in prospect, perhaps they are actually less emotionally satisfying than pornography or unaided masturbation. Perhaps those who seek out prostitutes in order to relieve anxiety and depression almost always feel more anxious and depressed afterward. Perhaps the kind of companionship that prostitutes provide typically leaves the customer feeling even more lonely and isolated than before the transaction. If so, the interests that customers have in the freedom to purchase sexual services have less weight, and it is less likely that their rights are violated by abolitionist policies.

It is also possible that patronizing prostitutes commonly undermines a client's capacity for love and friendship and interferes with important relationships, such as his relationship to his wife. If so, there are paternalistic reasons given by the interests of clients to restrict access to prostitutes, which may outweigh or balance whatever interests clients have in the legal opportunity to obtain these services.[14]

Suppose, though, that some men really do need the services of prostitutes in order to feel good about themselves and about their lives. Suppose that these interests decisively outweigh whatever paternalistic reasons there are to restrict access on behalf of clients. Suppose, too, that impermissive abolitionist policies do not substantially reduce underage prostitution or sex trafficking, or that they do not reduce them much more than well-enforced permissive abolitionist or impermissive regulationist policies do. Then, I think, there is a good case to be made that impermissive abolitionist policies, such as the policy of Sweden, violate the rights of some clients, and therefore must not be adopted.

If prostitution is harmful in the ways that I described in chapter 1, and paternalistic reasons can justify the government in adopting policies that limit adult sexual freedom, then there is a case to be made for the Swedish policy of impermissive abolition. This policy, however, prohibits a person from purchasing sexual services from anyone, regardless of age or personal situation, and this makes this policy hard to justify. Because young people commonly fail to understand the long-term negative consequences of their actions, there are good reasons for them to want to be protected from opportunities and incentives to engage in self-destructive conduct. As a person grows older, however, her experience of the world grows and her ability to reason well about what is best for her improves, as does her ability to resist manipulative pressure from others. This does not invalidate the paternalistic reasons for the government to adopt policies that protect older women against self-destructive sex work, because a person might still reason poorly as an adult about what is best for her and might still be vulnerable to destructive forms of manipulation. These facts, however, do reduce the weight of these paternalistic reasons relative to the reasons that there are for other adults to want their sexual freedom not to be restricted, which is why an impermissive policy of abolition might violate the rights of some clients.

Even if the rights of clients, however, would be violated by impermissive abolition, it is doubtful that their rights would be violated by a permissive abolitionist policy or by an impermissive regulationist policy. A permissive abolitionist policy does not criminalize the purchase of sexual services as such; it criminalizes only certain ways of obtaining these services, such as kerb crawling. An impermissive regulationist policy does not criminalize the purchase of sexual services as such; it criminalizes only the purchase of sexual services from persons under a certain age. Both policies would therefore allow those individuals who need to acquire sexual services in order to feel good about themselves and their lives to do so legally. A permissive abolitionist policy would allow a person legally to acquire such services via newspaper and Internet advertisements. An impermissive regulationist policy would permit brothels, escort services, and "massage parlors" as well. Because these policies do not threaten the most important interests of clients, it is doubtful that they violate the burdens principle on this ground.

Some might argue that even permissive abolitionist policies violate the rights of customers because they deprive them of opportunities for a certain kind of fun: the opportunity to buy sex on the street, for example, or in a brothel. Many laws, however, deprive people of opportunities for fun, including laws that prohibit skateboarding in parking garages, drag racing on public roads, flashing and other forms of exhibitionism, smoking cigarettes in bars and restaurants, and drinking alcoholic beverages while walking down the street. The mere fact that a law deprives people of an opportunity for fun is not a decisive objection to it. This is partly because in any free society there are many other opportunities for fun. If one opportunity is blocked, plenty of other opportunities remain, and the loss of this one opportunity is not great. The loss of an opportunity for a particular kind of fun is a serious loss only if this particular kind of fun plays an important and irreplaceable role in enabling a person to enjoy life. This does not seem true of the particular kind of fun that is involved in picking up a streetwalker or in visiting a brothel. So it is doubtful that permissive abolition violates anyone's rights on this ground.

Some might think that kerb crawling laws and other laws prohibiting outdoor purchase violate the rights of customers simply by imposing on them the risk of arrest and conviction for pursuing a kind of recreational amusement. We do not, however, generally take the risk of criminal liability to be a sufficient objection to a law that prohibits a form of conduct when there are good reasons for this law. If the penalties for kerb crawling and related activities are too harsh, it makes sense to object to these penalties on this ground. These laws, however, need not be enforced by harsh penalties. They might be enforced primarily by warnings backed up by misdemeanor charges and fines.

The burden of criminal liability on customers can also be lightened in other ways. In many jurisdictions one can avoid paying a traffic ticket fine and nullify the record of the ticket by going to driving school. Likewise, San Francisco has required those arrested for patronizing prostitutes to go to "johns' school," where customers learn more about prostitution, about why the women do it, about how unenjoyable it is for them to do, and about how destructive it is for them in other ways.[15] A policy of this kind, which provides those arrested for patronizing prostitutes with an opportunity to avoid conviction, might lighten the burden of criminal liability enough to be justified by the benefit of reducing the harm caused by doing sex work on the streets.

In some ways a policy of impermissive regulation with a high age limit would be more burdensome than a permissive policy of abolition. Although impermissive regulation would impose no penalties for kerb crawling or other forms of outdoor solicitation as such, it would still impose penalties for engaging in these activities in certain areas, as part of the zoning restrictions that a policy of regulation imposes. This policy might also impose criminal penalties for hiring anyone under twenty-one or twenty-five for sex work, which would significantly limit the persons a client could legally hire for sex work. These limitations, however, also do not seem unduly burdensome. Impermissive regulation allows those who truly *need* to purchase sexual services to do so. If a man prefers the sexual company of young people, he has the legal opportunity to pursue them noncommercially. If, then, a high age limit is necessary to protect young people adequately from incentives to make harmful choices, the burdens imposed by this policy seem consistent with the burdens principle, too.

V. The Burdens on Families

Prohibition arguably violates the rights of sex workers. Impermissive abolition arguably violates the rights of customers. Neither permissive abolition nor impermissive regulation violates *their* rights. Do these policies violate the rights of others?

If a man is arrested for patronizing a prostitute on the street or for patronizing an underage prostitute, this can have a bad effect on his family. It may upset his spouse or partner and she (or he) might be strongly motivated to leave the relationship as a consequence. This might be a bad thing for both of them, because this relationship might otherwise be a good one. It might be bad for their children, too. Furthermore, an arrest might result in the loss of a job, which would harm those who depend on this man's income. These are objections not only to prohibition and impermissive abolition, but also to any permissive abolitionist policy that criminalizes outdoor purchase and to any regulationist policy that makes it illegal to purchase sex from anyone under twenty-one or twenty-five.

A traditional argument for prostitution laws is that they are necessary to protect the family members of men tempted to go to prostitutes. This would be a good argument if prostitutes were responsible for the spread of serious sexually transmitted diseases to unwitting partners. For reasons given in the introduction, however, it is unclear that the legal availability of prostitutes significantly increases the risk of serious disease to unwitting third parties. Some might argue that prostitution laws are nonetheless necessary to protect the family by reducing adultery. If, however, prostitution does not contribute significantly to the spread of deadly disease, prostitution laws arguably threaten the interests of family members more than they protect them. This is because a man's family is far more likely to be torn apart by an arrest for patronizing a prostitute than by a clandestine encounter that is unknown to anyone but the participants.

In any case, the burden of criminal liability on the customer and the consequent threat to families can be significantly lightened by restrained policies of enforcement. If a client visits a brothel or uses an escort agency and the owner or manager is arrested, this client is at risk of being exposed, with consequent harm to his family. This risk, however, is significantly reduced if the police and the courts adopt a policy of not releasing the names of clients to the public when the owner of a brothel or escort agency is charged. If a man is arrested for kerb crawling, this poses a threat to his family. Detectives on vice squads, however, can be instructed by their superiors to "go easy on family men," to give only warnings at first, and to issue citations only when doing so is necessary to prevent the system of enforcement from seeming like an empty sham. If there is an opportunity to avoid conviction by going to johns' school, then not even a citation need result in unwanted publicity. How burdensome a policy of permissive abolition or impermissive regulation is depends, then, on how it is enforced. If the policy is enforced wisely, the burden on families can be reduced sufficiently to be justified by the goal of reducing self-destructive sex work.

VI. Rights and Policies

Prohibition arguably violates the rights of sex workers in limiting their sexual autonomy. Impermissive abolitionist policies arguably violate the rights of customers in limiting their sexual freedom. Whether these policies violate anyone's rights in these ways depends on how much they do to reduce the risk to young women of self-destructive sex work when enforced by mild penalties and also on the degree to which clients are benefited by sexual services. If a prohibitionist policy does much more than any less restrictive feasible alternative to reduce self-destructive sex work even when enforced with mild penalties, this policy might not violate the rights of sex workers after all, because it might then not violate the burdens principle. If sex work does not provide genuine psychological benefits to clients or an impermissive abolitionist policy does much more to reduce self-destructive sex work than any less restrictive feasible alternative, then this policy might not violate the rights of clients to sexual freedom. Even if these policies, however, *do* violate the rights of sex workers and clients, neither a permissive policy of abolition nor a strong regulation does. Nor do these policies violate the rights of anyone else. This is the claim so far.

This claim rests on a number of assumptions that might reasonably be questioned. It rests on the assumption that the burdens principle provides the correct individualistic test for whether a person's rights are violated by a policy that limits his liberty or opportunities. It also rests on a number of substantive judgments about the relative weight of burdens, which rest on substantive judgments about the relative weight of individuals' reasons for preferring their situations under various policies. Because all of these assumptions might be questioned, a reader might wonder what the arguments of the previous sections are supposed to have shown.

I have argued that prostitution laws *in some form* are compatible with the rights of sex workers, clients, and others on one general account of our rights to liberty, given certain substantive judgments about the relative weight of burdens. The modest goal of this argument is to show that one may coherently defend prostitution laws in some form while claiming to take individuals' rights to liberty seriously. This is coherent because the burdens principle is defensible as the correct individualistic test for whether a policy violates a person's rights in limiting his liberty, and because the relevant substantive judgments about burdens are also coherent and defensible. Someone might also coherently reject the burdens principle and these judgments about burdens. At this point we must consider in greater depth what the best account of rights is and what can be said for and against these judgments about burdens. All I hope to have shown so far is that an intellectually conscientious person might sincerely and coherently defend significant legal restrictions on prostitution while taking seriously the idea that individuals have rights to liberty and while accepting individualism as the correct framework for reasoning about our rights.

Even if I am right, however, that neither a policy of permissive abolition nor a policy of strong regulation violates anyone's rights to liberty, it does not directly follow that the government ought to adopt these policies because the costs of these policies, properly considered, might nonetheless outweigh their benefits. If a policy does not impose a burden on anyone that is substantially worse than the worst burden anyone would bear in its absence, then it does not violate the burdens principle, and so does not violate anyone's rights on this ground. This policy, however, might still be objectionable on at least three other grounds. First, it might impose a burden on someone that is *slightly* worse than the worst burden anyone would bear in its absence. Second, although the worst burdens on either side are equivalent, more people might be burdened by this policy than are benefited by it. Third, although the worst burden someone bears in the absence of a policy is slightly worse than the worst burden anyone would bear as a result, many more people might be burdened by this policy than are benefited by it. An individualistic principle such as the burdens principle entails that whether or not the government ought to adopt a policy cannot be settled by aggregative reasoning alone. The burdens principle, however, also allows aggregative considerations to play a role in justifying government policies. So even if a policy does not violate the burdens principle, its aggregated costs might still outweigh its aggregated benefits, and the government might therefore not be justified in adopting this policy, all things considered.

In chapter 1 I identified the ways in which prostitution is thought to be harmful to the women who do it. I did not, however, say anything about the proportion of women who are harmed by this work. I simply said, vaguely, that prostitution is "commonly harmful." One scholar has suggested that only about one-quarter of the women who do sex work are much worse off as a result. About half are slightly worse off. A quarter are better off.[16] Suppose this is true. The fact that only a quarter of sex workers are much worse off as a result of doing this work does not imply that prostitution laws violate anyone's rights, because prostitution laws might nonetheless substantially reduce the risk to some vulnerable women of doing this work to their own detriment. If, however, a quarter of the women who do this work are benefited by it and only a quarter of women are substantially harmed by it, this is clearly relevant to whether the policy is justified, all things considered, and so to whether the government ought adopt it.

Some may think that the government is justified in adopting a policy provided that the majority supports it and it violates no one's rights. I reject this view. If the costs of a policy are significantly greater than its benefits, then the legislature is not justified in adopting this policy even if a majority supports it and even if it violates no one's rights. If a legislator does not support a policy that his constituents support, then he might be voted out of office. If his likely opponent in the upcoming election will do more harm than good, these facts might provide a good reason for him to support this policy, even if it is not the best one. The fact that a legislature adopts a policy is also a good reason for the police and the courts to enforce it, provided that it is constitutional. These facts alone, however, do not justify the *legislature* in adopting the policy. The legislature is justified in adopting a policy only if it is the best policy, all things considered.

How, then, should we weigh the costs and benefits of a policy to determine whether the government should adopt it? I do not think we have a satisfactory model. Hedonistic act utilitarianism provides the simplest theory, but it is not easy to apply to actual cases, because we cannot ordinarily tell how much pleasure and pain will result from a given policy. This theory also assumes that pleasure and pain are the only consequences relevant to our evaluation of government policy, which is probably false. If we adopt a nonhedonistic form of utilitarianism instead or a nonutilitarian consequentialism that takes into account consequences other than gains or losses in human welfare, it is even less clear how to assign numbers to the relevant positive and negative consequences and so how to weigh costs and benefits arithmetically.

Whatever the correct way, though, to reason about the relative costs and benefits of government policies, it might warrant the conclusion that neither permissive abolition nor the strongest form of impermissive regulation considered here is the best policy, all things considered. Perhaps the kind of impermissive regulation that Germany and the Netherlands adopt is better. Or perhaps the best policy is a regulationist policy that is more restrictive than the Dutch and German policies, but less restrictive than any form of prohibition or abolition.

Suppose the government prohibits the purchase of sexual services from anyone under twenty-one and the employment of anyone under twenty-one by a sex business (with more than one employee). A reasonable objection is that this policy would provide inadequate protection to adolescent girls because it would be too easy for them to pretend that they are twenty-one and for sex businesses and customers to take advantage of this. Perhaps, though, this risk could be effectively reduced by imposing strict liability on the employment of someone for sexual services, so that reasonable mistakes of age would provide no legal excuse for employing someone under twenty-one. The law might permit the purchase of sex only from those with a valid identification showing the seller to be at least twenty-one. Perhaps this policy could be effectively and ethically enforced by police decoys. This policy would provide more opportunities to make money through sex work to those young women for whom sex work is an advisable choice; it would provide more choices for customers and would thereby reduce the risk to families; and it would provide more entrepreneurial opportunities for those in the sex business. On the other hand, this policy, if effectively enforced, might still significantly reduce the risk to young women of self-destructive sex work by making their services too risky to employ. If a stronger policy of regulation with an age limit of twenty-five does not violate anyone's rights, neither does this one. Perhaps this policy is the best policy, all things considered.

Perhaps, though, the best policy is significantly more restrictive than this. Perhaps the best policy, all things considered, is to prohibit brothels and escort services, prohibit purchase on the street, *and* prohibit purchase from anyone under twenty-five. As I said in chapter 1, my goal here is not to defend any particular policy on prostitution as the best one, all things considered. Public policy judgments of this kind are best left to the experts. My aim here is simply to establish, given a number of assumptions, that some paternalistic restrictions on prostitution violate no one's rights. If so, then paternalistic prostitution laws in *some* form are compatible in principle with taking our rights to liberty seriously, and so with liberalism.

VII. Rights and Paternalism

I have now explained why I do not believe that either a permissive form of abolition or a strong form of impermissive regulation would violate the rights of sex workers, clients, or others, assuming that this policy protects vulnerable young women in the way I have supposed. Some might still think that this policy violates the rights of these vulnerable young women in being paternalistic toward them. So before concluding this chapter I should connect what I have said about rights in this chapter with what I said about paternalism in the previous chapter.

In chapter 3 I held that a policy is paternalistic toward a person if (a) this policy limits this person's liberty or opportunities; (b) the strongest reason for limiting this person's liberty or opportunities in this way is that this policy benefits this person; and (c) the way in which this policy limits this person's liberty or opportunities cannot be justified as benefiting anyone else. For the purpose of this discussion I will suppose that both the policies of permissive abolition and of impermissive regulation are paternalistic in this sense: they limit the opportunities of young people to sell sexual services; the strongest reason for these policies is that they benefit these young people; and these policies cannot be justified as benefiting others.

In chapter 3 I also distinguished *hard* and *soft* forms of paternalism. A policy is a form of hard paternalism if (a) this policy is paternalistic toward someone in the sense just defined and (b) this policy limits this person's liberty or opportunities in a way that he or she opposes. A policy is a form of soft paternalism if (a) this policy is paternalistic toward someone and (b) this policy does not limit this person's liberty or opportunities in ways that he or she opposes. Hard paternalism is commonly thought to threaten individuals' rights in a way that soft paternalism does not. If, however, the burdens principle were the only valid test of rights violations, there would be little reason to believe that hard paternalism always violates a person's rights or that soft paternalism never does.

To see how a soft paternalistic policy might violate the burdens principle, imagine someone who wants the government to make his marital decisions for him because he believes he is bad at choosing a suitable mate. If the strongest reasons for the government to make these decisions is to protect this person from his own bad marital decisions and this policy cannot be justified as benefiting anyone else, this policy would be a form of paternalism, and it would be a form of soft paternalism because this person wants the government to adopt this policy. Given the importance, however, of freedom of marital choice, it is arguable that the (objective) reasons for this person to prefer his situation when the government does not oversee his life in this way nonetheless have substantially greater weight than the reasons there are for him to want it to do so. If so, then this policy violates the burdens principle even though it is a form of soft paternalism.

A hard paternalistic policy, on the other hand, might not violate the burdens principle. Imagine a law that requires motorcyclists under the age of twenty-one to wear a helmet but permits older motorcyclists not to wear one. Suppose that the strongest reason for this law is that it protects the health and safety of motorcyclists under twenty-one and that it cannot be justified as benefiting anyone else. Suppose, too, that this law cannot be justified unless the following benefits are counted in its favor: its benefits in health and safety to persons under twenty-one who do not want this kind of protection. Then this policy is a form of hard paternalism. There is little reason, though, to believe that this policy violates the burdens principle. This is because the freedom to ride without a helmet when one is under twenty-one is not very important and the risks to those under twenty-one of riding without a helmet are significant. Consequently, the reasons for the intended beneficiaries of this policy to want the government to adopt it arguably have greater weight than their reasons to want the government not to adopt it, despite their opposition to it. If these reasons do have greater weight, this policy does not violate the burdens principle, although it is a form of hard paternalism.

Identifying a paternalistic policy as hard or soft does not therefore suffice to determine whether it violates the burdens principle and so whether it violates someone's rights on this ground. Which kinds of hard paternalism, then, violate a person's rights? In chapter 3 I endorsed the following general principle of antipaternalism: if (a) a person has achieved at least that degree of ability at prudential reasoning that we normally expect from a fully mature adult in our society, and if (b) a government policy limits the liberties or opportunities of this person in a way that he or she opposes, and if (c) the liberties or opportunities it limits are important ones for this person to have, and if (d) this person's wish to do what this policy prohibits or aims to discourage does not result from psychosis, acute emotional distress, or ignorance of grave demonstrable consequences, then the government may not adopt this policy unless it can be fully justified without counting any benefit to this person in its favor. If this principle is valid, then it constitutes a limited right against hard paternalism.

What is the connection, though, between this principle of antipaternalism and the burdens principle? If the burdens principle were the *only* basis of our rights, then this principle of antipaternalism would constitute a right only if every policy that violates this principle also violates the burdens principle. This may not be true. Even if a liberty is important, the reasons for a mature person who is adequately informed to want this liberty to be limited against his will might have substantial weight. Although these reasons might nonetheless always be outweighed by the reasons for this person to want this important liberty not to be limited, these reasons might not always have *substantially greater weight* than the reasons there are for him to prefer his situation when this liberty is limited. If not, this principle of antipaternalism cannot be grounded on the burdens principle. On what grounds, then, is it valid?

Rights to liberty are valid moral principles that limit the reasons that can justify the government in limiting our liberty. Some of these rights are grounded on the kind of individualism that the burdens principle represents, but not all rights are justified in this way. Some are grounded instead on valid generalizations about reasons, which hold correctly that reasons of a certain kind are insufficient to justify government policies of a certain kind. This is the kind of claim on which my principle of antipaternalism is based.

The burdens principle is proposed as a test of whether a policy that sacrifices the liberty of one person for the benefit of *another* person violates the first person's rights, a test that is structured to allow adequate room for aggregative considerations. The issue of paternalism is whether a person's rights are violated by a policy that sacrifices his liberty for his *own* benefit. When we evaluate whether a paternalistic policy is justifiable, the antiaggregative considerations that motivate individualism are absent. Furthermore, in evaluating paternalism, there is no need to adjust our individualistic framework, as the burdens principle does, to allow adequate room for aggregative considerations. This is because a limitation of someone's liberty that could be justified by its aggregate benefits to others would not, by definition, *be* a paternalistic policy in the relevant sense. When assessing the permissibility of paternalism, it therefore makes sense to set the individualistic framework aside and ask directly whether paternalism is ever morally justifiable.

I suppose that a policy that is paternalistic toward someone is morally justifiable provided that the reasons for this person to want the government to limit his liberty or opportunities in this way have greater weight than the reasons for him to want the government not to limit his liberty or opportunities in this way. When this is the case, the government is justified in limiting a person's liberty for his own good. Assuming, then, that this is sometimes the case, not all forms of paternalism violate our rights. If, however, a policy violates my principle of antipaternalism, then I believe that this policy is not justifiable in this way. When a liberty is important, and when a person wishes to exercise this liberty, and when this person is mature, adequately informed and reasoning sanely, then the reasons for him to prefer his own situation when this liberty is not limited against his will always have greater weight than any reason there is for him to prefer his situation when this liberty is limited. Hence no policy that violates this principle of antipaternalism is justifiable. If this principle is valid, it makes sense to regard it as a right, and so to hold that there is a general, if qualified, right against paternalism, even if this principle cannot be grounded on the burdens principle.

In this chapter I have considered whether prostitution laws violate the rights of persons other than those these laws are intended to benefit. I have suggested that prohibition might violate the rights of sex workers for whom sex work is an advisable choice. Does it also violate the rights of sex workers for whom sex work is *not* an advisable choice? Yes and no. Prohibition deprives people of the liberty to sell sexual services and in doing so restricts their sexual freedom. Because sexual autonomy is an important component of a person's control over her own life, sexual freedom is an important liberty. So if a mentally mature person opposes this legal restriction and would, in the absence of this restriction, choose to do this work with knowledge of the consequences while sane and not emotionally distressed; and prohibiting this person from doing sex work could not be justified as benefiting anyone else; then prohibiting this person from doing sex work would violate my principle of antipaternalism, and so would violate this right. It would violate this right and so would be objectionably paternalistic toward her even if, as matter of fact, sex work is not an advisable choice for this person. If, however, a person is mentally immature, or would choose to do this work only as a result of mental illness, emotional distress, or ignorance of grave demonstrable consequences, then, even if prohibiting this person from doing sex work could not be justified as benefiting anyone else, this policy would not violate my principle of antipaternalism, and so would not violate this right.

Abolitionist and impermissive regulationist policies, in contrast, do not prohibit anyone from selling sexual services. So they do not deprive sex workers or would-be sex workers of any important liberty. These policies reduce a person's opportunities to make money through sex work, but these opportunities are not sufficiently important in economically advanced nations to constitute a violation of my principle of antipaternalism. So neither abolitionist nor regulationist policies violate *this* right. Abolitionist policies might still violate the rights of *others*, customers in particular. But, I have argued, neither a permissive abolitionist policy nor a strong impermissive regulationist policy would violate anyone's rights. From this I conclude that if the empirical assumptions of the paternalistic argument for prostitution laws are sound, significant restrictions on prostitution can be justified by this argument consistent with a due respect for everyone's rights to liberty, and so consistent with the fundamental principles of liberalism.

5

Government Neutrality and Perfectionism

Paternalistic prostitution laws are not all objectionably paternalistic. They are not moralistic, and not all of them violate someone's rights. This is the argument so far. Some may believe that paternalistic prostitution laws are still objectionably *perfectionist.* They may also believe that government paternalism, government moralism, and government perfectionism are all wrong for the same reason: they violate the principle that the government should be as neutral as possible toward different conceptions of a good life, which some have suggested is essential to liberalism.[1] Given that my aim here is to show that paternalistic prostitution laws are compatible with liberalism, I should now address this objection, either by explaining why the principle of neutrality permits paternalistic prostitution laws or by explaining why this principle is not essential to liberalism.

The policies of permissive abolition and impermissive regulation defended in the previous chapters *tolerate* prostitution, but they also *discourage* it. They tolerate prostitution by not criminalizing all commercial sexual transactions. They discourage it by reducing the opportunities or incentives to do this work. Neither permissive abolition nor impermissive regulation violates anyone's rights in violating the burdens principle, I have argued. If, however, policies that seek to discourage prostitution in this way violate a valid principle of government neutrality, an important objection to paternalistic prostitution laws remains.

In this chapter I address this objection in the following way. I argue that the principle of government neutrality is best understood to rule out certain reasons for the government to limit individual liberty, and that this constraint on reasons permits the paternalistic reasons for prostitution laws that I have identified. Some may prefer to interpret the principle of neutrality in a different way, so that it rules out these paternalistic reasons. On this interpretation, however, the principle of neutrality is neither valid nor essential to liberalism.

I. The Possibility of Neutrality

One way to deal with the objection that prostitution laws violate the principle of government neutrality is to deny that this principle is valid. One way to dispute its validity is to claim that government neutrality toward conceptions of a good life is impossible. The impossibility of neutrality might be defended in the following way. Some people are serial killers, who believe that the best life involves killing others for fun. If the government prohibits murder, it expresses the view that this conception of the good life may not be pursued and makes it more difficult to live according to this conception. It therefore fails to be neutral between this conception of a good life and others. Every legitimate government, however, must prohibit murder. So no legitimate government can be neutral toward all conceptions of a good life. Neutrality is therefore impossible.

Despite the apparent persuasiveness of this objection, I think there is a good answer to it. This is that the government is neutral in the relevant sense when it adopts only those policies that can be fully justified by neutral reasons. Assuming that murder laws can be fully justified by neutral reasons, this policy is neutral in the relevant sense. In what way are these reasons neutral? This is not so easy to say, but for now we can say that a neutral reason is one that the principle of neutrality allows as a legitimate reason for government policy.

In endorsing the principle of neutrality, liberal theorists have intended to exclude as illegitimate a number of different reasons for the government to limit individual liberty, which we can identify by a list. Nonneutral reasons, we can say for now, are the reasons on this list; neutral reasons are reasons not on this list. Here is a list of nonneutral reasons for the government to limit individual liberty that one might arrive at by reflecting on the reasons that defenders of neutrality have meant to exclude:

1. A person's conception of a good life is false, or contains false propositions about what is good or valuable.
2. By expressing some belief or attitude, a person makes it more likely that someone else will form a false evaluative belief, about politics, religion, philosophy, science, art, or about how best to live.
3. By engaging in an activity, a person will displease God (or a god), or create distance between himself and God (or some god), or make himself worse off in the afterlife.

4. By pursuing a goal or by engaging in an activity, a person will live a life that is less than the best or most excellent life that he or she could have led.
5. By pursuing a goal or by engaging in an activity, a person will not develop and exercise her higher human capacities as fully as possible throughout her life, or as fully as she might have.
6. What a person wishes to do is intrinsically wrong or bad, or wrong or bad independent of its negative effects on anyone.
7. The goals a person wishes to pursue or the activities she wishes to engage in are inherently worthless.
8. By pursuing a goal or by engaging in an activity, a person becomes less admirable.
9. Others disapprove of the goals a person wishes to pursue or the activities she wishes to engage in.
10. The activities a person wishes to engage in are shameful, base, ignoble, or degrading in having one of these qualities.
11. What a person wishes to do, or be, or become, or have, or create is ugly or otherwise aesthetically objectionable.
12. By doing something, a person fails to treat with due care or respect something precious, such as the capacity for sexual intimacy, or sacred, such as potential human life.

If the principle of neutrality is understood to permit only policies that can be justified by reasons that are not on this list, then clearly neutrality in the relevant sense is possible, because it is possible for the government to adopt only policies that can be justified by reasons that are not on this list.

Some critics of neutrality, however, have doubted its possibility for a different reason, which is that any plausible conception of political justice or system of principles of political justice must be grounded on some view of what is good for people. Although this is true, it does not entail that neutrality in the relevant sense is impossible.

To see why, it is helpful to distinguish two different levels of neutrality, legislative and foundational. The legislative principle of neutrality is that the government should not adopt a policy unless it can be justified by neutral reasons. The foundational principle of neutrality is that a principle of political justice or a principle of liberty (such as the principle of legislative neutrality) is valid only if it can be justified without making any assumptions about what kinds of life are best for people.[2] Some may think that *foundational* neutrality is impossible because no plausible system of principles could be justified without making *some* assumptions about what kinds of life are best for people. Even if this is true, however, it implies nothing with respect to the possibility of *legislative* neutrality. This is because the correct view of the best human life might warrant the principle of legislative neutrality as a valid principle of political justice even if it provides a nonneutral foundation for this principle.[3] It is also possible that the foundational principle of neutrality is valid although the legislative principle is not valid, because a neutral foundation might identify decisive reasons to reject the principle of legislative neutrality.[4] The possibility and desirability of legislative neutrality is therefore a separate issue from the possibility and desirability of foundational neutrality.

No leading contemporary political philosopher, so far as I know, has claimed that foundational neutrality is essential to liberalism. What some have suggested is that liberalism is committed to a principle of legislative neutrality. For this reason I now set aside the question of whether *foundational* neutrality is possible and desirable, to focus on the objection to paternalistic prostitution laws that they violate a valid principle of *legislative* neutrality.

If the principle of legislative neutrality is understood to permit the government to limit liberty only in those ways that can be justified without reference to any of the nonneutral reasons on the above list, and the paternalistic argument of chapter 1 is sound, then prostitution laws are compatible with the principle of legislative neutrality. This is because the reasons for prostitution laws that this argument identifies are not on the above list. The principle of legislative neutrality does exclude certain reasons of degradation, and the paternalistic argument for prostitution laws presupposes that prostitution is degrading in *some* sense. But, as I indicated in the discussion of Rawls and Dworkin in chapter 2,[5] the sense in which the argument for prostitution laws presupposes that prostitution is degrading is not the sense in which reasons of degradation are ruled out by the principle of legislative neutrality.

This approach, however, to defending the neutrality of paternalistic prostitution laws clearly presupposes a particular conception of what reasons are neutral and nonneutral, and some may question this conception. They may believe that the paternalistic reasons for prostitution laws *ought* to be placed on the above list of nonneutral reasons, and that it is arbitrary to omit them. So I want to explain why this is not arbitrary.

II. The Neutrality of Paternalistic Reasons

Whether it is arbitrary to exclude the paternalistic reasons for prostitution laws from the above list of nonneutral reasons depends partly on what *makes* a reason nonneutral. Do the paternalistic reasons for prostitution laws share a property with all the other nonneutral reasons on the above list that would warrant counting them as nonneutral too? If not, it is not arbitrary to exclude them from this list. What property is it, then, that makes a reason nonneutral?

On one possible analysis, a reason is nonneutral if and only if it implies that someone's conception of the good life is false or unsound. To give this a bit more structure, we might say that a reason is nonneutral if and only if taking it as sufficient to justify the government in limiting someone's liberty implies that a belief that someone has about the best life for her to lead is incorrect. If preventing the harm that commonly results from prostitution is sufficient to justify prostitution laws in some form, then, it seems, someone must be making a mistake about what is best for her: those who are choosing to do this work self-destructively. So, on this account of what makes a reason nonneutral, paternalistic prostitution laws do seem to violate the principle of neutrality.

This analysis, however, fails to identify as nonneutral some of the reasons that defenders of neutrality have clearly meant to exclude. Consider, for example, the reason to prohibit homosexual sodomy that a majority disapproves of it. By this I do not mean the procedural fact that a majority of voters have voted for some ballot proposition prohibiting homosexual sodomy; I mean the nonprocedural psychological fact that most people (in their heads) disapprove of homosexual sodomy (if this is a fact). Although this is one of the reasons that defenders of neutrality such as Dworkin have meant to exclude,[6] taking majority disapproval to be a good reason to prohibit a form of conduct does not imply that any belief that someone has about the best life for her to lead is incorrect (not at least if *imply* has its normal logical meaning). There is no inconsistency in holding that in a democracy government officials are justified in prohibiting some form of private conduct by the fact that the majority disapproves of it even if no one is making an error in believing that this activity is part of the best life for her. Hence there is no inconsistency in holding that majority disapproval is a sufficient reason to prohibit a form of private conduct while also holding that a conception of the good life that recommends this conduct is correct.

Despite this defect, this analysis may come closer than any other to capturing what makes a reason nonneutral. So perhaps we should say that, despite what some defenders of neutrality have suggested, majority disapproval is not a *nonneutral* reason. It is a bad reason of some other kind. The only nonneutral reasons, strictly speaking, are those that imply (loosely speaking) that someone is wrong about the best life for her. This does not explain what *all* the reasons on the above list have in common, but perhaps it explains what most of them have in common.

If, however, the principle of neutrality is properly interpreted to rule out paternalism in this way, this raises two further difficulties. First, if some kinds of paternalism are permissible, as I argued in the previous two chapters, then the principle of neutrality is invalid. Second, most leading contemporary liberal theorists believe that some kinds of paternalism are permissible. So if the principle of neutrality rules out paternalism, it makes little sense to hold that the principle of neutrality is essential to liberalism.

Rawls clearly allows the permissibility of some kinds of paternalism in *A Theory of Justice*.[7] Hart allows the permissibility of paternalism in his famous response to Lord Devlin.[8] Dworkin allows the permissibility of paternalism in *Life's Dominion*, where he allows that the government might permissibly interfere with suicide attempts by depressed young people.[9] Thomas Nagel allows the permissibility of paternalism in his oft-cited "Moral Conflict and Political Legitimacy."[10] Joseph Raz in *The Morality of*

Freedom allows that paternalism can be justified, as protecting or promoting personal autonomy.[11] Even Joel Feinberg, who is perhaps the best known contemporary antipaternalist, allows that *some* forms of paternalism are permissible because he allows paternalistic interference with choices that are "substantially involuntary," and he endorses an unusually demanding test of full voluntariness, one that renders many acts substantially involuntary that we would ordinarily think of as voluntary.[12]

Because so many leading liberal theorists believe that some kinds of paternalism are permissible, it makes sense to ask whether there is an interpretation of the principle of neutrality that permits paternalism. I think there is. On this interpretation, the principle of neutrality prohibits any policy that limits individual liberty unless this policy can be justified by reasons that are not on the above list of nonneutral reasons. Because this list does not include every paternalistic reason, some paternalistic policies are permitted by this principle.

This interpretation of neutrality, however, raises another difficult question, which is, what makes this a principle of *neutrality*? If there were a morally relevant property that all the reasons on the above list possess that is not also possessed by any neutral reason, there would be a good answer. When we try to identify such a property, however, we discover that this is not so easy.

Consider the following proposal: neutral reasons are constituted by human interests; nonneutral reasons are not constituted by human interests. This might seem like a nonstarter. Aren't neutral reasons impartial reasons, and aren't interests inherently partial? This analysis, however, is naturally reached if we understand the principle of neutrality as a philosophical descendent of Mill's harm principle. Suppose that Mill's harm principle is defensible only if harm is construed broadly to include any injury to a legitimate interest. Suppose, too, that the extreme antipaternalism of Mill's harm principle is indefensible. Something interesting remains, which might be worth defending: the principle that the government is justified in limiting a person's liberty against his will only to protect the legitimate interests of individuals. I will call this the legitimate interests principle. The principle of neutrality, on one understanding, is a version of this legitimate interests principle. It includes this principle, but adds a particular interpretation of legitimate interests: legitimate interests are interests constituted by neutral reasons. Which reasons are neutral? A simple answer is the one under consideration: neutral reasons are those constituted by real or genuine interests. To illustrate, the fact that people have an interest in continuing to live is a neutral reason for laws prohibiting murder, but the fact that murder is "an intrinsic evil" is a nonneutral reason (assuming that *intrinsic evils* are states of affairs that make the world a worse place independently of their having a negative impact on anyone's interests—as might be true, for example, of the intentional abortion of a first-trimester fetus[13]).

As an analysis, however, of the distinction between neutral and nonneutral reasons, this interest-based account is unsatisfactory because some genuine interests provide reasons that seem nonneutral. Consider, for example, the interests that children have in being educated by adults who do not teach them to believe things that are highly improbable and for which there is no good evidence. This seems like a genuine interest, but as a reason for the government to prohibit the teaching of biblical literalism in private religious schools, it seems like a nonneutral reason.

A natural response is that *this* reason is nonneutral because the interest in question is not sufficiently weighty to justify the government in prohibiting the teaching of biblical literalism. So perhaps we should identify the neutral reasons for a policy only with those interests that are sufficiently weighty to justify the government in adopting it.

If this is the correct understanding of the distinction between neutral and nonneutral reasons, then it is possible to defend the claim that the principle of neutrality permits paternalism. We can argue that people sometimes have interests in having less liberty or fewer opportunities, and that these interests are sometimes sufficiently weighty to justify the government in adopting policies that limit their liberty or reduce their opportunities, even against their will.

Not everyone, however, will be satisfied with this account of the distinction between neutral and nonneutral reasons. One cause for dissatisfaction is that an insufficiently weighty interest might constitute a neutral reason. To see this, consider some real or genuine interest that you believe is sufficient to justify the government in limiting some liberty, an interest that strikes you as providing a perfectly neutral reason. Now consider this interest as a justification for some other policy that it supports but fails to justify. This interest might still strike you as a neutral reason for this policy even though it is insufficient to justify it. To illustrate, suppose that murder laws are justified as protecting our interests in not being unwillingly killed. This seems like a perfectly neutral reason. Suppose, though, that this interest fails to justify a law prohibiting all recreational driving, even though this law would also reduce our risk of being unwillingly killed. According to the analysis under consideration, this interest constitutes a nonneutral reason for laws that prohibit recreational driving. If, however, our interest in not being unwillingly killed counts as a neutral reason for murder laws, it seems that it should also count as a neutral reason for laws prohibiting recreational driving.

Some may be unconvinced by this objection. They may feel perfectly comfortable holding that the neutral reasons for a policy are constituted only by those human interests that provide sufficient justification for this policy, whereas nonneutral reasons include all the other reasons that might be given for this policy. If this is correct, then there is a simple answer to the question of what all the nonneutral reasons on the above list have in common with each other that they do not have in common with any neutral reason, which is that none of these reasons is constituted by an interest that is sufficiently weighty to justify the government in limiting someone's liberty. Assuming, then, that some paternalistic reasons are constituted by sufficiently weighty interests, as I believe, this explains why some paternalistic reasons are neutral.

Others, however, may not believe that the distinction between sufficiently weighty interests and other reasons provides a plausible account of the intuitive distinction between neutral and nonneutral reasons. I am sympathetic to this view for the reason given above. If, however, we reject this account of the distinction, how are we to explain the difference between neutral and nonneutral reasons? Elsewhere I have considered a number of possible analyses of this difference and have found that they all fail to track the intuitive distinction between them.[14] From this I have tentatively concluded that there is no morally relevant property that all nonneutral reasons have in common that they do not also share with some neutral reasons. This might strike you as incredible. How is it, then, that we are able to pick out neutral and nonneutral reasons and roughly agree on which are neutral or nonneutral? I think there is an answer. The principle of neutrality was originally advanced as a way of unifying a number of more specific principles of liberty—principles of freedom of expression, freedom of worship, sexual freedom, and other important liberties. In fact, these more specific principles of liberty have less in common with each other than the unifying idea of neutrality suggests. We have nonetheless learned to make the distinction between neutral and nonneutral reasons on the basis of our beliefs about what reasons these other more specific principles of liberty permit and exclude. So although we are able to make an intuitive distinction between neutral and nonneutral reasons, this intuitive distinction fails to track any essential or constant difference between them.

Liberal theorists of rights have been drawn to the principle of (legislative) neutrality primarily for theoretical reasons. This principle seems to unify and explain the validity of a number of separate principles of liberty that they have endorsed: the government may not prohibit the expression of a political opinion for the reason that it is false or offensive; the government may not prohibit a form of worship for the reason that the religious beliefs on which it is based are false; and the government may not limit these and other important liberties for the reasons that I identified in chapter 2 as moralistic. What all these illegitimate reasons have in common, one might think, is that the government would fail to be neutral toward different conceptions of a good life if it were to limit individual liberty for these reasons. If so, the principle of neutrality offers a unified explanation of *why* all these reasons are illegitimate. This explanation is that when the government limits individual liberty for these reasons, it unfairly favors some pursuits of happiness over others and so treats its citizens unfairly.

If, however, there is no morally relevant property that all and only nonneutral reasons have in common, then the principle of neutrality cannot play this unifying role in the theory of rights. For one thing, if there is no morally relevant property that all and only nonneutral reasons have in common, there is no common property that can explain why all and only these reasons are illegitimate in violating the principle of neutrality. Second, if there is no morally relevant common property that all and only nonneutral reasons have in common, there is no simple and identifiable way in which the government would fail to act impartially or fairly in adopting policies for these reasons, and the idea of neutrality, with its implicit commitment to fairness and impartiality, fails to explain *why* all these reasons are illegitimate.

Despite these theoretical shortcomings, the principle of legislative neutrality might be valid. Suppose one interprets this principle, as I do, to state that the government may not adopt a policy that limits anyone's liberty or opportunities unless this policy can be justified by neutral reasons. If it is not possible to identify a morally relevant property that all and only nonneutral reasons have in common, then the content of this principle of legislative neutrality is theoretically indeterminate until we specify its content by a list of nonneutral reasons. It is nonetheless possible to specify the content of this principle by such a list, which we can construct by reflecting on the kinds of reasons that defenders of neutrality have meant to exclude. We can then say that unless a government policy is justified by reasons that are not on this list of nonneutral reasons, it is unjustifiable and the government should not adopt it. If so, then the principle of legislative neutrality, so interpreted, is valid.

In my view, neutrality is a failed theory of what all the nonneutral reasons on the above list have in common. There is still something right in the idea of neutrality, which is that none of the reasons on the list can on their own, either singly or in combination with each other, justify the government in limiting any important individual liberty; the government is justified in limiting important liberties only by neutral reasons or reasons that are not on this list.[15] If there is no morally relevant property that all and only reasons on this list have in common that they do not also share with some neutral reasons, then it is not clear why we should call this a principle of *neutrality*. So I will not call it that. I will call it the *postneutrality principle* instead.

I think the postneutrality principle captures what is right in the idea of neutrality. If so, then it is possible to reconcile paternalistic prostitution laws with what is right in the idea of neutrality. For one thing, the postneutrality principle permits paternalistic reasons for prostitution laws. For another, it governs only reasons for limiting *important* liberties, and not all prostitution laws limit important liberties. Some may doubt the coherence of this position. They may think that any plausible explanation of why the postneutrality principle is valid must entail, at least loosely speaking, that the kind of paternalism that prostitution laws involve is impermissible. So I now explain in greater depth why it is coherent to endorse both the postneutrality principle and the permissibility of paternalism.

III. The Individualistic Conception of Political Justification

The postneutrality principle can be grounded on an individualistic conception of political justification that can be grounded on the kind of contractualist moral theory that Scanlon has proposed. This argument makes a number of assumptions and draws a number of inferences that might reasonably be questioned, but I will not defend these assumptions or inferences at length here. My aim is not prove that the postneutrality principle is valid. It is to explain how one might coherently endorse this principle while also endorsing some paternalistic prostitution laws.

The first crucial assumption of this argument is that Scanlon's contractualism provides the correct framework for reasoning about whether a principle of liberty is valid. The second crucial assumption is that this framework warrants a general principle of political justification that I will call the *individualistic conception*. According to this conception, a reason can justify the government in limiting an important liberty only if it meets three conditions: (1) it is a personal reason; (2) there is sufficient epistemic reason for government officials to accept the proposition that constitutes this personal reason; and (3) this personal reason is not decisively outweighed by any personal reason against the government limiting individual liberty in this way. A personal reason for a government policy is a reason for someone to prefer his or her own situation when the government has this policy; an impersonal reason for a government policy is a reason to prefer the world when the government has this policy, but not one's own situation in this world.[16] There is sufficient epistemic reason for a government official to accept a proposition as part of the justification for a coercive government policy if and only if the information that is available to this government official warrants belief in this proposition. The third crucial assumption of this argument is that all the nonneutral reasons on the above list, either singly or in combination, violate at least one of these three conditions. Some reasons on this list are impersonal reasons; some are constituted by propositions that there is insufficient epistemic reason for government officials to accept; and the rest, although they are personal reasons for which there is sufficient evidence, are decisively outweighed by personal reasons for the government not to limit liberty in the relevant way. If these three crucial assumptions are sound, then the postneutrality principle is valid.

This position is consistent with holding that some paternalistic prostitution laws are justifiable. According to the individualistic conception of political justification, a reason can justify the government in limiting an important liberty only if it satisfies the three conditions identified above. If this conception of political justification is what grounds the postneutrality principle, it makes sense to hold that a reason is permitted by the postneutrality principle if it satisfies all three conditions. I believe that some paternalistic reasons for prostitution laws do satisfy these three conditions: they identify personal reasons of sufficient weight to justify some restrictions of individual liberty, and they are constituted by propositions that there is sufficient epistemic reason for government officials to accept. Because this position is consistent with the argument just sketched for the postneutrality principle, it makes sense to hold that although the postneutrality principle is valid, the government may adopt some paternalistic prostitution laws.

Within contractualism, a principle of liberty is valid if and only if no one could reasonably reject it as properly regulating government policy.[17] A person can reasonably reject a principle of liberty if the reasons for him to prefer his own situation when this principle is not observed by the government decisively outweigh everyone's reasons to prefer his or her own situation when the government does observe this principle. The only reasons relevant to assessing whether a principle of liberty may be reasonably rejected are personal reasons:[18] reasons for individuals to prefer their own situations when this principle is or is not generally observed.

The contractualist argument for the individualistic principle of political justification presupposes that no one may reasonably reject a principle that prohibits the government from limiting an important liberty unless there is a reason to do so that satisfies the three conditions identified by the individualistic principle of political justification. If a liberty is important, there is a weighty reason for someone to prefer his situation when the government does not limit this liberty and so a weighty personal reason for the government not to limit it. If there is a weighty personal reason for the government not to limit a liberty, there is a weighty personal reason to reject a principle that permits the government to limit it. If there are also personal reasons to want the government to limit this liberty, then there are also personal reasons to reject a principle that prohibits the government from limiting this liberty. The only reasons, however, that could warrant someone in rejecting a principle that prohibits the government from limiting an important liberty are those personal reasons that are not decisively outweighed by the personal reasons to want the government not to limit this liberty. So no one can reasonably reject condition (3) of the individualistic principle of sufficient reason.

There are reasons for us to prefer our own situations when the government has the authority to coordinate social action to promote impersonal values that we care about, and when we have the opportunity to express our respect for impersonal values through the political process. So there are personal reasons for us to reject a general principle that prohibits the government from limiting liberty in ways that can be justified only by impersonal reasons. When a liberty is important, however, there are weighty personal reasons to reject a principle that allows the government to limit this important liberty, and these reasons outweigh the personal reasons to want the government to have the authority to limit this important liberty for impersonal reasons. They also outweigh every impersonal reason to want the government to have this authority. So no one can reasonably reject condition (1) of the individualistic principle of political justification.

Whenever there is a good reason for us to prefer our situations when the government limits a liberty, there is a personal reason for the government to limit this liberty, and a personal reason to reject a principle that prohibits the government from limiting this liberty. When, however, there is insufficient epistemic reason for someone to accept a proposition, this proposition does not constitute a good personal reason for him to reject a principle that prohibits the government from limiting this liberty. If there is sufficient epistemic reason for someone to accept a proposition that constitutes a reason for him to prefer his situation when the government limits a liberty, then, I assume, sufficient evidence for this proposition can be made available to government officials that would warrant them in accepting this proposition, too. So if the information *available* to government officials fails to warrant them in accepting a proposition that constitutes a personal reason to limit an important liberty, then, I assume, there is insufficient epistemic reason for a person to accept this proposition as a reason for him to prefer his situation when this liberty is limited. If there is insufficient reason for him to accept this proposition as a reason for him to prefer his situation when this liberty is limited, this is not a good reason for him to reject a principle that prohibits the government from limiting this liberty. So no one can reasonably reject condition (2) of the individualistic principle of political justification.

This contractualist argument for the individualistic principle of political justification makes a number of assumptions and draws a number of inferences that might reasonably be questioned. Because, however, these assumptions and inferences are all consistent with the claim, made in chapter 3, that someone could reasonably reject a principle that prohibits all forms of paternalism, it is coherent to hold within a contractualist framework both that the individualistic principle of political justification is valid and that paternalism is permissible. One might also reasonably question the assumption that the postneutrality principle is warranted by the individualistic principle of political justification. Because, however, this assumption is also consistent with the claim that contractualism permits paternalism, it is also coherent to hold both that the postneutrality principle is valid and that paternalism is permissible. Within the contractualist framework one may therefore coherently endorse both the postneutrality principle and paternalistic prostitution laws.

IV. Hard Paternalism and External Preferences

Not everyone will be convinced by this attempt to reconcile the permissibility of paternalistic prostitution laws with what seems right in the principle of legislative neutrality. Some may think that the kinds of prostitution laws that I have defended must involve some kind of hard paternalism and that, properly interpreted, the principle of neutrality must prohibit hard paternalism. There is nothing in the individualistic principle of political justification that rules out hard paternalism, but one might conclude from this that this principle of political justification fails to ground what is right in the principle of neutrality. There is a better explanation, some may think, one that implies that hard paternalism is always wrong.

One reason to think that hard paternalism is inconsistent with neutrality is suggested by Dworkin's early work on rights. Dworkin held that the principle of neutrality prohibits any policy that can be justified, if at all, only as satisfying "external preferences."[19] External preferences, as initially defined by Dworkin, are preferences about others' shares of opportunities and resources; personal preferences are preferences about one's own share of resources.[20] If this is the correct interpretation of neutrality, and paternalistic prostitution laws could be justified only as satisfying external preferences, this would explain why these laws are ruled out by the principle of neutrality.

The premise is false, though, that paternalistic prostitution laws can be justified only as satisfying external preferences. If a legislator supports a prostitution law for the reason that it will benefit young people by reducing their opportunities to do self-destructive sex work, he does not act to satisfy the preferences of his constituents, external or otherwise; he acts for the reason that this policy will benefit vulnerable young people. To be sure, in supporting this legislation, a legislator would act on his *own* external preferences—his own preferences regarding the distribution of opportunities and resources to others. A conscientious legislator, however, should *always* act to satisfy his *own* external preferences, provided, of course, they are based on sound moral reasoning. We would regard as completely corrupt a legislator who sought only to satisfy his own personal preferences in legislating, for he would then vote for or against legislation only to increase (or, if he is strangely self-denying, to decrease) his own share of resources and opportunities. The principle of neutrality cannot be interpreted, then, to prohibit legislators from supporting policies that satisfy their *own* external preferences; it can be interpreted to prohibit legislators only from supporting policies for the reason that they satisfy the external preferences of their constituents. This constraint, however, permits legislative support of paternalistic prostitution laws, because a legislator might support such policies not to satisfy the preferences of his constituents, but simply to make some people better off.

Implicit, however, in the external preference interpretation of neutrality is another interpretation of neutrality that might seem to provide a better argument against hard paternalism. On this interpretation, the principle of neutrality prohibits not only policies that can be justified, if at all, only as satisfying external preferences, but also any policy that cannot be fully justified as satisfying personal preferences. The government may not adopt a policy, in other words, unless it can be fully justified as satisfying desires that individuals have about their own share of goods.[21] I will call this the *personal preference principle.*

Hard paternalism refers loosely to any policy that cannot be justified unless its benefits to those who oppose it are counted in its favor. So it might seem that hard paternalism, by definition, cannot be justified as satisfying personal preferences. If a policy that limits a person's liberty is justified as satisfying personal preferences, then either this policy is not paternalistic, because it is justified as satisfying the personal preferences of persons other than those whose liberty is limited by it, or, although paternalistic, it is not a form of *hard* paternalism, because it is justified as satisfying the personal preferences of those who *want* their liberty to be limited in this way. Interpreted to require observance of the personal preference principle, the principle of neutrality would therefore seem to prohibit all forms of hard paternalism. In truth, however, the personal preference principle excludes hard paternalism only on a specific interpretation, one that is open to serious objection.

According to Dworkin, the personal preference principle emerges as an implication of the principle of equal concern and respect when the latter principle is understood to operate as a constraint on preference utilitarianism, taken as a general "background theory" of what justifies the government in adopting coercive policies.[22] Preference utilitarianism directs the government to act so as to maximize the satisfaction of desires. This way of justifying government policy is compatible with the principle of equal concern and respect, Dworkin maintains, only if the satisfaction of external preferences is not counted in favor of coercive policies. This, according to Dworkin, is because equal concern and respect requires the *equal* counting of *personal* preferences and counting the satisfaction of external preferences in favor of a policy will result in the overcounting or undercounting of personal preferences: overcounting if the external preferences are positive or benevolent; undercounting if the external preferences are negative or malevolent. The personal preference principle is thus warranted as a constraint on government policy when preference utilitarianism is taken as the correct background theory of policy justification and when the principle of equal concern and respect operates as a constraint on this background theory.

Even if this course of argument is sound,[23] however, the personal preference principle excludes hard paternalism *only on a specific interpretation* of this principle: that coercive government policies are justified only as satisfying personal preferences that are both *present* and *actual*.

Hard paternalistic policies can be understood in the following way: they go against the present wishes of a person so that he will be better off in the future. If a person's future self wants it to be the case that he did not have a liberty or opportunity in the past, then a policy that deprives his younger, present self of a liberty might therefore be justified as satisfying the personal preferences of his future self, even though it is a form of hard paternalism as enforced against his present, younger self. What makes a paternalistic policy *hard* is that it is justified as benefiting someone who does not now want it. If present-Jones wants a liberty, but its limitation is justified as benefiting future-Jones, then it is justified as benefiting Jones even though Jones does not now want it. In this way, hard paternalistic policies might be justified consistent with the personal preference principle. So the personal preference principle excludes hard paternalism only if it is interpreted to hold that government policies can be justified only as satisfying *present* personal preferences.

It is also true that the personal preference principle excludes hard paternalism only if it is interpreted to mean that government policies can be justified only as satisfying *actual* personal preferences. A person might not want to have a liberty or opportunity if he were thinking clearly about his welfare or if he were adequately informed. So a hard paternalistic policy might be justified as satisfying a person's *hypothetical* personal preferences even if it cannot be justified as satisfying his *actual* personal preferences. The personal preference principle thus excludes hard paternalism only on the assumption that coercive government policies can be justified only as satisfying a person's *actual* personal preferences.

Dworkin's double-counting argument, however, warrants the "actual and present preference" interpretation of the personal preference principle only if a person's utility or welfare consists solely in satisfaction of his present and actual desires. Well-known preference utilitarians hold, to the contrary, that a person's welfare consists in the satisfaction of his *hypothetical* desires: the desires he would have if well-informed and thinking clearly.[24] They also hold that a person's welfare consists partly in the satisfaction of desires he will have in the future, and does not consist only in the satisfaction of the desires that he has at present.[25] If a person's utility consists in the satisfaction of his hypothetical preferences and of some of his future preferences, then preference utilitarianism cannot yield via Dworkin's argument the interpretation of the personal preference principle that is necessary to exclude hard paternalism.

To this observation we may now add familiar doubts about desire-satisfaction theories of welfare in general. Hypothetical desire-satisfaction theories of welfare are more plausible than actual desire-satisfaction theories, but they might still be incorrect because a person might not desire for himself, even under good conditions, what there is good reason for him to desire. Those who are convinced by this objection are commonly drawn instead to an "objective list" or "substantive good" account of well-being.[26] According to this kind of view, a person's welfare consists in his having certain substantive goods, the value of which for him is not fundamentally a matter of what he desires, or would desire under certain conditions, but is fundamentally a matter of the good reasons there are for him to desire these things. If substantive good theories of individual welfare are correct, then desire satisfaction theories are not, and preference utilitarianism is not the best form of utilitarianism. If preference utilitarianism is not the best form of utilitarianism, it is not the correct background theory, and the validity of the personal preference principle cannot be established by the course of reasoning sketched above. Moreover, if a substantive good theory of welfare is correct, there is little reason to believe that hard paternalism is never justified. According to a substantive good theory, an activity might be bad for a person even if she actually desires to engage in it. So a person might be benefited by a policy that prohibits her from doing what she wants to do. Some forms of hard paternalism might therefore be warranted as making a person better off. This observation is sometimes made as an objection to substantive good theories, but it has at least as much force as an objection to any unqualified antipaternalism.

More recently Dworkin has offered a different view of individual welfare as the basis for ruling out those forms of hard paternalism that he regards as being most objectionable. According to this view, which Dworkin labels the *constitutive view*, something can be good for us—it can contribute to our welfare and make our lives go better for us—only if we endorse it as good.[27] A career in the military, for example, does not make a person better off unless he endorses this career as something that it would be good for him to have. The constitutive view seeks to preserve an important idea in the actual desire theory of welfare, namely, that something cannot be good for us unless we see it as being good for us. The constitutive view, however, is more sophisticated than the actual desire view, because it allows that how good a state of affairs is for us depends not only on our actual attitude toward it, on whether we desire it or think it is good, but also on its objective worth, on whether it is objectively desirable or good. The constitutive view thus combines appealing elements of both objective list and desire-satisfaction views.

The constitutive view might be challenged. One might believe, for example, that the development and exercise of our higher human capacities, such as the capacity for practical reasoning, is intrinsically good for us even if we do not actually value it. Even if the constitutive view is correct, however, it poses no objection to the kind of hard paternalism that permissive abolitionist or impermissive regulationist policies on prostitution might involve.

If the constitutive view is correct, it rules out one kind of paternalism: forcing a person to live in a way that he does not see as being good for him. This is because, according to the constitutive view, a person *cannot* benefit by being forced to live in a way that he does not see as good for him. Neither permissive abolitionist nor impermissive regulationist policies, however, force anyone to live a life that they think is bad. Nor do they prevent someone who believes that prostitution is part of the best life for her from doing this work, and so from living in accordance with her own judgments. These policies only make it more difficult for some people to make money by doing this work and so reduce the incentives to do it.

Neither, then, Dworkin's early work on rights nor his more recent work on well-being warrants the conclusion that all forms of hard paternalism are wrong. Nor does Dworkin hold that all forms of hard paternalism are wrong. If a form of hard paternalism is employed so as to encourage a young person to make wise choices, it might be justifiable, Dworkin suggests, provided it allows adequate opportunities for this person to shape his or her own life as an adult.[28] I conclude that neither Dworkin's early work on rights nor his more recent work on well-being warrants the conclusion that we should regard all paternalistic reasons as nonneutral reasons. To the contrary, the claim that some paternalistic reasons should be regarded as neutral is supported by the fact that Dworkin and other leading defenders of neutrality allow that some paternalistic reasons are legitimate, even as reasons to interfere with a person's liberty against his wishes.[29]

To this we might add that one plausible explanation of why liberal theorists were drawn to the principle of neutrality in the first place presupposes that some paternalistic reasons are neutral. Many admirers of Mill, including Hart, Rawls, and Dworkin, have accepted the antimoralistic implications of Mill's harm principle, but they have doubted that paternalism is always wrong.[30] If paternalism is sometimes permissible, as most contemporary liberal theorists seem to believe,[31] then the principle of legislative neutrality is superior to Mill's harm principle as general principle of liberty, because it has the antimoralistic implications of Mill's harm principle without its extreme antipaternalism. This explanation of the appeal of neutrality makes sense, however, only if some paternalistic reasons are properly counted as neutral.

V. Perfectionism

Whether or not government neutrality makes sense as a political goal, the principle of legislative neutrality defended by Dworkin and others seems to contain a valid insight: that the nonneutral reasons on the above list cannot on their own, either singly or in combination, justify the government in limiting an important individual liberty. The primary purpose of this chapter is to show that one may coherently accept this insight while defending paternalistic prostitution laws in some form. Some may now object, however, that the paternalistic defense of prostitution laws that I have given is a *perfectionist* defense and that the principle of legislative neutrality, properly understood, rules out government perfectionism.

This is my response: if the postneutrality principle is valid, then certain kinds of government perfectionism are impermissible. If paternalistic prostitution laws involved these kinds of perfectionism, they would therefore be ruled out by this principle. These laws, however, do not involve these kinds of perfectionism.

The postneutrality principle identifies certain perfectionist reasons as insufficient to justify the government in limiting important liberties. These include the reasons for the government to limit an important liberty (a) that by pursuing a goal or by engaging in an activity a person will live a life that is less than the best or most excellent life that he or she could have led; (b) that by pursuing a goal or by engaging in an activity a person will not develop and exercise her higher human capacities as fully as possible throughout her life, or as fully as she might have; (c) that the goals a person wishes to pursue or the activities she wishes to engage in are inherently worthless; and (d) that by pursuing a goal or by engaging in an activity a person becomes less admirable. The paternalistic argument for prostitution laws does not presuppose the validity of any of these perfectionist reasons. So paternalistic prostitution laws are consistent with the antiperfectionism implicit in the postneutrality principle.

The term *perfectionism* is used in different ways. Sometimes it is used to refer to any objective list or substantive good conception of individual welfare.[32] At the beginning of chapter 3 I explained the distinction between objective and subjective conceptions of individual interests in the following way. According to an objective conception, a person has an interest in something if and only if there is good reason for her to want it. According to a subjective conception, a person has an interest in something if and only if she actually wants it (or would want it if she had the relevant empirical information), regardless of whether there is any good reason for her to want it. My defense of paternalistic prostitution laws, I said, presupposes an objective conception of human interests. If any objective conception of human interests is properly characterized as *perfectionist*, my defense of prostitution laws is therefore perfectionist in this sense.

Despite the fact, however, that the term *perfectionist* is sometimes used in this way, this terminological choice is inaccurate and misleading. To characterize a conception of human interests as perfectionist suggests that this conception holds that we have important human interests in achieving perfection or excellence, or in becoming admirable, or in leading exemplary lives. One might, however, consistently endorse an objective conception of human interests and reject these views. To illustrate, consider the philosophical hedonist position that pleasure is good for us independently of whether we want it; that only pleasure is intrinsically good for us; and that pleasures vary in value only according to intensity and duration and not according to the worth or excellence of their objects and not according to the worth or excellence of the capacities that are developed and exercised in experiencing these pleasures. This is an objective conception of human welfare, because it holds that pleasure is good for us independently of whether we desire it. However, it does not place any special value on perfection or excellence as key components of human welfare. So it would be inaccurate and misleading to characterize this conception of human welfare as perfectionist.[33]

It is likewise inaccurate and misleading to apply the term *perfectionist* to any conception of political justification that presupposes an objective conception of human interests. The term *perfectionist* suggests a conception of political justification according to which it is a legitimate aim of government policy to lead people to have the most perfect, most excellent, most admirable lives possible, and the government might therefore be justified in limiting a person's liberty or opportunities solely by the fact that this will lead them to have more excellent or admirable lives. Someone, however, who endorses an objective conception of interests might consistently deny this. Rawls, for example, holds that we have objective interests in the social conditions necessary for the full development and exercise of our two moral powers, our capacity for a conception of justice, and our capacity to form, revise, and rationally to pursue a conception of the good. Rawls does not hold, though, that it is a legitimate function of government to promote human excellence, or that the government is justified by this goal in limiting individual liberty. So it would be inaccurate and misleading to characterize his view as perfectionist on the ground that it contains an objective conception of human interests.

There is, in any case, nothing objectionable or illiberal in perfectionism if the term is meant only to refer to an objective conception of interests. So defending paternalistic prostitution laws against the charge that they are perfectionist in *this* sense is not necessary in order to show that they are consistent with liberalism.

There is, however, another way in which my paternalistic argument for prostitution laws might seem perfectionist. In chapter 1 I identified as a key reason for prostitution laws that prostitution commonly interferes with the ability to have healthy, stable, supportive, mutually respectful intimate relationships. If so, then prostitution interferes with the development and exercise of the capacity for love and friendship, which is one of our higher human capacities. Other writers, too, have argued that prostitution is objectionable partly because it interferes with the development and exercise of the higher human capacities of those who do it. Thus Maude Miner argues that in prostitution "women are held in moral and spiritual bondage which deadens and destroys their highest powers."[34] On one understanding, perfectionist views hold that "the objective goods are those that are elements in an ideal of a perfect human life, one which fully realizes the distinctive and essential characteristics of human nature."[35] So if the claim that prostitution commonly damages the capacity for love and friendship were an essential part of the paternalistic case for prostitution laws, this argument might be characterized as perfectionist on this ground.

This use of the term *perfectionist*, however, is also misleading. The paternalistic case that I have presented for prostitution laws assumes that people have important interests in developing and exercising their capacities for love and friendship and that prostitution commonly interferes with their doing so. It holds that partly for this reason, the government ought to adopt policies that reduce the amount of prostitution that is done. This argument, however, does not assume that the government has an obligation to ensure that citizens achieve *perfection* or that they lead their *best* lives possible. It assumes only that the government has an obligation to protect certain important interests in developing and exercising our higher human capacities. This argument also does not assume that citizens have important interests, which the government must try to protect, in developing and exercising their higher human capacities to the *highest possible* degree. It assumes only that we have important interests in developing and exercising these important capacities to a sufficient degree, above a certain threshold. Finally, it makes sense to believe that developing and exercising our capacities for love and friendship is good for us without also believing that it is good for us *because* it is an "element in an ideal of a perfect human life." So this argument for prostitution laws does not presuppose that human *perfection* is a legitimate goal of government policy. It presupposes only that it is legitimate for the government to adopt policies that put individuals in a better position to achieve important human goods.

If, however, someone insists on using the term *perfectionist* to describe this kind of argument for prostitution laws, then we should respond that there is nothing objectionable or illiberal in this kind of perfectionism either. If it is appropriate to rely on an objective conception of interests in defending government policy, and we have objective interests in living in a social environment in which we are more likely to develop and exercise our higher human capacities to a sufficient degree, and this environment will be promoted by government policies that do not deprive us of important liberties, then we have legitimate interests in the government adopting these policies, whether or not these interests are characterized as perfectionist.

In this connection it is worth noting that Rawls, who accepts the antiperfectionism implicit in the postneutrality principle, also acknowledges the political legitimacy of our interests in developing some of our higher human capacities. Rawls assumes that we have important interests in developing and exercising two moral powers—a capacity for a conception of the good and a capacity for a sense of justice—and that a democratic government must therefore recognize and protect certain basic liberties as necessary to secure the social conditions needed for the adequate development and full and informed exercise of these two moral powers.[36] Rawls assumes, too, that the development and exercise of the capacity for a conception of a good is itself a constitutive part of our good.[37] So his argument for basic liberty is that the recognition and protection of basic liberties by the government is necessary for us to develop and exercise certain higher human capacities, which is partly constitutive of our good. If, however, our interests in developing and exercising the two moral powers provide a legitimate basis for government policy, it seems that our interests in developing and exercising other higher human capacities might also provide a legitimate basis.

It is true that Rawls's moral powers play an essential role in social cooperation, and in our reasoning about what to do in our own lives and about what government policies to support, in a way that our other higher capacities do not. So there is no inconsistency in holding that the two moral powers are relevant to evaluating government policy in a way that our other higher capacities are not. Moreover, it is one thing to cite our interests in developing our higher capacities as reasons for *protecting* liberty, as Rawls does, and another to cite them as reasons for *restricting* liberty, as I do. We should not, however, make too much of these differences.

The two moral powers are not our only higher capacities, and they are not the only important ones. So there is no reason to suppose that our interests in developing our two moral powers are the only ones relevant to evaluating government policy. Furthermore, the assumption that our interests in developing and exercising other higher human capacities are important and relevant to government policy might be necessary to explain why some liberties are basic even within Rawls's framework. Many of us would say that sexual and marital freedoms are basic liberties. In what way, though, are they necessary for the full development and exercise of the two moral powers? They are not necessary simply to *deliberate* about the right and the good. Are they necessary, then, for people to live the life they would choose if they were permitted to live any life they wanted? The problem with this explanation is that many other liberties that we do not consider basic are likewise necessary.[38] So it seems that in order to explain why sexual and marital freedoms are basic liberties, we must explain how, although they are not necessary for deliberation about the right and the good, they are nonetheless necessary for the full development and exercise of the two moral powers in a way that other (nonbasic) liberties are not. Perhaps the best explanation is that these liberties are necessary fully to develop and exercise the capacities for love and friendship in a way that other liberties are not.

It is, admittedly, one thing to cite our capacities as reasons to protect liberty, and another to cite them as reasons to restrict it. This might seem to mark an important difference between Rawls's position on basic liberties and my position here on paternalistic prostitution laws. Sometimes, however, it is necessary for the government to *restrict* liberty in order to secure the social conditions necessary for the full development and exercise of our two moral powers. For instance, protecting the freedom of speech necessary to develop our powers necessarily involves limiting the freedom to drown out speech. Given, then, that we have genuine interests in developing and exercising higher human capacities other than the two moral powers, and given that securing the social conditions necessary for the full development and exercise of our two moral powers sometimes requires the restriction of liberty, it is hard to see why the interests we have in developing our other higher capacities *never* provide legitimate reasons for policies that restrict individual liberty.

To sum up the argument of this chapter, there is something right in the idea of neutrality, which is captured by the postneutrality principle. This principle, however, permits some paternalistic prostitution laws. The postneutrality principle prohibits certain kinds of perfectionism, but it does not rule out the kind of perfectionism that paternalistic prostitution laws involve. So paternalistic prostitution laws are consistent with what is right in the idea of neutrality, and the goal of neutrality does not present a serious objection either to permissive abolitionist policies or to impermissive regulationist policies.

Conclusion

As an occupation and as a way of life, prostitution seems less than ideal. If our children chose this occupation, we would be sorry and would worry that we had failed as parents. If we had worked as prostitutes as adolescents or young adults, we would likely regret this earlier phase of our lives and wish that we had entered adulthood in some other way. For this reason it may seem that the government should adopt policies that discourage prostitution. It is not, however, generally the government's business to tell people how to lead their own lives or to impose the personal moral beliefs of the majority on an unconventional minority. So it may seem to the contrary that government policies should be neutral on the morality of prostitution and should respect the sexual and economic freedom of consenting adults as fully as possible.

These conflicting attitudes toward prostitution laws raise a general question about the proper role of government in guiding our lives, a question that has been asked since Plato. Some hold that because one of the proper functions of government is to promote human well-being and development, the government should sometimes adopt coercive policies with the aim of leading people to choose better lives. Others hold, to the contrary, that because a democratic government is a government of all the people, and people disagree about what kinds of life are best, a democratic government should be as neutral as possible toward different conceptions of a good life, and should not presume that one way of life is better than another. It would be an error, though, to conclude that whether prostitution laws are justifiable depends on which of these two general views of government is correct. This is because the principle of neutrality allows the government to adopt policies to protect people from harm—even harm that results partly from their own choices—and leading advocates of prostitution laws argue that prostitution harms the women who do it.

This prompts another question, which is, what kinds of harm can justify the government in limiting individual liberty? Or, more accurately, what kinds of harm are such that the good of preventing or reducing them justifies the government in limiting our liberty? Looking at our own political culture, we find at least two different answers. One, which I call *civil libertarianism*, is that, because the only legitimate function of government is to protect our rights, the government should not prohibit an activity unless it violates someone's rights. Assuming that the voluntary sale and purchase of sex violate no one's rights, the government should not prohibit them. Another view, which I call *progressivism*, is that because a central function of government is to promote human well-being and human development, the government is sometimes justified in limiting individual liberty to reduce harm even when this policy is not necessary to protect anyone's *rights* from being violated. If prostitution laws are necessary to protect people from harm—even self-inflicted harm—they might therefore be warranted even if prostitution violates no one's rights.

Some may find it difficult to see anything progressive about prostitution laws. From the civil libertarian point of view, they can seem to be nothing more than an illegitimate imposition by the government of the majority's prejudices about improper sexual conduct. The most active opponents of prostitution and its legalization today, however, are left-leaning feminists who see prostitution as a form of violence against women; they are not sexual traditionalists or religious conservatives. Looking back into the history of American and British prostitution laws, we find that some of the most influential opponents of legalizing prostitution in the early twentieth century were social progressives, such as Jane Addams, who also actively advocated female suffrage, racial equality, and worker health and safety legislation.[1]

Civil libertarian and progressive principles have clashed on other policies, and the civil libertarian position has not always been the correct one. Consider again *Lochner v. New York*,[2] in which the U.S. Supreme Court struck down a New York law limiting the number hours a week that someone could work in a bakery. Early-twentieth-century progressives supported such legislation as necessary to protect the health and safety of workers, but the Supreme Court took the civil libertarian position that because a bakery owner does not violate a bakery employee's rights by paying him to work more than sixty hours a week, the New York law violated the constitutional rights of bakery workers and owners in limiting their freedom of contract. The progressives' position on worker health and safety now appears to many of us to have been the correct one. Why not think they were also right about prostitution?

Civil libertarianism and progressivism are both deeply rooted in our political culture. Both contain important truths and recognize important values that must be carefully considered in evaluating laws that limit individual liberty. Neither always supports the most defensible policy, and they conflict, not only over prostitution laws and worker health and safety legislation, but over many other policies as well, including drug and gun control, gambling regulations, and in a different way over antidiscrimination law and child education law. How, then, is this conflict to be resolved as a matter of principle?

A century and a half ago John Stuart Mill sought to resolve this conflict in the following way. Human well-being and development will be best promoted over time, he argued, if society adopts and observes the principle that the government is justified in limiting a person's liberty only to protect *others* from being harmed.[3] As Mill saw it, traditional progressives, in urging legislation aimed at discouraging private vices, such as intemperance, prostitution, and gambling were adopting a strategy that was self-defeating in the long run. This kind of public interference in private affairs, Mill thought, would ultimately thwart human development, which is what traditional progressives aimed ultimately to promote in advocating these policies.

Even if Mill's harm principle were valid, however, its policy implications would be less clear than Mill seems to have supposed. This principle does not directly rule out any particular policy; it rules out only certain *reasons* for policies—those that might be labeled *paternalistic* or *moralistic*. Because any policy for which there are paternalistic or moralistic reasons might be justified by nonpaternalistic and nonmoralistic ones, Mill's principle does not directly rule out any policy. Consider alcohol prohibition, which Mill opposed but which other nineteenth-century progressives such as Susan B. Anthony and William Lloyd Garrison supported.[4] Alcohol prohibition might be justified, not as protecting the problem drinker from his own temptation to drink, nor as combating the moral vice of intemperance, but as protecting the heavy drinker's family from violence and neglect. If so, alcohol prohibition would be compatible with Mill's principle, despite what he says against it in *On Liberty*.[5]

Contemporary liberal theorists such as Ronald Dworkin suggest a different way of resolving the tension between civil libertarianism and progressivism.[6] First, we should abandon those aspects of traditional progressivism that strike us as moralistic, and abandon, too, those aspects of civil libertarianism, such as strong protections of freedom of contract and property rights, that are characteristic of an earlier laissez-faire ideology. Second, we should adopt those progressive goals that can be interpreted as aimed at achieving greater equality, particularly equality of opportunity, and combine these egalitarian goals with a civil libertarianism that advocates strong protection only of certain basic liberties, such as freedom of expression, political liberty, religious liberty, and sexual and reproductive freedoms. Dworkin and other contemporary liberal egalitarians are sharply critical of the Supreme

Court's decision in *Lochner v. New York* on the grounds that it gave too much weight to freedom of contract, which is not of fundamental moral importance, and that it did not give enough weight to the egalitarian goal of improving the situation of workers. They are also sharply critical, however, of other traditional progressive goals, such as promoting temperance and discouraging prostitution because, in their view, these goals are moralistic, not egalitarian.

The sense, however, in which policies like alcohol prohibition and prostitution laws are moralistic is obscure. Heavy drinking is highly correlated with violence, accidental injury, and property crime. If alcohol prohibition were to reduce heavy drinking, it might therefore be defended nonmoralistically as reducing harm. Contemporary feminist opponents of prostitution argue that for most of those who engage in it, prostitution is a horrible experience, one that inflicts a lasting psychological trauma from which it is difficult ever fully to recover, and that this harm would increase if prostitution were fully legalized. If so, it makes little sense to dismiss prostitution laws as inherently moralistic—any more than it makes sense to dismiss worker health and safety laws in this way.

Liberal political philosophy from Mill to Dworkin has been characterized by the statement of general principles of liberty, such as Mill's harm principle[7] and Dworkin's principle of neutrality.[8] Although these principles are commonly taken to imply that prostitution and drug laws and other policies of this kind are morally objectionable, this is an illusion. General principles of liberty such as Mill's harm principle and Dworkin's principle of neutrality rule out certain reasons for government action as illegitimate or otherwise inadequate. If a policy can be justified by reasons other than those these principles rule out, it is permitted by these principles. As a result, no one is warranted in concluding that these policies are unjustifiable until he or she considers *all* the reasons that might reasonably be given for them and explains why *none* of these reasons is sufficient to justify this policy in some form. In evaluating policies such as drug and prostitution laws, we must therefore go beyond Mill's harm principle and Dworkin's principle of neutrality. We must identify the general forms of moral reasoning that are appropriate to evaluating policies of this kind, and consider whether the strongest arguments for them succeed in justifying them within this framework.

When civil libertarian and progressive orientations conflict on a particular policy, I suggest that we directly compare the reasons that individuals have to prefer their situations with this policy in place and their reasons to prefer their situations without this policy. Because what reasons there are depends on the facts, we must first determine to the best of our ability what the empirical consequences of the policy alternatives are likely to be. We must then determine to the best of our ability which reasons have greater moral weight, the reasons of individuals to want the government to adopt this policy or their reasons to want the government not to adopt it. If the reasons for someone to want the government not to adopt a legal restriction decisively outweigh the reasons for anyone to want the government to adopt it, then this restriction violates her moral rights and the government may not adopt it. If this is not the case, however, then the government may justifiably adopt this restriction, provided that its benefits outweigh its costs.

In some cases this course of reasoning will warrant policies that a civil libertarian would favor; in other cases it will not. As a consequence there is no sound and informative general answer to the question of what kinds of harm can justify the government in limiting individual liberty. The government is justified in adopting a policy that limits individual liberty in order to prevent or reduce a kind of harm provided that this policy violates no one's rights and its benefits outweigh its costs. Whether this is true depends not on the *kind* of harm at issue, but on the weight of individuals' reasons to want to avoid this harm and the weight of individuals' reasons not to want their liberty to be restricted by policies that would reduce it.

American political philosophy often centers on the nature of democracy. What is it? What are its fundamental principles? What government policies do these principles permit or require? Both Dworkin and John Rawls, for example, have defended their egalitarian theories of economic justice as being more faithful to democracy than less egalitarian alternatives.[9] Justices Breyer and Scalia of the U.S. Supreme Court have both defended their competing approaches to constitutional interpretation as being more faithful to democracy.[10] Such disagreement reveals that there are different ways of understanding democracy and tensions between different democratic values. One of these tensions is between what Benjamin Constant called "the liberty of the ancients" and "the liberty of the moderns."[11] Another is between what Isaiah Berlin called "negative liberty" and "positive liberty."[12] Another is the one identified here between civil libertarianism and progressivism. In this book I have been concerned with how to resolve this third tension consistent with the fundamental principles of democracy. Because I believe the fundamental principles of democracy are the fundamental principles of liberalism, I have been concerned with how to resolve this tension consistent with the fundamental principles of liberalism.

The central theoretical claim of this book is that if the empirical assumptions of the paternalistic argument for prostitution laws are sound, then prostitution laws *in some form* can be justified by this argument consistent with our rights to liberty and so consistent with liberalism. A policy of prohibition that categorically prohibits the sale of sexual services arguably violates a right to sexual autonomy of those who choose, or would choose, to do this kind of work. If so, this policy is incompatible with liberalism. A policy of abolition that categorically prohibits the purchase of sexual services arguably violates a right to sexual freedom of those who benefit from these services. If so, this policy is incompatible with liberalism. A permissive policy of abolition, however, that permits the purchase of sexual services, but prohibits brothels and reduces the legal opportunities to purchase sexual services in other ways, violates no one's rights, not at least on certain defensible assumptions. Nor does a strong policy of impermissive regulation that prohibits hiring anyone under twenty-five for sexual services. These policies are therefore compatible with liberalism.

To defend this claim, I have now made a number of arguments. In chapter 1 I presented a harm-based argument for prostitution laws, and in chapter 2 I explained why this argument is not moralistic. Although this argument is paternalistic, I argued in chapter 3 that the kind of paternalism involved is morally permissible. Although some prostitution laws arguably violate individuals' rights to liberty, I argued in chapter 4 that on certain defensible assumptions, neither a permissive policy of abolition nor a strong impermissive policy of regulation does. In chapter 5 I then argued that these policies are also compatible with what is right in the idea that a democratic government should be neutral toward different conceptions of a good life and that they are not objectionably perfectionist. The purpose of these arguments is to show that paternalistic prostitution laws in some form are compatible in principle with liberalism.

Obviously this depends, however, on what liberalism is. Liberalism, as I understand it, is constituted primarily by a principle of liberty: that the government may not limit individual liberty for insufficient reason, when this principle is interpreted by a certain kind of view about what reasons are insufficient. Because liberal theorists regard many different reasons as insufficient, and because those who regard themselves as liberal do not completely agree on which reasons these are, it is impossible to specify completely the content of this principle of liberty in a way that would gain universal assent. Any recognizably liberal view, however, will accept the following specific principles of liberty. First, the government may not prohibit political, scientific, scholarly, religious, or artistic expression when there is no reason to do so other than that the beliefs expressed are incorrect, or believed to be incorrect, or that their expression will lead others to form incorrect beliefs, or that their expression is upsetting or offensive to other citizens or to government officials. Second, the government may not prohibit a religious practice when there is no reason to do so other than that it is incorrect, or that it will have bad consequences for a person in the afterlife, or that government officials or other citizens disapprove of it. Third, the government may not deprive a person of political liberty, such as the freedom to vote or run for office, or any of the other liberties just mentioned, when there is no reason to do so other than this person is of a certain race, gender, religious belief, ethnicity, national origin, sexual orientation, and so on. Fourth, the government may not limit important individual liberties, including sexual and reproductive freedoms, unless there is some reason to do so other than the reasons I identified in chapter 2 as moralistic. A liberal view might allow the government to limit relatively *unimportant* liberties for moralistic reasons. No recognizably liberal view, however, will permit the government to limit the most important liberties for these reasons.

One might think that any recognizably liberal view must also endorse a strong principle of antipaternalism, according to which the government is never justified in limiting a person's liberty or opportunities against her wishes solely by the fact that she will be better off as a consequence. I do not believe that this principle is valid or that it is essential to liberalism. Nor do I believe that any leading contemporary liberal theorist of rights endorses this strong principle of antipaternalism.[13] I do believe, however, that *some* principle of antipaternalism is valid and essential to liberalism. In chapter 3 I identified a principle of antipaternalism that I think is valid. Perhaps it, or something like it, is essential to liberalism.

Although liberalism, as I understand it, is constituted primarily by a principle of liberty, other principles are also essential, including a principle of adequate opportunity, a principle of personal security, and a principle of equality before the law. The essential principle of adequate opportunity is that everyone must have an adequate opportunity to pursue desirable social positions and wealth. The essential principle of personal security is that the criminal and civil law must adequately protect the personal security of everyone within its jurisdiction: their lives, physical safety, personal space, and property. The essential principle of equality before the law is that the government must not recognize or enforce any system of second-class citizenship of the kind created by caste systems or Jim Crow laws. Because there may be reasonable disagreement on what adequate opportunity and the adequate protection of personal security involve, as well, perhaps, as what equality before the law requires, there might be different liberal views. Nonetheless, any recognizably liberal view will accept these three principles on some defensible interpretation.

Any view is genuinely liberal that endorses on some defensible interpretation all four of the principles that I have just identified—of liberty, adequate opportunity, personal security, and equality before the law. Any view that rejects one or more of these principles, or endorses them only on an indefensible interpretation, is not genuinely liberal. When I claim that paternalistic prostitution laws in some form are compatible in principle with liberalism I am claiming that these laws do not in every form violate these four constitutive principles of liberalism on every defensible interpretation.

To establish, however, that paternalistic prostitution laws are compatible with liberalism, one must show more than this. One must also show that paternalistic prostitution laws in some form might be justified within the moral framework that provides the best foundation for these constitutive principles of liberalism or the best explanation of their validity. I believe that Scanlon's contractualism, or some view that is similarly individualistic, provides the best account of why these principles are valid.[14] If so, and it is possible to justify paternalistic prostitution laws in some form within this framework, then these laws are compatible not only with the four constitutive principles of liberalism just identified, but also with the grounds of these principles. I believe this is true.

In the previous chapter I sketched how a *postneutrality* principle of liberty can be grounded on contractualism. If so, then the principle of antimoralism discussed in chapter 2 can also be grounded in this way, because the postneutrality principle entails this principle of antimoralism, at least in some form. I believe that the burdens principle presented in chapter 4 can also be grounded on Scanlon's contractualism because no one could reasonably reject the general principle of liberty that the government may not limit individual liberty in ways that violate the burdens principle. I also believe that no one could reasonably reject the principle of antipaternalism that I endorsed in chapter 3. Finally, I believe that no one could reasonably reject any of the specific principles of liberty just mentioned in connection with the liberal principle of liberty. All of these principles, however, permit paternalistic prostitution laws in some form.

Do paternalistic prostitution laws nonetheless violate some *other* principle of liberty that could not be coherently rejected if all the principles I have mentioned are valid and contractualism provides the best foundation for them? I do not think so. Although paternalistic prostitution laws would violate a principle that prohibits all forms of paternalism, there is no reason to believe that this principle is warranted by contractualism, for the reasons given in chapter 3. To this I would add that if prostitution is commonly harmful in the ways that I have supposed, and if having more opportunities to make money by doing this work is not important in the relevant sense to sex workers, and if having more opportunities to have paid sex is not important in the relevant sense to clients, and if having the legal opportunity to hire people to work in a sex business is not important in the relevant sense to entrepreneurs in the sex industry, then someone could reasonably reject any principle of liberty that requires the full decriminalization of prostitution. I conclude that if contractualism is the correct foundation of liberalism and if the empirical assumptions of the argument of chapter 1 are sound, then permissive abolitionist or impermissive regulationist policies on prostitution are compatible in principle with liberalism, even if they are paternalistic.

Perhaps Scanlon's contractualism does not provide the best foundation for the principles that I take to be essential to liberalism. Perhaps something like Dworkin's principle of equal concern and respect provides a better foundation. Or perhaps some consequentialist theory does. If so, and if this other foundation entails that all paternalistic prostitution laws are illegitimate, even if the empirical assumptions of chapter 1 are sound, then paternalistic prostitution laws would not be compatible in principle with liberalism after all. There is no reason, though, to believe that any plausible general foundation for the specific rights to liberty that we regard as being constitutive of liberalism would have this implication. So I do not believe that prostitution laws are incompatible in principle with liberalism on any plausible view of its moral foundations.

Thomas Nagel has recently characterized a liberal as someone who believes that there are certain questions on which the government does not properly take a stand. What is the best kind of life for humans to live? What religious beliefs are true? What kinds of sexual conduct are best or most fitting? A true liberal, according to Nagel, holds that it is illegitimate for the government to take an official position on such matters, because doing so is unnecessary, divisive, and disrespectful to those who disagree.[15] I agree with Nagel that the government should not take an official position on these matters. It would be a mistake to infer from this, however, that prostitution laws are incompatible with liberalism. One might think that if the government should not take a position on the *morality* of prostitution, then prostitution should be *legalized*, but this is a non sequitur. The inference makes sense only on the assumption that immorality is the only reason for prostitution laws, and this is not the only reason. A much stronger reason is that that more people will be harmed in lasting ways if prostitution is legalized. If this is true and we are justified in believing it, then prostitution laws in some form are compatible with liberalism.

Notes

Introduction

1. For some case studies that support the conclusion that sex work is generally voluntary, see Alexa Albert, *Brothel: Mustang Ranch and Its Women* (New York: Random House, 2001), pp. 68–167; Arlene Carmen and Howard Moody, *Working Women: The Subterranean World of Street Prostitution* (New York: Harper and Row, 1985), pp. 101–104; Frederique Delacoste and Priscilla Alexander, eds., *Sex Work: Writings by Women in the Sex Industry* (Pittsburgh, Pa.: Cleis Press, 1987); Claude Jaget, ed., *Prostitutes—Our Life* (Bristol, U.K.: Falling Wall Press, 1980), pp. 57–174, especially 157–158; Kate Millet, "Prostitution: A Quartet for Female Voices," in Vivian Gornick and Barbara K. Moran, *Woman in Sexist Society: Studies in Power and Powerlessness* (New York: Basic Books, 1971), pp. 21–69 (J's and M's testimony); Eleanor Miller, *Street Women* (Philadelphia: Temple University Press, 1986), pp. 35–117; Julia O'Connell Davidson, *Prostitution, Power and Freedom* (Cambridge, U.K.: Polity Press, 1998), pp. 105–106; Roberta Perkins and Garry Bennett, *Being a Prostitute* (London: George Allen and Unwin, 1985), pp. 57–147; Joanna Phoenix, *Making Sense of Prostitution* (London: Macmillan Press, 1999), pp. 73–124; C. H. Rolph, ed., *Women of the Streets* (London: Secker and Warburg, 1955), pp. 137–180; Teela Sanders, *Sex Work: A Risky Business* (Cullompton, U.K.: Willan, 2005), p. 46; Karen Sharpe, *Red Light, Blue Light: Prostitutes, Punters, and the Police* (Brookfield, Vt.: Ashgate, 1998), pp. 168–169; Jess Stern, *Sisters of the Night* (New York: Julian Messner, 1956); Patricia Whelehan, *An Anthropological Perspective on Prostitution: The World's Oldest Profession* (Lewiston, N.Y.: Edwin Mellen Press,

2001), p. 166. Some sociologists (and one historian) who conclude that entry into prostitution or remaining in prostitution is generally voluntary are Nanette J. Davis, "Prostitution: Identity, Career, and Legal-Economic Enterprise," in James M. Henslin and Edward Sagarin, eds., *The Sociology of Sex: An Introductory Reader* (New York: Schocken Books, 1978), pp. 195–222, at p. 196; Erich Goode, *Deviant Behavior* (Englewood Cliffs, N.J.: Prentice-Hall, 1994), p. 205; George Kneeland, *Commercialized Prostitution in New York* (Montclair, N.J.: Patterson Smith, [1913] 1969), p. 104; Charles H. McCaghy and Charles Hou, "Taiwan" in Nanette J. Davis, ed., *Prostitution: An International Handbook on Trends, Problems and Policies* (London: Greenwood Press, 1993), pp. 273–299, at pp. 287, 294; Maude Miner, *Slavery of Prostitution: A Plea for Emancipation* (New York: Garland, 1987; Macmillan Co., 1916), pp. ix, 103–104, citation is to the Garland edition; Ruth Rosen, *The Lost Sisterhood: Prostitution in America. 1900–1918* (Baltimore: Johns Hopkins University Press, 1982), p. xiv; and Ine Vanwesenbeeck, *Prostitutes' Well-Being and Risk* (Amsterdam: VU University Press, 1994), pp. 19–31.

2. Roger Matthews, *Prostitution, Politics and Policy* (New York: Routledge-Cavendish, 2008), p. 31.

3. Ibid., p. 81.

4. Ibid., p. 83.

5. See, for example, Melissa Farley, *Prostitution and Trafficking in Nevada: Making the Connections* (San Francisco: Prostitution Research and Education, 2007), pp. 100, 172; and Sheila Jeffreys, "Challenging the Adult/Child Distinction in Theory and Practice on Prostitution," *International Journal of Feminist Politics* 2, no. 3 (2000): 359–379, at pp. 368–369.

6. See, for example, Farley, *Prostitution and Trafficking in Nevada*, p. 98; Evelina Giobbe, "Prostitution: Buying the Right to Rape," in A. W. Burgess, ed., *Rape and Sexual Assault III: A Research Handbook* (New York: Garland Press, 1991), pp. 143–160; Cecilie Hoigard and Liv Finstad, *Backstreets: Prostitution, Money, and Love*, trans. Katherine Hanson, Nancy Sipe, and Barbara Wilson (University Park: Pennsylvania State University Press, 1992), pp. 178–180; Sheila Jeffreys, *The Idea of Prostitution* (Melbourne: Spinifex, 1997), p. 151; Matthews, *Prostitution, Politics and Policy*, pp. 30–31; JoAnn L. Miller, "Prostitution in Contemporary America," in Elizabeth Grauerholz and Mary A. Koralewski, eds., *Sexual Coercion: A Sourcebook on Its Nature, Causes, and Prevention* (Lexington, Mass.: Lexington Books, 1991), pp. 47, 54; and Janice G. Raymond, "Ten Reasons for *Not* Legalizing Prostitution and a Legal Response to the Demand for Prostitution," in Melissa Farley, ed. *Prostitution, Trafficking, and Traumatic Stress* (Binghamton, N.Y.: Haworth Maltreatment and Trauma Press, 2003), pp. 315–332, at pp. 324–325.

7. See, for example, Raymond, "Ten Reasons for *Not* Legalizing Prostitution," p. 325; and Hoigard and Finstad, *Backstreets*, pp. 200–202.

8. For this characterization of prostitution, see Melissa Farley et al., "Prostitution in Five Countries: Violence and Post-Traumatic Stress Disorder," *Feminism and Psychology* 8 (1998): 405–426, at p. 405; Evelina Giobbe, "Confronting the Liberal Lies about Prostitution," in Dorchen Leidholdt and Janice G. Raymond, eds., *Sexual Liberals and the Attack on Feminism* (New York: Pergamon Press, 1990), pp. 67–81, at p. 80; Hoigard and Finstad, *Backstreets*, pp. 114, 200; Kelly Holsopple, "Pimps, Tricks, and Feminists,"

Women's Studies Quarterly 27 (1999): 47–52, at p. 49; and Martin Monto, "Holding Men Accountable for Prostitution," *Violence Against Women* 4 (August 1998): 505–517, at p. 509.

9. See Giobbe, "Buying the Right to Rape," pp. 150–58, and Hoigard and Finstad, *Backstreets*, pp. 114–117, 200–201.

10. Some might prefer the term *parentalist*, which is more accurate, but I use the term *paternalist*, despite its patriarchal overtones, because it is the term standard in the relevant philosophical literature.

11. Barbara Milman, "New Rules for the Oldest Profession: Should We Change Our Prostitution Laws?" *Harvard Women's Law Journal* 3 (1980): 1–82, at pp. 24–25.

12. See Dorchen Leidholdt, "Prostitution: A Modern Form of Slavery," in Donna M. Hughes and Claire Roche, eds., *Making the Harm Visible: Global Sexual Exploitation of Women and Girls* (Kingston, R.I.: Coalition Against Trafficking in Women, 1999), pp. 49–55, who writes, "when prostitution is legitimized as sex work, the values and dynamics of prostitution spill over into other areas of society, influencing the valuation and treatment of girls and lowering their status" (p. 54). See, too, Giobbe, "Confronting the Liberal Lies about Prostitution," p. 77; Debra Satz, "Markets in Women's Sexual Labor," *Ethics* 106 (October 1995): 63–85, at pp. 78–81; and Christina Stark, "Stripping as a System of Prostitution," in Jessica Spector, ed., *Prostitution and Pornography: Philosophical Debate about the Sex Industry* (Stanford, Calif.: Stanford University Press, 2006), pp. 40–49, at p. 47.

13. Elizabeth Anderson, *Value in Ethics and Economics* (Cambridge, Mass.: Harvard University Press, 1993), pp. 154–155. For related arguments, see Margaret Jane Radin, *Contested Commodities* (Cambridge, Mass.: Harvard University Press, 1996), pp. 132–136; and Charles Winick and Paul M. Kinsie, *The Lively Commerce* (Chicago: Quadrangle Books, 1971), p. 190.

14. For the classic argument against regulation as an effective means of preventing disease, see Abraham Flexner, *Prostitution in Europe* (Montclair, N.J.: Patterson Smith, [1914] 1969), pp. 204–264.

15. See, for example, Deborah R. Brock, *Making Work, Making Trouble: Prostitution as a Social Problem* (Toronto: Toronto University Press, 1998), pp. 148–150; Goode, *Deviant Behavior*, p. 207; Matthews, *Prostitution, Politics and Policy*, pp. 2–3; and Vanwesenbeeck, *Prostitutes' Well-Being and Risk*, p. 38.

16. See Sophie Day, "Prostitute Women and AIDS: Anthropology," *AIDS* 2 (1988): 421–428; and Judith Porter and Louis Bonilla, "Drug Use, HIV, and the Ecology of Street Prostitution," in Ronald Weitzer, ed., *Sex for Sale: Prostitution, Pornography and the Sex Industry* (New York: Routledge, 2000), pp. 103–121, at p. 104. But for the view that sex work might play a significant role in HIV transmission independent of intravenous drug use, see Jacquie Astemborski et al., "The Trading of Sex for Drugs or Money and HIV Seropositivity among Female Intravenous Drug Users," *American Journal of Public Health* 84 (March 1994): 382–387.

17. Margaret A. Baldwin, "Split at the Root: Prostitution and Feminist Discourses of Law Reform," *Yale Journal of Law and Feminism* 5 (1992): 47–119, at pp. 49, 50.

Chapter 1

1. Melissa Farley and Howard Barkan, "Prostitution, Violence, and Posttraumatic Stress Disorder," *Women and Health* 27 (1998): 37–49, at p. 45.

2. Some empirical studies and discussions that support these claims about the negative effects of prostitution are Wendy Chapkis, *Live Sex Acts: Women Performing Erotic Labor* (New York: Routledge, 1997), pp. 92–96; John F. Decker, *Prostitution: Regulation and Control* (Littleton, Colo.: Rothman, 1979), pp. 203–210; Melissa Farley, "'Bad for the Body, Bad for the Heart': Prostitution Harms Women Even if Legalized or Decriminalized," *Violence Against Women* 10 (October 2004): 1087–1125, at pp. 1104–1109; Evelina Giobbe (a.k.a. Sarah Wynter, founder of WHISPER: Women Hurt in Systems Prostitution Engaged in Revolt), "Prostitution: Buying the Right to Rape," in Ann Wolbert Burgess, ed., *Rape and Sexual Assault III: A Research Handbook* (New York: Garland, 1991), pp. 143–160, at pp. 150–158; Judith Lewis Herman, "Hidden in Plain Sight: Clinical Observations on Prostitution," in Melissa Farley, ed., *Prostitution, Trafficking, and Traumatic Stress* (Binghamton, N.Y.: Haworth Maltreatment and Trauma Press, 2004), pp. 1–13, at pp. 6–7; Cecilie Hoigard and Liv Finstad, *Backstreets: Prostitution, Money and Love*, trans. Katherine Hanson, Nancy Sipe, and Barbara Wilson (University Park: Pennsylvania State University Press, 1992), pp. 50–84, 106–123; Joan J. Johnson, *Teen Prostitution* (Danbury, Conn.: Franklin Watts, 1992), pp. 18–19; Lisa A. Kramer, "Emotional Experiences of Performing Prostitutes," in Farley, *Prostitution, Trafficking, and Traumatic Stress*, pp. 187–197; Sven-Axel Mansson and U-C. Hedin, "Breaking the Matthew Effect—On Women Leaving Prostitution," *International Journal of Social Welfare* 8, no. 1 (1999): 67–77, at p. 72; Roger Matthews, *Prostitution, Politics and Policy* (New York: Routledge-Cavendish, 2008), pp. 37, 81; Neil McKeganey and Marina Barnard, *Sex Work on the Streets* (Philadelphia: Open University Press, 1996), pp. 82–98; Kate Millett, "Prostitution: A Quartet for Female Voices," in Vivian Gornick and Barbara K. Moran, eds., *Woman in Sexist Society: Studies in Power and Powerlessness* (New York: Basic Books, 1971), pp. 21–69, particularly the testimony of J and M; Julia O'Connell Davidson, *Prostitution, Power and Freedom* (Cambridge, U.K.: Polity Press, 1998), pp. 102–103, 206–210; Roberta Perkins and Garry Bennett, *Being a Prostitute* (Winchester, Mass.: Allen & Unwin, Inc., 1985), pp. 109, 112, 113, 123–124, 131; Joanna Phoenix, *Making Sense of Prostitution* (London: Macmillan Press, 1999), pp. 131–136; Janice G. Raymond, "Ten Reasons for *Not* Legalizing Prostitution and a Legal Response to the Demand for Prostitution," in Farley, *Prostitution, Trafficking, and Traumatic Stress*, pp. 315–332, at pp. 324–326; Ruth Rosen, *The Lost Sisterhood: Prostitution in America, 1900–1918* (Baltimore: Johns Hopkins University Press, 1982), pp. 97–100; Jess Stern, *Sisters of the Night* (New York: Julian Messner, 1956), pp. 151–163; Ine Vanwesenbeeck, *Prostitutes' Well-Being and Risk* (Amsterdam: VU University Press, 1994), pp. 106–110, 147–152; and D. Kelly Weisberg, *Children of the Night: A Study of Adolescent Prostitution* (Lexington, Mass.: Lexington Books, 1985), pp. 111–113, 116–117.

3. Hoigard and Finstad, *Backstreets*, p. 201. Cf. pp. 112, 116, 132.

4. Pat Barker, *Blow Your House Down* (London: Virago Press, 1984), p. 82; Nanette J. Davis, "From Victims to Survivors: Working with Recovering Street Prostitutes," in Ronald Weitzer, ed., *Sex for Sale: Prostitution, Pornography and the Sex Industry* (New York: Routledge, 2000), pp. 139–155, at p. 151; Hoigard and Finstad, *Backstreets*, pp. 51, 79; Matthews, *Prostitution, Politics and Policy*, p. 81; Alexandra K. Murphy and Sudhir A. Venkatesh, "Vice Careers: The Changing Contours of Sex Work in New York City," *Qualitative Sociology* 29 (2006): 129–154, at p. 148; Adele Weiner, "Understanding the Social Needs of Streetwalking Prostitutes," *Social Work* 41 (1996): 97–105, at p. 98.

5. For a good description of this course of thought, see O'Connell Davidson, *Prostitution, Power and Freedom*, p. 69. See, too, Hoigard and Finstad, *Backstreets*, pp. 47–50; Eileen McLeod, *Women Working: Prostitution Now* (London: Croom Helm, 1982), p. 26; Phoenix, *Making Sense of Prostitution*, pp. 107–109; and Stern, *Sisters of the Night*, p. 147.

6. For the characterization of prostitution as an addiction, see Deborah R. Brock, *Making Work, Making Trouble: Prostitution as a Social Problem* (Toronto: Toronto University Press, 1998), p. 109; Ronald B. Flowers, *The Prostitution of Women and Girls* (London: McFarland, 1998), p. 28; Claude Jaget, ed., *Prostitutes—Our Life* (Bristol, U.K.: Falling Wall Press, 1980), p. 159; Johnson, *Teen Prostitution*, pp. 106–107; Millet, "Prostitution: A Quartet for Female Voices," p. 52; Murphy and Venkatesh, "Vice Careers," p. 142; O'Connell Davidson, *Prostitution, Power and Freedom*, p. 69; Karen Sharpe, *Red Light, Blue Light: Prostitutes, Punters, and the Police* (Brookfield, Vt.: Ashgate, 1998), p. 168; Stern, *Sisters of the Night*, p. 156; Weisberg, *Children of the Night*, p. 111.

7. See Teela Sanders, *Sex Work: A Risky Business* (Cullompton, U.K.: Willan, 2005), p. 48; Sharpe, *Red Light, Blue Light*, p. 34.

8. Hoigard and Finstad, *Backstreets*, pp. 79–82.

9. See Arlene Carmen and Howard Moody, *Working Women: The Subterranean World of Street Prostitution* (New York: Harper and Row, 1985), pp. 84–85; Melissa Farley, *Prostitution and Trafficking in Nevada: Making the Connections* (San Francisco: Prostitution Research and Education, 2007), p. 57; Flowers, *Prostitution of Women and Girls*, p. 51; and Hoigard and Finstad, *Backstreets*, pp. 77–81.

10. For some related statistics, see Farley, *Prostitution and Trafficking in Nevada*, p. 97.

11. Jane Addams claims the average age is 16–18 in *A New Conscience and an Ancient Evil*, introduction by Katherine Joslin (Chicago: University of Illinois Press, [1912] 2002), p. 64; Nanette J. Davis reports that the average age of girls in her study was 17.3, with an age range of fourteen to twenty-five, "Prostitution: Identity, Career, and Enterprise," in James M. Henslin and Edward Sagarin, eds., *The Sociology of Sex: An Introductory Reader* (New York: Schocken Books, 1978), pp. 195–222, at p. 201; Evelina Giobbe reports that the average age is estimated to be fourteen and a half, "Juvenile Prostitution: Profile of Recruitment," in Ann Wolbert Burgess, ed., *Child Trauma I: Issues and Research* (New York: Garland Press, 1992), pp. 117–130, at p. 117; Hoigard and Finstad say that the average age of the first trick of those in their study was fifteen and a half, *Backstreets*, p. 15; Charles H. McCaghy and

Charles Hou report three studies that identify different average ages of entry into prostitution in Taiwan, but each confirms that many girls start before age eighteen, "Taiwan" in Nanette J. Davis, ed., *Prostitution: An International Handbook on Trends, Problems and Policies* (London: Greenwood Press, 1993), pp. 273–299, at p. 286; Matthews, *Prostitution, Politics and Policy*, p. 32, concludes that "the majority first become involved under the age of eighteen"; Mimi H. Silbert says that 78 percent of sex workers in her study of 200 San Francisco sex workers reported that they started prostitution as juveniles and that 68 percent were sixteen or younger when they started, "Prostitution and Sexual Assault: Summary of Results," *The International Journal for Biomedical Research* 3 (1982): 69–71, at p. 70; and the Vice Commission of Chicago identified "the average age of entrance to life" as eighteen, *The Social Evil in Chicago* (New York: Arno Press, [1911] 1970), p. 169.

12. Silbert reports an eight-month difference between the average age of starting prostitution and the average age of starting to work regularly in Mimi H. Silbert, *Sexual Assault of Prostitutes: Phase One* (Washington, D.C.: National Institute of Mental Health, National Center for the Prevention and Control of Rape, 1980), p. 39. Cited in Weisberg, *Children of the Night*, pp. 156–157.

13. This is dubbed "scarlet letter syndrome" by Giobbe, "Prostitution: Buying the Right to Rape," pp. 156–157. See, too, Mansson and Hedin, "Breaking the Matthew Effect," p. 73.

14. Patricia Whelehan, *An Anthropological Perspective on Prostitution: The World's Oldest Profession* (Lewiston, N.Y.: Edwin Mellen Press, 2001), p. 49.

15. Sanders, *Sex Work*, pp. 121–127, 147.

16. Murphy and Venkatesh, "Vice Careers," p. 145; Sanders, *Sex Work*, pp. 131–133.

17. For a poignant description of the emotional challenges faced by mothers who are (legal) prostitutes, see Alexa Albert, *Brothel: Mustang Ranch and Its Women* (New York: Random House, 2001), pp. 89–93. See, too, Sanders, *Sex Work*, p. 123. But for a more positive picture, see Whelehan, *Anthropological Perspective on Prostitution*, p. 160.

18. Some sex workers, however, do express pride in the fact that they are helping people as providers of a kind of therapy. See, for example, Albert, *Brothel*, pp. 104–106, and Murphy and Venkatesh, "Vice Careers," pp. 141–142.

19. For a good discussion of the beneficial opportunities that prostitution creates for some people, see Phoenix, *Making Sense of Prostitution*, pp. 75–100, and also Gail Pheterson, ed., *Vindication of the Rights of Whores* (Seattle: Seal Press, 1989), pp. 160, 168–169. Relatively positive portrayals of sex work can also be found in Albert, *Brothel*, pp. 68–167 (but see Daisy's remarks on p. 234); Murphy and Venkatesh, "Vice Careers," pp. 141–142; O'Connell Davidson, *Prostitution, Power and Freedom*, pp. 88–106 (discussion of Desiree); and Whelehan, *Anthropological Perspective on Prostitution*, pp. 167–175.

20. See Brock, *Making Work, Making Trouble*, p. 13. In the novel *Blow Your House Down*, pp. 28–30, 33–41, 45–53, Pat Barker makes vivid in her description of Brenda's situation how streetwalking, despite its many

negative aspects, can seem on balance to be the best choice for a single working-class mother of small children, given the alternative of exhausting, disgusting work in a chicken factory.

21. Jennifer James, "The Prostitute as Victim," in Jane Roberts Chapman and Margaret Gates, eds., *The Victimization of Women* (Beverly Hills: Sage, 1978), pp. 175–201, at p. 177; Silbert, "Prostitution and Sexual Assault," p. 70; Nobuho Tomita, "Japan," in Davis, ed., *Prostitution*, pp. 176–190, at p. 182; Weisberg, *Children of the Night*, p. 153.

22. Flowers, *Prostitution of Women and Girls*, p. 47; Matthews, *Prostitution, Politics and Policy*, p. 36; Murphy and Venkatesh, "Vice Careers," p. 135; Silbert, "Prostitution and Sexual Assault," p. 70; Stern, *Sisters of the Night*, p. 147; Weisberg, *Children of the Night*, pp. 112–113.

23. Gail Sheehy, *Hustling: Prostitution in Our Wide Open Society* (New York: Delacorte Press, 1973), p. 6; Hoigard and Finstad, *Backstreets*, pp. 47–50; Jaget, *Prostitutes*, pp. 159–160; Sharpe, *Red Light, Blue Light*, pp. 71–73, 168; and Stern, *Sisters of the Night*, p. 147.

24. See Barker, *Blow Your House Down*, p. 48; Matthews, *Prostitution, Politics and Policy*, pp. 11, 74–75; Sanders, *Sex Work*, p. 156.

25. Phoenix, *Making Sense of Prostitution*, pp. 108–109.

26. See Barker, *Blow Your House Down*, p. 48; and Hoigard and Finstad, *Backstreets*, p. 49.

27. Albert, *Brothel*, p. 157; Farley, *Prostitution and Trafficking in Nevada*, p. 149; Sheehy, *Hustling*, p. 5; and Charles Winick and Paul M. Kinsie, *The Lively Commerce* (Chicago: Quadrangle Books, 1971), p. 287. The latter identify this as "perhaps the least desirable feature of prostitution." Because, however, it is at least as true of other occupations like film actress and photography model, this cannot explain what is uniquely bad about prostitution. Norma Jean Almodovar points out that an advantage of prostitution, compared to acting in pornographic films, is that a woman does not have to be young, in shape, and good-looking to succeed as a prostitute. See Norma Jean Almodovar, "Porn Stars, Radical Feminists, Cops and Outlaw Whores: The Battle between Feminist Theory and Reality, Free Speech and Free Spirits," in Jessica Spector, ed., *Prostitution and Pornography: Philosophical Debate about the Sex Industry* (Stanford, Calif.: Stanford University Press, 2006), pp. 149–174, at p. 160.

28. See Dorchen A. Leidholdt, "Prostitution and Trafficking in Women: An Intimate Relationship," in Farley, *Prostitution, Trafficking, and Traumatic Stress*, pp. 167–183, at p. 171; Phoenix, *Making Sense of Prostitution*, p. 109.

29. Students of prostitution policy who endorse this line of reasoning include Abraham Flexner, *Prostitution in Europe* (Montclair, N.J.: Patterson Smith, [1914] 1969), pp. 395–400; Hoigard and Finstad, *Backstreets*, pp. 182, 200–201; Roger Matthews, "Beyond Wolfenden? Prostitution, Politics and the Law," in Roger Matthews and Jock Young, eds., *Confronting Crime* (London: Sage, 1986), pp. 188–210, at p. 199; and Maude Miner, *Slavery of Prostitution: A Plea for Emancipation* (New York: Garland, 1987; Macmillan Co., 1916), p. 125, citation to Garland edition.

30. See, for example, Linda-Mary Banach and Sue Metzenrath, *Principles for Model Sex Industry Legislation* (Sydney: Scarlet Alliance, 2000), p. 1;

Kate DeCou, "U.S. Policy on Prostitution: Whose Welfare Is Served?" *Civil and Criminal Confinement* 24 (1998): 427–53, at p. 451.

31. See, for example, Banach and Metzenrath, *Principles for Model Sex Industry Legislation*, p. 4; Lars Ericsson, "Charges Against Prostitution: An Attempt at a Philosophical Assessment," *Ethics* 90 (April 1980): 335–366, at 343–344, 356, 362, 363, 366; and Decker, *Prostitution: Regulation and Control*, pp. 301–302.

32. Matthews, *Prostitution, Politics and Policy*, p. 109.

33. For the observation that prostitution is stigmatized in the Netherlands despite its permissive official policy, see Katherine Gregory, *The Everyday Lives of Sex Workers in the Netherlands* (New York: Routledge, 2005), p. 163. See, too, Claire Sterk-Elifson and Carole A. Campbell, "The Netherlands," in Davis, ed., *Prostitution*, pp. 191–206, at pp. 192, 200, 203, 204, who suggest that the stigma is best explained by Calvinist morality and not by the fact that prostitution was not recognized by the government as a legal profession until 1988 (p. 204). For further observations of the stigma in the Netherlands, see Chapkis, *Live Sex Acts*, pp. 152–153, 204; Pheterson, *Vindication of the Rights of Whores*, pp. 85, 88; and Vanwesenbeeck, *Prostitutes' Well-Being and Risk*, pp. 6, 9. For the observation that prostitution remains stigmatized in Germany, despite the fact that it has been legal since 1927, see Annette Jolin, "Germany," in Davis, ed., *Prostitution*, pp. 129–156, at pp. 129, 150. For the view that there has been little change in attitudes toward prostitution in Portugal since 1982, when it was decriminalized, see Gilbert Geis, "Portugal," in Davis, ed., *Prostitution*, pp. 225–242, at p. 240. For the observation that prostitution is "a highly stigmatized profession" in Taiwan even though brothel prostitution is legal and licensed, and prostitution itself is everywhere decriminalized, see McCaghy and Hou, "Taiwan," p. 274. For the observation that prostitution is "still treated with a general attitude of moralistic shunning in [the former] Yugoslavia despite the fact that there were no laws regulating prostitution as such, see Vesna Nikolic-Ristanovic, "Yugoslavia," in Davis, *Prostitution*, 351–372, at p. 352. Daniella Dana observes that in Italy prostitution is so stigmatized that many believe that it is illegal even though it is not, "Italy," in Joyce Outshoorn, ed., *The Politics of Prostitution: Women's Movements, Democratic States, and the Globalization of Sex Commerce* (New York: Cambridge University Press, 2004), pp. 165–184, at p. 167. Albert observes that "brothel prostitution in Nevada is still a very stigmatized business (despite its legal status) and that most licensed prostitutes and customers conceal their practices from loved ones," *Brothel* (author's note).

34. See Joyce Outshoorn, "Voluntary and Forced Prostitution: The 'Realistic Approach' of the Netherlands," in Outshoorn, ed., *The Politics of Prostitution*, pp. 185–204, at pp. 198–199.

35. Scott Anderson makes this point in "Prostitution and Sexual Autonomy: Making Sense of the Prohibition of Prostitution," *Ethics* 112 (July 2002): 748–780, at p. 762

36. See ibid, pp. 762–763, for an illuminating list of some further consequences of "treating sex as just another use of the body in commerce."

37. Alan Wertheimer makes a similar point about laws that prohibit statutory rape in *Consent to Sexual Relations* (New York: Cambridge University Press, 2003), p. 220.

38. Chapkis, *Live Sex Acts*, pp. 94–95. For some similar descriptions, see Erich Goode, *Deviant Behavior* (Englewood Cliffs, N.J.: Prentice-Hall, 1994), pp. 202–203; and Millet, "Prostitution: A Quartet for Female Voices," pp. 52–54 (J's testimony).

39. Arlie Hochschild presents a nuanced account of the emotional labor that flight attendants performed in the days before economy travel and how psychologically taxing this work was. She certainly does not suggest, however, that this work was as psychologically taxing as sex work. See Arlie Hochschild, *The Managed Heart* (Berkeley: University of California Press, 1983), pp. 185–198.

40. See Giobbe, "Prostitution: Buying the Right to Rape," p. 158.

41. Chapkis, *Live Sex Acts*, p. 116. See, too, Giobbe, "Prostitution: Buying the Right to Rape," p. 158.

42. A vivid account of the difficulties in maintaining normal boundaries in doing sex work and the psychological costs of failing to do so is given in Vicki Funari, "Naked, Naughty, Nasty: Peep Show Reflections," in Jill Nagle, ed., *Whores and Other Feminists* (London: Routledge, 1997), pp. 19–35. Although Funari worked in a peep show and not as a prostitute, her experience is illuminating.

43. See Chapkis, *Live Sex Acts*, pp. 98–99, 119–120. Nor does legalization help. See Matthews, *Prostitution, Politics and Policy*, p. 107.

44. Chapkis, *Live Sex Acts*, p. 120.

45. Ibid., p. 114.

46. See, for example, Stern, *Sisters of the Night*, p. 4.

47. Some prostitutes say they sometimes enjoy sex with some of their clients. See, for example, Albert, *Brothel*, pp. 132–137; Jaget, *Prostitution*, p. 128; and Sanders, *Sex Work*, p. 145. Many prostitutes, however, say they do not enjoy the sex, or enjoy it only rarely, and some regard the enjoyment of sex with a client as contemptible. For some expressions of this last attitude, see Albert, *Brothel*, pp. 133–136, and Hoigard and Finstad, *Backstreets*, p. 71.

48. For a good example of the kind of self-deception common among customers, see Albert, *Brothel*, pp. 120–122.

49. For a similar conclusion, see Catherine Benson and Roger Matthews, "Street Prostitution: Ten Facts in Search of a Social Policy," *International Journal of the Sociology of Law, 1995* 23 (1995): 395–415, who write that advocates of decriminalization "all fail to recognize that the stigma which is associated with prostitution is not solely a consequence of legal regulation, but rather it is the legal regulation which is a function of social stigmatization" (p. 398).

50. Winick and Kinsie, *Lively Commerce*, p. 287.

51. Pheterson, *Vindication of the Rights of Whores*, p. 107.

52. Cited in Laurie Bell, ed., *Good Girls/Bad Girls: Feminists and Sex Trade Workers Face to Face* (Toronto: Seal Press, 1987), p. 129. For a similar comment (perhaps the same one), see Pheterson, *Vindication of the Rights of Whores*, pp. 180–181. See, too, ibid., p. 178, for the observation that prostitutes tend to paint a sunnier picture of their work in public than the underlying reality warrants.

53. Annie Sprinkle, "We've Come a Long Way—And We're Exhausted!" in Nagle, *Whores and Other Feminists*, pp. 66–69, at p. 67.

54. Chapkis, *Live Sex Acts*, p. 1.
55. Ibid., p. 78.
56. Ibid., p. 73. I have been unable to find a passage in which Hoigard and Finstad make this claim, but see *Backstreets*, p. 132, for a statement that comes close.
57. Chapkis, *Live Sex Acts*, p. 78.
58. Ibid., p. 227.
59. See Wertheimer, *Consent to Sexual Relations*, pp. 217–218.
60. See Allie C. Kilpatrick, *Long-Range Effects of Child and Adolescent Sexual Experience: Myths, Mores, Menaces* (Hillsdale, N.J.: Lawrence Erlbaum, 1992), pp. xvii, 37–41, 45, 115–116.
61. For a recent example of this usage, see *Purchasing Sexual Services in Sweden and the Netherlands: Legal Regulation and Experiences*, Norwegian Ministry of Justice and Police Affairs report series 2004 (G-0367), abbreviated English version, at http://www.regjeringen.no/upload/kilde/jd/rap/2004/0034/ddd/pdfv/232216-purchasing_sexual_services_in_sweden_and_the_nederlands.pdf., p. 47. Chapkis, *Live Sex Acts*, p. 8, also uses the terms this way. See, too, Harry Benjamin and R. E. L. Masters, *Prostitution and Immorality* (New York: Julian Press, 1964), pp. 372–376. Laurie Shrage, *Moral Dilemmas of Feminism: Prostitution, Adultery and Abortion* (London: Routledge, 1994), pp. 82–87, 158–161, uses the terms *prohibition, regulation,* and *decriminalization* in this way, but uses the term *feminist regulationism* instead of *abolitionism.*
62. Note that I would also characterize as a form of prohibition a policy that makes sale, but not purchase, a crime, although this would be an "incomplete" form of prohibition.
63. For a useful compendium of U.S. prostitution laws, see Richard A. Posner and Katharine B. Silbaugh, *A Guide to American Sex Laws* (Chicago: University of Chicago Press, 1996), pp. 155–187.
64. The term *abolition* was originally used in the late nineteenth century to express opposition to the policy of *regulation.* In this context it referred not to the abolition of *prostitution* but to the abolition of brothels and, more specifically, to the repeal of the specific policy of regulation recently adopted by the British government in the Contagious Diseases Acts (1864), which was the object of fierce criticism. Nineteenth-century British "abolitionists" like Josephine Butler opposed this policy of regulation because, in their view, it licensed too much unwarranted police intrusion into the liberty of prostitutes and into the liberty of women generally, because it allowed the police to require health inspections of any woman walking on the street they suspected of prostitution. The term *abolition* was thus originally used in this historical context specifically to mean opposition to this particular policy of regulation, but it soon came to express opposition to official toleration generally or to any regulationist policy. See Alan Hunt, *Governing Morals: A Social History of Moral Regulation* (Cambridge, U.K.: Cambridge University Press, 1999), p. 102. Not surprisingly, however, the term was also soon used to express opposition to prostitution as such or to endorse the goal of ending it. This usage was further supported by the fact that prostitution was commonly regarded as a kind of "white slavery," which ought to be "abolished," as "black slavery" had been abolished in the United States by

the Thirteenth Amendment. The "white slavery" idea was fostered by the widespread belief that many prostitutes were the victims of kidnapping, threats, and fraud, but it was supported, too, by the widespread belief that this kind of life involved a kind of spiritual and mental bondage. Here I use the term *abolition* more narrowly to refer to a particular kind of legal restriction on prostitution.

65. Street Offences Act 1959, 7 & 8 Eliz 2. c. 57.

66. Sexual Offences Act 1985, Eliz. 2. c. 44.

67. Note that I would categorize the kind of civil penalties that Linda Hirshman and Jane Larson endorse in *Hard Bargains* as a form of impermissive regulation. Although they favor decriminalizing adult sexual commerce, they propose allowing prostitutes of all ages to recover civil damages in the way that sweatshop laws allow those they have employed to sue, as a way of deterring clients and agents and so as a way of reducing prostitution. See Linda R. Hirshman and Jane E. Larson, *Hard Bargains* (New York: Oxford University Press, 1998), p. 289.

68. See Matthews, *Prostitution, Politics and Policy*, p. 102, but this argument against prohibition has long been recognized. See, for example, Vice Commission of Chicago, *Social Evil in Chicago*, p. 46.

69. Elizabeth Vorenberg and James Vorenberg, "The Biggest Pimp of All," *Atlantic* (January 1977): 27–38. Note, though, that if the government were to legalize prostitution and to tax income from sex work, as the Vorenbergs seem to advocate, then the government would arguably be acting even more like a pimp, as Matthews observes in *Prostitution, Politics and Policy*, p. 107.

70. Some have questioned, however, whether sex workers are likely to organize effectively given the anarchical temperament of many sex workers. See, for example, Albert, *Brothel*, p. 160.

71. But these experiences seem to bother some prostitutes more than others. See Sharpe, *Red Light, Blue Light*, pp. 144–146.

72. See Matthews, "Beyond Wolfenden?" p. 204. Vorenberg and Vorenberg also concede that prohibition may have this effect, "The Biggest Pimp of All," p. 37.

73. See, for example, Jaget, *Prostitution*, pp. 117–118.

74. See note 19.

75. See Laura Miller, "Prostitution," *Harper's Bazaar* 3400 (March 1995): 208–210, at p. 209.

76. See Matthews, *Prostitution, Politics and Policy*, pp. 48, 101; and Priscilla Pyett and Deborah Warr, "Women at Risk in Sex Work: Strategies for Survival" *Journal of Sociology* 35, no. 2 (1999): 183–197, at p. 195.

77. See note 11.

78. Mimi H. Silbert and Ayala M. Pines, "Sexual Child Abuse as an Antecedent to Prostitution," *Child Abuse and Neglect* 5 (1981): 407–411, conclude from Silbert's study that most prostitutes have been sexually abused as children. Different explanations are possible, however. According to one hypothesis, the experience predisposes a person to abusive and exploitive sexual relationships and so predisposes a person to prostitution. According to another hypothesis, the experience makes it more likely that a person will run away from home and then turn to prostitution out of financial need.

79. See Hoigard and Finstad, *Backstreets*, p. 205; and Sheila Jeffreys, "Challenging the Adult/Child Distinction in Theory and Practice on Prostitution," *International Journal of Feminist Politics* 2, no. 3 (2000): 359–379, at pp. 365–367.

80. See Mary Sullivan and Sheila Jeffreys, "Legalization: The Australian Experience," *Violence against Women* 8, no. 9 (2002): 1140–1148, at p. 1142, for the claim that prostitution has increased dramatically since being legalized in Victoria, Australia.

81. See Jeffreys, "Challenging the Adult/Child Distinction," pp. 362–363; and Raymond, "Ten Reasons for *Not* Legalizing Prostitution," p. 321.

82. See Albert, *Brothel*, p. 61.

83. See Dorchen A. Leidholdt, "Prostitution and Trafficking in Women: An Intimate Relationship," in Farley, *Prostitution, Trafficking, and Traumatic Stress*, pp. 167–183, at pp. 179–180; and Raymond, "Ten Reasons for *Not* Legalizing Prostitution," pp. 317–318. Both Leidholdt and Raymond have been co-executive directors of the Coalition Against Trafficking in Women. A causal connection between trafficking and local legal markets in prostitution is also recognized in *Report of the Special Body of Experts of Traffic in Women and Children* (Advisory Committee of the League of Nations, Document C.52.M.52 1927), pp. 14–16, 41, 47, and in *Study on Traffic in Persons and Prostitution 50–57* (United Nations Department of Economic and Social Affairs, ST/SOA/SD/8, U.N. Publ. Sales No. 59.IV.5, 1959), pp. 5, 6, 9. The observation that legal brothels or "licensed houses" create the demand for trafficking is also strongly endorsed in Flexner, *Prostitution in Europe*, p. 185. The prediction that legalization increases trafficking also seems to be confirmed by an observed increase in illegal trafficking that has followed the legalization of brothels in Amsterdam. See Marlise Simons, "Amsterdam Tries Upscale Fix for Red-Light District Crime," *New York Times*, February 24, 2008, p. 10. See, too, Matthews, *Prostitution, Politics and Policy*, p. 106, who also associates a rapid increase in trafficking with legalized brothels.

84. Note here that much of what is called "trafficking" by antiprostitution activists does not involve force or fraud and so does not satisfy this definition. Much of what is called trafficking involves instead a kind of voluntary debt bondage. See Matthews, *Prostitution, Politics and Policy*, p. 39.

85. See Pheterson, *Vindication of the Rights of Whores*, p. 101, for some observations along these lines.

86. Seana Shiffrin offers an argument of this kind for the unconscionability doctrine in contract law in "Paternalism, Unconscionability Doctrine, and Accommodation," *Philosophy & Public Affairs* 29 (Summer 2000): 205–250.

87. See act on prohibiting the purchase of sexual services, Swedish Code of Statutes (SFS 1998: 408).

88. "Since the introduction of the legislation prostitution has, according to official estimates, decreased by 50 per cent and equally significantly, it has slowed down the rate of recruitment of young women into prostitution. It is also believed that the approach of criminalizing male clients has deterred traffickers with the consequence that the number of women trafficked into Sweden is relatively low compared to neighboring countries," Matthews, *Prostitution, Politics, and Policy*, p. 113. See, too, Julie Bindel and Liz Kelly,

A Critical Examination of Responses to Prostitution in Four Countries: Victoria, Australia; Ireland; the Netherlands, and Sweden (London: London Metropolitan University, 2003) p. 25; and Gunilla Ekberg, "The Swedish Law that Prohibits the Purchase of Sexual Services," *Violence Against Women* 10, no. 10 (2004): 1187–1218, at pp. 1193–1194, 1199–1200. For another relatively optimistic assessment that the criminalization of purchase is likely reduce demand for sexual services, see Ronald Weitzer, "Prostitution Control in America: Rethinking Public Policy," *Crime, Law and Social Change* 32 (1999): 83–102, at pp. 95–97.

89. For a sympathetic discussion of the different nonpathological motives men have for visiting prostitutes, see Elizabeth Bernstein, "The Meaning of the Purchase: Desire, Demand, and the Commerce of Sex," *Ethnography* 2, no. 3 (2001): 389–420, at pp. 397–404.

90. See, for example, Farley, *Prostitution and Trafficking in Nevada*, p. 208.

91. For skepticism as to whether regulation is ever sufficiently well-enforced to control underage prostitution adequately, see Jeffreys, "Challenging the Adult/Child Distinction," p. 372.

92. For informed skepticism as to whether there is much more trafficking under the Dutch policy, see Ronald Weitzer, "The Growing Moral Panic over Prostitution and Sex Trafficking," *The Criminologist* 30, no. 5 (September/October 2005): 1–5, at p. 4.

93. For a discussion of policies that would help women to leave prostitution that do not involve criminalizing the sale or purchase of sexual services, see Jody Williams, "Barriers to Services for Women Escaping Nevada Prostitution and Trafficking," in Farley, *Prostitution and Trafficking in Nevada*, pp. 159–172.

94. Matthews, *Prostitution, Politics and Policy*, p. 26.

95. For a grim description of the ways in which brothel owners control the lives of their workers in Nevada's legalized brothels (and also take half of their fee), see Farley, *Prostitution and Trafficking in Nevada*, pp. 16–19. See, too, Chapkis, *Live Sex Acts*, pp. 98–99; Phoenix, *Making Sense of Prostitution*, p. 142; and Raymond, "Ten Reasons for *Not* Legalizing Prostitution," p. 320.

96. Bindel and Kelly, *Critical Examination of Responses*, p. 16; Matthews, *Prostitution, Politics and Policy*, p. 108.

97. Matthews, *Prostitution, Politics and Policy*, p. 108; McKeganey and Barnard, *Sex Work on the Streets*, p. 20; Miner, *Slavery of Prostitution*, p. 16; Sharpe, *Red Light, Blue Light*, pp. 152–153, 157; Whelehan, *Anthropological Perspective on Prostitution*, p. 48.

98. See Albert, *Brothel*, p. 52.

99. Ibid., p. 75.

100. Hoigard and Finstad, *Backstreets*, pp. 170–171; Millett, "Prostitution: A Quartet for Female Voices," pp. 65–67; and Phoenix, *Making Sense of Prostitution*, pp. 147–149, 156–159.

Chapter 2

1. For an explanation of what is wrong with prostitution that does not rely on the inherent preciousness of sex, but relies instead on the close

relation between a person's self and her sexuality, see Carole Pateman, *The Sexual Contract* (Stanford, Calif.: Stanford University Press, 1988), pp. 189–218, esp. pp. 206–208, For a critique of Pateman's argument, see Sibyl Schwarzenbach, "Contractarians and Feminists Debate Prostitution," *NYU Review of Law and Social Change* 28 (1991): 103–130, at pp. 112–117.

2. See introduction, note 8.

3. 539 U.S. 558, 590 (2003).

4. Ronald Dworkin, *Sovereign Virtue* (Cambridge, Mass.: Harvard University Press, 2000), p. 282.

5. John Rawls, *A Theory of Justice* (Cambridge, Mass.: Harvard University Press, 1971), p. 331.

6. Catharine A. MacKinnon, *Sex Equality* (New York: Foundation Press, 2001), p. 1395.

7. Claude Jaget, ed., *Prostitutes—Our Life* (Bristol, U.K.: Falling Wall Press, 1980), p. 113.

8. Bob Herbert, "City as Predator," *New York Times*, September 4, 2007.

9. Cecilie Hoigard and Liv Finstad, *Backstreets: Prostitution, Money, and Love,* trans. Katherine Hanson, Nancy Sipe, and Barbara Wilson (University Park: Pennsylvania State University Press, 1992), p. 63.

10. Dorchen Leidholdt and Jessica Neuwirth, "Memorandum of Law of APNE AAP and Eighteen Other Organizations as Amici Curiae," *Alliance for Open Society International and Open Society Institute v. United States Agency for International Development*, Civil Action No. 05-CV-8209, United States District Court for the Southern District of New York, p. 4.

11. Evelina Giobbe, "Prostitution: Buying the Right to Rape," in Ann W. Burgess, ed., *Rape and Sexual Assault III: A Research Handbook* (New York: Garland Press, 1991), pp. 143–160, at p. 151.

12. D. Kelly Weisberg, *Children of the Night: A Study of Adolescent Prostitution* (Lexington, Mass.: Lexington Books, 1985), p. 99.

13. See Ronald Dworkin, *Life's Dominion* (New York: Vintage Books, 1994), p. 96.

14. See Giobbe, "Buying the Right to Rape."

15. See John Stuart Mill, *On Liberty*, ed. Elizabeth Rapaport (Indianapolis: Hackett, 1978), p. 9; H. L. A Hart, *Law, Liberty, and Morality* (Stanford, Calif.: Stanford University Press, 1963), pp. 4–6, 30–34.

16. For the view that the motive or intent of an act is not generally relevant to its moral permissibility, see T. M. Scanlon, *Moral Dimensions: Permissibility, Meaning and Blame* (Cambridge, Mass.: Harvard University Press, 2008), pp. 12–20.

17. See, for example, Hart, *Law, Liberty, and Morality*, pp. 4–6.

18. Joel Feinberg, *The Moral Limits of the Criminal Law, Vol. I: Harm to Others* (New York: Oxford University Press, 1984), p. 12.

19. See, for example, Lars Ericsson, "Charges against Prostitution: An Attempt at a Philosophical Assessment," *Ethics* 90 (April 1980): 335–366, at pp. 337–339, 342–344; and David A. J. Richards, "Commercial Sex and the Rights of the Person," *Sex, Drugs, Death and the Law* (Totowa, N.J.: Rowman and Littlefield, 1982), pp. 84–153, at pp. 94–95.

20. Kate Millet, "Prostitution: A Quartet for Female Voices," in Vivian Gornick and Barbara K. Moran, eds., *Woman in Sexist Society: Studies in*

Power and Powerlessness (New York: Basic Books, 1971), pp. 21–69, at p. 68 (J's testimony).

21. See, for example, Richards, "Commercial Sex and the Rights of the Person," and "Drug Use and the Rights of the Person," in *Sex, Drugs, Death and Law*, pp. 157–212.

22. Mill, *On Liberty*, pp. 95, 98.

23. Douglas Husak and Peter de Marneffe, *The Legalization of Drugs* (New York: Cambridge University Press, 2005).

24. Jane Addams, *A New Conscience and an Ancient Evil*, introduction by Katherine Joslin (Chicago: University of Illinois Press, [1912] 2002), p. 99.

25. Maude Miner, *Slavery of Prostitution: A Plea for Emancipation* (New York: Garland, 1987; Macmillan Co., 1916), pp. 307–308, citation to the Garland edition.

26. Vice Commission of Chicago, *The Social Evil in Chicago* (New York: Arno Press, [1911] 1970), p. 3, citation to 1970 edition.

27. Ibid. p. 6.

28. Ibid. p. 43.

29. Ibid. p, 47.

30. Ibid. p. 105.

31. Edwin R. A. Seligman, *The Social Evil* (New York: G. P. Putnam's Sons, [1900] 1912), p. 21, citation to 1912 edition.

32. John Stuart Mill, *Utilitarianism*, ed. George Sher (Indianapolis: Hackett, 1979), pp. 8–11.

33. Walter Lippmann, *A Preface to Politics* (New York: Mitchell Kennerley, 1914), p. 124. See, too, pp. 127, 132, 135, and 158.

34. Ibid., p. 135.

35. Ibid., p. 135.

36. Mark Thomas Connelly, *The Response to Prostitution in the Progressive Era* (Chapel Hill: University of North Carolina Press, 1980), p. 88.

37. Ruth Rosen, *The Lost Sisterhood: Prostitution in America. 1900–1918* (Baltimore: Johns Hopkins University Press, 1982), pp. xii, 13, 16, 19, 36, and 37.

38. Ibid., pp. xiv, xvii, 6, 62, 64, 83, 110, 111, 128, 134, 172, 173, and 175.

39. John Decker, *Prostitution: Regulation and Control* (Littleton, Colo.: Rothman, 1979), p. 20.

40. Ibid., p. 300.

41. See chapter 1, p. 33.

42. The Canadian Badgley Committee seems to have accepted this argument, for instance. See Deborah R. Brock, *Making Work, Making Trouble: Prostitution as a Social Problem* (Toronto: Toronto University Press, 1998), p. 106. Note that Brock infers from her own assumption that "the existence of a prohibitive law rarely affects people's conduct" that Canadian prostitution laws are moralistic. "What the law really accomplishes," she writes, "is symbolic, in establishing society's moral code, and is punitive (and professedly 'rehabilitative'), toward those who transgress it" (p. 116). Brock, however, does not defend her assumption that the law is ineffective, or explain why she thinks prostitution laws are less effective and so more functionally moralistic than the criminal law in general.

43. Ronald Weitzer, "The Politics of Prostitution in America," in Ronald Weitzer, ed., *Sex for Sale* (New York: Routledge, 2000), pp. 159–180, at p. 163.

44. Note, too, that even if Americans think that prostitution is immoral only because it is sinful or intrinsically wrong, it does not directly follow that this belief is the best explanation for American prostitution laws. This is because a majority might think that a form of conduct is immoral and yet not believe that it ought to be prohibited. This appears to be the position of a majority of Americans on abortion, for example. See Dworkin, *Life's Dominion*, pp. 13–14. Hence even if most Americans believe that prostitution is immoral on moralistic grounds, American prostitution *laws* might not be moralistic, because a majority might support these laws only because they believe that sex work is bad for the women who do it, in which case the primary motive for these laws would be paternalistic and not moralistic.

45. See Yvonne Svanstrom, "Criminalizing the John—A Swedish Gender Model?" in Joyce Outshoorn, ed., *The Politics of Prostitution: Women's Movements, Democratic States, and the Globalization of Sex Commerce* (New York: Cambridge University Press, 2004), pp. 225–244, at pp. 239–243.

46. *R. v. Mara and East*, [1996] 105 C.C.C. (3d) 156 (Dubin, C.J.O), cited in MacKinnon, *Sex Equality*, p. 1397.

Chapter 3

1. John Stuart Mill, *On Liberty*, ed. Elizabeth Rapaport (Indianapolis: Hackett, 1978), p. 9; Joel Feinberg, "Legal Paternalism," *Rights, Justice, and the Bounds of Liberty* (Princeton, N.J.: Princeton University Press, 1980), pp. 110–129, at p. 118.

2. R. Barri Flowers, *The Prostitution of Women and Girls* (London: McFarland, 1998), p. 47; Mimi H. Silbert, "Prostitution and Sexual Assault: Summary of Results," *International Journal for Biomedical Research* 3 (1982): 69–71, at p. 70.

3. Flowers, *Prostitution of Women and Girls*, p. 47; Silbert, "Prostitution and Sexual Assault," p. 70; Jess Stern, *Sisters of the Night* (New York: Julian Messner, 1956), p. 147; D. Kelly Weisberg, *Children of the Night: A Study of Adolescent Prostitution* (Lexington, Mass.: Lexington Books, 1985), pp. 112–113.

4. I do not mean to suggest here that all valid paternalistic arguments are autonomy-protecting arguments. The paternalistic argument for prostitution laws presented in chapter 1 is a welfare-promoting argument, not an autonomy-protecting one. The point here is simply that it is false that all autonomy-protecting reasons for limiting liberty are nonpaternalistic reasons, and that it therefore makes no sense to argue that paternalistic reasons are illegitimate because none are autonomy protecting.

5. 198 U.S. 45 (1905).

6. The main points of this section are drawn from my article "Avoiding Paternalism," *Philosophy & Public Affairs* 34 (Winter 2006): 68–94.

7. Mill, *On Liberty*, p. 9.

8. Two recent discussions of paternalism that stress the centrality of motive are Douglas N. Husak, "Legal Paternalism," in Hugh LaFollette, ed., *The Oxford Handbook of Practical Ethics* (New York: Oxford University Press, 2003), pp. 387–412; and Seana Valentine Shiffrin, "Paternalism,

Unconscionability Doctrine, and Accommodation," *Philosophy and Public Affairs* 29 (Summer 2000): 205–250.

9. Mill, *On Liberty*, p. 9.

10. Loc. cit.

11. Loc. cit.

12. See Cecilie Hoigard and Liv Finstad, *Backstreets: Prostitution, Money and Love*, trans. Katherine Hanson, Nancy Sipe, and Barbara Wilson (University Park: Pennsylvania State University Press, 1992), p. 199; Kate Millet, "Prostitution: A Quartet for Female Voices," in Vivian Gornick and Barbara K. Moran, eds., *Woman in Sexist Society: Studies in Power and Powerlessness* (New York: Basic Books, 1971), pp. 21–69, at p. 41 (M's testimony); and Janice G. Raymond, "Ten Reasons for *Not* Legalizing Prostitution and a Legal Response to the Demand for Prostitution," in Melissa Farley, ed., *Prostitution, Trafficking, and Traumatic Stress* (Binghamton, N.Y.: Haworth Maltreatment and Trauma Press, 2003), pp. 315–332, at pp. 325–326.

13. One study found that only about a quarter of women involved in street prostitution supported decriminalization, and that almost three-quarters advocated some form of state regulation. See Roger Matthews, *Prostitution, Politics and Policy* (New York: Routledge-Cavendish, 2008), p. 4.

14. Mill, *On Liberty*, p. 9.

15. Note that on this interpretation Mill's principle would rule out even the relatively permissive Dutch policy of regulation, assuming that this policy could be justified only as benefiting some girls against their will, because this policy prohibits the sale of sex work by persons under eighteen, which is older than the age at which people are legally permitted to consent to sex and to be employed (sixteen).

16. Mill, *On Liberty*, p. 10.

17. J. S. Mill, *Utilitarianism*, ed. George Sher (Indianapolis: Hackett, 1979), p. 7.

18. Mill, *On Liberty*, p. 81.

19. Ibid., p. 74.

20. See Hoigard and Finstad, *Backstreets*, pp. 50–84, 106–123.

21. Mill, *On Liberty*, p. 10.

22. See Mill's discussion of the "higher faculties" in relation to the "higher pleasures" in *Utilitarianism*, pp. 8–11; Mill's discussion of "individuality" in connection to human development in *On Liberty*, pp. 53–71; and the quotation from Wilhelm von Humboldt in the epigram to *On Liberty*.

23. Mill, *On Liberty*, pp. 3–9, 54, 66–69.

24. Ibid., pp. 53–59, 61–65.

25. Ibid., p. 65.

26. See http://www.anniesprinkle.org.

27. Mill, *On Liberty*, p. 84.

28. It is sometimes suggested both by critics of prostitution laws and by critics of pornography that it is "inconsistent" for the government to prohibit prostitution while permitting the production and distribution of pornography. This is incorrect. It is consistent to believe that both policies are justified because there are relevant differences between prostitution and the production of pornography, some of which are identified in this paragraph.

29. Lars Ericsson, "Charges against Prostitution: An Attempt at a Philosophical Assessment," *Ethics* 90 (April 1980): 335–366, at p. 343.
30. Ibid., p. 342.
31. Ibid., p. 343.
32. Ibid., p. 344.
33. Ibid., p. 344.
34. Ibid., p. 344.
35. Martha Nussbaum, "Whether from Reason or Prejudice: Taking Money for Bodily Services," *Sex and Social Justice* (New York: Oxford University Press, 1999), pp. 276–298.
36. Ibid., pp. 288–295.
37. Ibid., pp. 288–295.
38. See, for example, Evelina Giobbe, "Confronting the Liberal Lies About Prostitution," in Dorchen Leidholdt and Janice G. Raymond, eds., *The Sexual Liberals and the Attack on Feminism* (New York: Pergamon Press, 1990), pp. 67–81; Giobbe, "Prostitution: Buying the Right to Rape," in Ann Wolbert Burgess, ed., *Rape and Sexual Assault III: A Research Handbook* (New York: Garland, 1991), pp. 143–160, at pp. 150–158; Hoigard and Finstad, *Backstreets*, pp. 50–84, 106–123; Joan J. Johnson, *Teen Prostitution* (Danbury, Conn.: Franklin Watts, 1992), pp. 18–19; Millett, "Prostitution: A Quartet for Female Voices," pp. 21–69; Ine Vanwesenbeeck, *Prostitutes' Well-Being and Risk* (Amsterdam: VU University Press, 1994), pp. 106–110, 147–152; and Weisberg, *Children of the Night*, pp. 111–113, 116–117. Note, too, that this argument for prostitution laws is endorsed in Catharine A. MacKinnon, *Sex Equality* (New York: Foundation Press, 2001), chapter 10: 1381–1512, and that Mackinnon cites much of the same material.
39. Nussbaum, "Whether from Reason or Prejudice," p. 290.
40. Ibid., pp. 290–291.
41. David A. J. Richards, "Commercial Sex and the Rights of the Person," *Sex, Drugs, Death, and the Law: An Essay on Overcriminalization* (Totowa, N.J.: Rowman and Littlefield, 1982), pp. 84–153.
42. Ibid., pp. 112–113.
43. Ibid., p. 113.
44. Ibid., p. 114.
45. Ibid., p. 114.
46. Ibid., p. 112.
47. Ibid., p. 113.
48. Ibid., p. 113.
49. See Rochelle L. Dalla, "Exposing the 'Pretty Woman' Myth: A Qualitative Examination of the Lives of Female Streetwalking Prostitutes," *Journal of Sex Research* 37, no. 4 (2000): 344–353, at p. 348; Vanwesenbeeck, *Prostitutes' Well-Being and Risk*, pp. 21–24.
50. As Roger Matthews observes, child prostitutes and victims of parental neglect and child sexual abuse "may at 18 be more dependent, more unable to make rational and informed choices and suffer greater levels of victimization than at any previous point in their lives." See *Prostitution, Politics and Policy*, pp. 53–54.
51. John Rawls, *A Theory of Justice* (Cambridge, Mass.: Harvard University Press, 1971), p. 249.

52. Ibid., p. 12. For a different kind of contractualist defense of hard paternalism that reaches the same conclusion, see Gerald Dworkin "Paternalism," in Rolf Sartorius, ed., *Paternalism* (Minneapolis: University of Minnesota Press, 1983), pp. 19–34.

53. Rawls, *Theory of Justice*, pp. 92–95, 142–143.

54. T. M. Scanlon, *What We Owe to Each Other* (Cambridge, Mass.: Harvard University Press, 1998), p. 4.

55. Richards, "Commercial Sex and the Rights of the Person," p. 114.

56. Note, though, that some kinds of hard paternalism would be permitted by libertarianism. If people actually consent, as Ulysses does, to give the government the authority to limit their liberty in certain ways against their will for their own good, *these* forms of hard paternalistic interference would be compatible with libertarianism.

Chapter 4

1. See *Caesar's Health Club v. St. Louis County*, 565 S.W. 2d 783, 786 (1978), cert. denied 439 U.S. 955 (1978); and Richard Posner and Katharine B. Silbaugh, *A Guide to American Sex Laws* (Chicago: University of Chicago Press, 1996), p. 156.

2. See *Loving v. Virginia*, 388 U.S. 1, 12 (1967).

3. John Rawls, "The Basic Liberties and Their Priority," *Political Liberalism* (New York: Columbia University Press, 1993), pp. 289–371.

4. John Rawls, *A Theory of Justice* (Cambridge, Mass.: Harvard University Press, 1971), p. 244.

5. In "Rights, Reasons, and Freedom of Association," in Amy Gutmann, ed., *Freedom of Association* (Princeton, N.J.: Princeton University Press, 1998), pp. 145–173, I explain at greater length why I believe that neither the democratic theory nor Rawls's two moral powers theory of basic liberty provide a satisfactory complete account of basic liberty.

6. See Rawls, *Theory of Justice*, pp. 11–12.

7. See Ronald Dworkin, *Taking Rights Seriously* (Cambridge, Mass.: Harvard University Press, 1978), pp. 180, 272–273.

8. See, for example, Dworkin's defense of a constitutional right to abortion in *Life's Dominion* (New York: Vintage Books, 1993), pp. 148–178.

9. T. M. Scanlon, *What We Owe to Each Other* (Cambridge, Mass.: Harvard University Press, 1998), p. 4.

10. Ibid., pp. 229–230.

11. See ibid., pp. 218–223, for the distinction between personal and impersonal reasons.

12. See introduction, note 1.

13. See Norma Jean Almodovar, "Porn Stars, Radical Feminists, Cops, and Outlaw Whores," in Jessica Spector, ed., *Prostitution and Pornography: Philosophical Debate about the Sex Industry* (Stanford, Calif.: Stanford University Press, 2006), pp. 149–174, at p. 161; R. Barri Flowers, *The Prostitution of Women and Girls* (London: McFarland & Company, 1998), pp. 128–129; Richard Goodall, *The Comfort of Sin: Prostitutes and Prostitution in the 1990s*

(Kent, U.K.: Renaissance Books, 1995), p. 70; Cecilie Hoigard and Liv Finstad, *Backstreets: Prostitution, Money, and Love*, trans. Katherine Hanson, Nancy Sipe, and Barbara Wilson (University Park: Pennsylvania State University Press, 1992), p. 30; Margaretha Jarvinen, *Of Vice and Women: Shades of Prostitution, Scandinavian Studies in Criminology*, vol. 13, trans. Karen Leander (Oslo: Scandinavian University Press, 1993), p. 21; Sven-Axel Mansson, "Men's Practices in Prostitution: The Case of Sweden," in Bob Pease and Keith Pringle, eds., *A Man's World? Changing Men's Practices in a Globalized World* (London: Zed Books, 2001), pp. 135–149, at p. 142; Eileen McLeod, *Women Working: Prostitution Now* (London: Croom Helm, 1982), pp. 83–84; Roger Matthews, *Prostitution, Politics and Policy* (New York: Routledge-Cavendish, 2008), p. 25; Martin A. Monto, "Why Men Seek Out Prostitutes," in Ronald Weitzer, ed., *Sex for Sale: Prostitution, Pornography and the Sex Industry* (New York: Routledge, 2000), pp. 67–83, at p. 81; and Ine Vanwesenbeeck, *Prostitutes' Well-Being and Risk* (Amsterdam: VU University Press, 1994), p. 33.

14. I thank Gilbert Harman for this observation.
15. See Monto, "Why Men Seek Out Prostitutes," pp. 69–71.
16. Vanwesenbeeck, *Prostitutes' Well-Being and Risk*, p. 147.

Chapter 5

1. As Ronald Dworkin argues in "Liberalism," *A Matter of Principle* (Cambridge, Mass.: Harvard University Press, 1985), pp. 181–204, at p. 191.
2. In "Liberalism, Liberty and Neutrality," *Philosophy and Public Affairs* 19 (Summer 1990): 253–274, at 253, I drew a similar, but not identical, distinction between "neutrality of grounds" (similar to "foundational neutrality") and "concrete neutrality" (similar to "legislative neutrality").
3. This appears to be Ronald Dworkin's mature position. See Dworkin, "Foundations of Liberal Equality," in Stephen Darwall, ed., *Equal Freedom* (Ann Arbor: The University of Michigan Press, 1995), pp. 190–306, at p. 209. There Dworkin says that he hopes to derive neutrality "as a theorem" from the general conception of human good he calls "the model of challenge" (p. 194).
4. This is the position I took in "Liberalism, Liberty, and Neutrality."
5. See chapter 2, p. 51.
6. See Dworkin, "Liberalism," p. 196.
7. John Rawls, *A Theory of Justice* (Cambridge, Mass.: Harvard University Press, 1971), p. 249.
8. H. L. A. Hart, *Law, Liberty, and Morality* (Stanford, Calif.: Stanford University Press, 1963), pp. 5, 32–34.
9. Ronald Dworkin, *Life's Dominion* (New York: Vintage Books, 1994), pp. 192–193.
10. Thomas Nagel, "Moral Conflict and Political Legitimacy," *Philosophy & Public Affairs* 16 (Summer 1987): 215–240, at p. 224.
11. Joseph Raz, *The Morality of Freedom* (New York: Oxford University Press, 1986), pp. 425–426.

12. See Joel Feinberg, "Legal Paternalism," *Rights, Justice, and the Bounds of Liberty* (Princeton, N.J.: Princeton University Press, 1980), pp. 110–129, at pp. 115–117.

13. See Dworkin's discussion in *Life's Dominion*, pp. 11–19, where he distinguishes the *detached* from the *derivative* objections to abortion.

14. "The Slipperiness of Neutrality," *Social Theory and Practice* 32 (January 2006): 17–34.

15. Note here that neutral reasons might include as elements claims that appear on the above list of nonneutral reasons. Neutral reasons, however, will always involve other elements that distinguish them from the reasons on this list of nonneutral reasons.

16. For the distinction between personal and impersonal reasons, see T. M. Scanlon, *What We Owe to Each Other* (Cambridge, Mass.: Harvard University Press, 1998), pp. 219–220.

17. This sentence applies Scanlon's contractualist theory of wrongness to principles of liberty. For a statement of the contractualist theory of moral wrongness itself, see ibid., p. 4.

18. Ibid., p. 220.

19. Dworkin, "Liberalism," p. 196.

20. Dworkin, *Taking Rights Seriously* (Cambridge, Mass.: Harvard University Press, 1978), pp. 234, 275.

21. See Dworkin, "Liberalism," p. 196.

22. See Dworkin, *Taking Rights Seriously*, pp. 274–276; and *A Matter of Principle*, pp. 359–365.

23. For the opinion that this derivation is not sound, see H. L. A. Hart, "Between Utility and Rights," *Columbia Law Review* 79 (1979): 828–846, at pp. 841–843.

24. See, for example, John C. Harsanyi, "Morality and the Theory of Rational Behavior," in Amartya Sen and Bernard Williams, eds., *Utilitarianism and Beyond* (New York: Cambridge University Press, 1982), pp. 39–62, at p. 55.

25. See, for example, R. M. Hare, *Moral Thinking* (New York: Oxford University Press, 1981), pp. 105–106.

26. For the term *objective list*, see Derek Parfit, *Reasons and Persons* (New York: Oxford University Press, 1984), p. 493. For the term *substantive good*, see T. M. Scanlon, "Value, Desire, and the Quality of Life," *The Difficulty of Tolerance* (New York: Cambridge University Press, 2003), pp. 169–186, at p. 173.

27. Ronald Dworkin, *Sovereign Virtue* (Cambridge, Mass.: Harvard University Press, 2000), pp. 248, 268.

28. Ibid., p. 269.

29. See Dworkin, *Life's Dominion*, pp. 192–193; and Ronald Dworkin, Thomas Nagel, Robert Nozick, John Rawls, Thomas Scanlon, and Judith Jarvis Thomson, "Assisted Suicide: The Philosopher's Brief," *New York Review of Books* 44 (March 27, 1997): 41–47, at pp. 46–47.

30. See Hart, *Law, Liberty, and Morality*, pp. 4–6, 31–33; Rawls, *Theory of Justice*, p. 249; Dworkin, *Life's Dominion*, pp. 192–193; and Dworkin et al., "Assisted Suicide," pp. 46–47.

31. See, too, Nagel, "Moral Conflict and Political Legitimacy," p. 224; Raz, *The Morality of Freedom*, pp. 425–426; and T. M. Scanlon, "A Theory of Freedom of Expression," *Difficulty of Tolerance*, pp. 16–25, at p. 20.

32. See, for example, Richard J. Arneson, "Equality and Equal Opportunity for Welfare," *Philosophical Studies* 56 (1989): 77–93, at p. 92; Arneson, "Liberalism, Distributive Subjectivism, and Equal Opportunity for Welfare," *Philosophy & Public Affairs* 19 (Spring 1990): 158–194, at p. 192; and George Sher, *Beyond Neutrality: Perfectionism and Politics* (New York: Cambridge University Press, 1997), pp. 8–9.

33. Note that Arneson has expressed doubt more recently about the accuracy of characterizing any objective conception of human interests as *perfectionist*. See Richard J. Arneson, "Opportunity for Welfare, Priority and Public Policy," in Steven Cullenberg and Prasanta K. Pattanaik, eds., *Globalization, Culture, and the Limits of the Market: Essays in Economics and Philosophy* (New Delhi: Oxford University Press, 2004), pp. 177–214, at p. 180.

34. Maude Miner, *Slavery of Prostitution: A Plea for Emancipation* (New York: Garland, 1987) (Macmillan Co., 1916), p. 308, citation to Garland edition.

35. Shelly Kagan, *Normative Ethics* (Boulder, Colo.: Westview Press, 1997), p. 40. See, too, Arneson, "Opportunity for Welfare, Priority and Public Policy," p. 180.

36. John Rawls, *Political Liberalism* (New York: Columbia University Press, 1993), pp. 74, 307–308.

37. Ibid, pp. 314–315.

38. See the discussion of Rawls's theory of basic liberty in chapter 4, p. 109.

Conclusion

1. See Jane Addams, *A New Conscience and an Ancient Evil*, introduction by Katherine Joslin (Chicago: University of Illinois Press, [1912] 2002), p. 109.

2. 198 U.S. 45 (1905).

3. John Stuart Mill, *On Liberty*, ed. Elizabeth Rapaport (Indianapolis: Hackett, 1978), pp. 9–10.

4. John J. Rumberger, *Profits, Power, and Prohibition: Alcohol Reform and the Industrializing of America, 1800–1930* (Albany, N.Y.: State University of New York Press, 1989), p. 39.

5. Mill, *On Liberty*, pp. 99–100.

6. See Ronald Dworkin, "Liberalism," *A Matter of Principle* (Cambridge, Mass.: Harvard University Press, 1985), pp. 181–204.

7. Mill, *On Liberty*, p. 9.

8. Dworkin, "Liberalism," p. 191.

9. See Ronald Dworkin, *Sovereign Virtue* (Cambridge, Mass.: Harvard University Press, 2000), pp. 1–3; and John Rawls, *Justice as Fairness: A Restatement* (Cambridge, Mass.: Harvard University Press, 2001), pp. 7, 13, 39, 46, 132, 133.

10. See Stephen Breyer, *Active Liberty* (New York: Alfred A. Knopf, 2005); Antonin Scalia, *A Matter of Interpretation* (Princeton, N.J.: Princeton University Press, 1997).

11. Benjamin Constant, "The Liberty of the Ancients Compared with That of the Moderns," *Benjamin Constant: Political Writings*, trans. and ed. Biancamaria Fontana (New York: Cambridge University Press, 1988), pp. 309–328.

12. Isaiah Berlin, "Two Concepts of Liberty," *Four Essays on Liberty* (New York: Oxford University Press, 1969), pp. 118–172, at pp. 122, 131.

13. See notes 7–11 in chapter 5.

14. See T. M. Scanlon, *What We Owe to Each Other* (Cambridge, Mass.: Harvard University Press, 1998), p. 4.

15. Thomas Nagel, "Progressive but Not Liberal," *New York Review of Books* 53 (May 25, 2006): 45–48.

Index

abolition. *See* prostitution, abolition of
abortion, 138, 181n8, 183n13
Addams, Jane, 59, 61, 155, 167n11
AIDS, 9, 20
alcohol prohibition, 156–157
Almodovar, Norma Jean, 169n27
Amsterdam, 20, 174n83
anarchism, 74, 87
Anthony, Susan B., 156
antidiscrimination law, 103, 105, 115, 156
antilegalization activists, 21, 31, 46, 95, 101, 120, 155
antimoralism, 149, 160
antipaternalism, 67, 148
   author's principle of, 67–73, 80, 129–131, 160–161
   Feinberg's principle of, 67, 138
   and liberalism, 4, 159–160
   Mill's principle of, 67, 77, 80–84, 138, 149
antipaternalists, 4, 10, 66, 72, 138
antiperfectionism, 150, 152
antiprostitution activists, 6–8, 58, 93, 98, 155, 174n84
autonomy
   commercial, 34, 115–116
   personal, 35, 105, 111, 115–117

   and paternalism, 66, 70–77, 88, 103, 138
   political, 34
   respect for, 5, 72–77
   sexual, 131
   and abolition, 38, 69
   and prohibition, 4, 33–35, 114–118, 125, 158

Backstreets, 96
Berlin, Isaiah, 158
Breyer, Stephen, 158
brothels
   illegal, 42
   legal, 41
   legalization of, 9, 18, 40–42, 93, 122, 170n33, 174n83, 175n95
   managers of, 20, 40–41, 124
   owners of, 7, 32, 40–41, 124, 175n95
   prohibition of, 4, 8, 29, 40, 128, 158
   prostitution inside, 40–41
   prostitution outside, 9, 41–42
   regulation of, 30, 40–42, 170n33, 172n64
   tolerance of, 58
   violence in, 41

burdens principle, 113–114,
    118–119, 122, 124–126,
    129–131, 133, 161
Butler, Josephine, 172n64

call girls, 41
Calvinism, 170n33
campaign finance laws, 26–27
Chapkis, Wendy, 25, 172n61
child prostitution, 19, 98, 180n50
civil libertarianism, 31, 49, 63,
    155–158
clients. *See* prostitutes, clients of
Coalition Against Trafficking in
    Women, 51, 174n83
Constant, Benjamin, 158
Contagious Diseases Acts, 172n64
contractualism, 105, 183n17
    and individualistic conception of
        political justification,
        141–144
    and liberalism, 160–161
    and paternalism 99–103, 144, 161
    and postneutrality principle,
        141–144, 160–161
COYOTE, 24
criminal law, justification of, 17,
    23, 26
customers. *See* prostitutes, clients of

debt bondage, 174n84
Decker, John, 62–63
decriminalization. *See* prostitution,
    decriminalization of
democracy, 38, 108, 137, 152, 154,
    158–159
Devlin, Patrick, 137
Dewey, John, 24
drug addiction, 50, 115
drug laws, 57, 88, 115–117,
    156–157
drug use, 15–16, 36, 88, 98, 115–117
drunk driving, 88
drunk driving laws, 78
Dworkin, Ronald
    on degradation, 49–53, 136
    and democracy, 158

    and equal concern and respect,
        112, 146, 161
    on external preferences, 145
    liberalism of, 57, 156–157, 182n1
    on majority disapproval, 137
    neutrality principle of, 157,
        182n3
    on paternalism, 137, 148–149
    and personal preference
        principle, 145–147
    on well-being, 148

emotional labor, 171n39
environmental protection laws,
    108, 120
Equality Now, 51
equality of opportunity, 109, 156
Ericsson, Lars, 56, 66, 92–94, 96
escort agencies. *See* escort services
escort services, 40–41, 122, 124, 128

Feinberg, Joel, 56, 67, 138
feminist theory, 10, 28
Finstad, Liv, 13, 23–25, 50, 84, 96,
    167n11, 169n29, 172n56
fornication, 47–49
freedom
    artistic, 116
    of association, 109
    of contract, 115, 155–157
    of expression, 4, 35, 67, 89, 109,
        113, 140, 153, 156, 159
    of marriage, 68, 86, 108, 110,
        129, 153
    of movement, 110
    of political speech, 107–108,
        110–111, 113, 140
    reproductive, 109, 156, 159,
        181n8
    sexual, 47–49, 154
        as basic liberty, 108–110, 153,
            156
        as important liberty, 4, 10,
            39–40, 52, 67, 131, 140, 159
        as right, 5, 120, 125, 158
    of worship, 4, 65, 67, 86,
        109–110, 140, 156, 159

Index   189

freedom of speech. *See* freedom of expression

Garrison, William Lloyd, 156
Giobbe, Evelina, 51–52, 166n2, 167n11, 168n13
Great Britain. *See* United Kingdom

Hart, H. L. A., 52, 55, 137, 149, 183n23
hedonism, 127, 150
Herbert, Bob, 50
HIV, 9, 165n16
Hochschild, Arlie, 171n39
Hoigard, Cecilie, 13, 23–25, 50, 84, 96, 167n11, 169n29, 172n56
homosexuality, 47, 49, 52, 67, 78, 90–91

immigration law, 18, 37–38
incest, 8, 19, 46–47
individualism, 57, 112–114, 125–126, 130, 160
individuality, 85–88, 103, 179n22
interests, 63, 84, 120, 153
  in autonomy, 111, 118
  of clients, 120–122
  impairment of, 97–99, 101
  in liberty, 102, 110, 116
  and neutral reasons, 138–140
  objective conception of, 66, 150–152, 184n33
  protection of, 9, 52, 55–56, 65, 76, 100, 109
  subjective conception of, 66, 150
  threats to, 27, 100–101

johns' school, 123, 125

kerb crawling, 29, 37, 42, 122–124

labor organizing, 32, 173n70
Las Vegas, 50
Lawrence v. Texas, 47
legal employment, age of, 18, 30, 82, 179n15

legalization. *See* prostitution, legalization of
legal moralism, 56
legal paternalism, 56
Leidholdt, Dorchen, 50, 174n83
liberalism, 4, 10–11, 158–162
  of Dworkin, 57, 156–158
  fundamental principles of, 22, 117, 132, 158–161
  and individual rights, 7, 114, 118, 128
  and neutrality, 133–134, 137–138
  and paternalism, 4, 10, 137–138, 159–161
  and perfectionism, 151–152
  of Rawls, 57, 158
libertarianism, 74, 102–103, 181n56
liberty
  of ancients, 158
  basic, 49, 51, 107–111, 152–153, 156
    theory of, 108–111, 153
  importance of, 68–70, 77, 101, 110, 116, 129–131, 143
  of moderns, 158
  negative, 158
  political, 116, 156, 159
  positive, 158
  religious, 107, 116, 156, 159
  theory of, 67
  value of, 4
Life's Dominion, 137
Lippmann, Walter, 61
Lively Commerce, 24
Lochner v. New York, 75, 81, 155, 157

MacKinnon, Catharine A., 50, 180n38
Mill, John Stuart, 52, 60, 66–67, 77, 156
  harm principle of, 57, 138, 149, 156–157
  liberty principle of, 80–83
  on paternalism, 83–87, 103–104
Miner, Maude, 59–61, 151, 169n29
mining, 92–93
moral disapproval, 55

moralism, 5, 46, 57–59, 121, 156–157, 177n42
    vs. paternalism, 55–64, 178n44
Morality of Freedom, 137–138
morals legislation, 53–54
motorcycle helmet laws, 66, 71, 88, 104, 129

Nagel, Thomas, 137, 161–162
neutrality
    toward conceptions of a good life, 5, 133, 140, 154, 159
    foundational, 135–136, 182n2
    legislative, 135–136, 140–141, 144, 149, 182n2
    possibility of, 134–136
    principle of, 5, 133–141, 144–145, 149, 155, 157
New Conscience and an Ancient Evil, 59
Newirth, Jessica, 51
New York, 75–76, 81, 155
New York City, 60
New York Times, 50
nude dancing, 88–89
Nussbaum, Martha, 66, 92, 94–96

On Liberty, 57, 80, 84, 156

parentalism, 165n10
paternalism, 65–106, 138, 141–144, 149, 165n10, 178n8
    and contractualism, 99–103, 144, 161
    definition of, 77–80
    hard, 71, 77, 86, 99–100, 102–103, 128–130, 144–148, 181n56
    and liberalism, 4, 10, 137–138, 159–161
    vs. moralism, 55–64, 178n44
    and neutrality 133–134, 137–138
    of prostitution laws, 4–7, 59, 107, 121, 133, 153, 161
    and rights, 128–132
    soft, 71, 86, 99–100, 128–129

paternalistic justification of prostitution laws. *See* prostitution laws, paternalistic argument for
peep shows, 171n42
perfectionism, 133, 149–153, 159, 184n33
pimps, 3, 7, 15, 20, 31, 41, 63, 173n69
Pines, Ayala M., 173n78
Plato, 154
pornography, 18, 88–89, 121, 179n28
postneutrality principle, 141–142, 144, 149, 152–153, 160–161
posttraumatic stress disorder, 8, 13
Preface to Politics, 61
privacy, 35, 104–105
Progressives, 61
progressivism, 155–158
prohibition. *See* prostitution, prohibition of
promiscuity, 45, 47–48, 55
prostitutes
    children of, 15, 32
    clients of, 7, 13, 19–20, 37, 39–40, 63, 70, 81, 85, 102, 107, 171n48, 175n89
        rights of, 120–124, 128, 132, 158
    as mothers, 15, 32, 168n17, 169n20
    rights of, 114–120, 131
prostitution
    abolition of, 12, 28–31, 59, 86, 95, 131, 133, 159
    defined, 29, 172–173n64
    effectiveness of, 39, 118–119, 174–175n88, 175n92
    and individuality, 85
    and Mill's principle, 81–83
    and neutrality, 153
    and paternalism, 63, 68–70, 74, 79, 84, 96, 107, 131, 148
    vs. regulation, 36–44
    and rights of clients, 120–124, 128, 132, 158

in Sweden, 38–40, 48, 69, 84
as an addiction, 14
age of entry into, 14, 37,
    167–168n11, 168n12
age restrictions of, 4, 18, 29–30,
    40, 42, 122–124, 127–128,
    159, 179n15
benefit of
  to clients, 39–40, 94, 111,
    120–121, 125, 168n18,
    175n89
  to prostitutes, 15, 115, 168n19,
    169n20, 169n27, 171n47
as a cause of
  crime, 7–8
  gender discrimination, 3, 7, 9,
    165n12
  sexually transmitted disease, 3,
    7, 9, 124, 165n16
as a choice, 5–7, 115
decriminalization of, 24–25, 81,
    173n67
  defined, 30
  effect of, 16, 23, 35–36, 65
  full, 16, 18, 21, 30–31, 38, 161
  in Germany, 18
  in Netherlands, 18
  and stigma, 18, 21, 170n33,
    171n49
as degrading, 49–53, 60, 62, 136
female, 12–13
feminist critics of, 3
harm of, 16, 36, 46, 64, 126–127,
    155
  physical, 10, 50, 60, 92
  psychological, 3, 10, 12–14, 22,
    26, 40, 48, 50–51, 60, 92,
    96–97, 117, 157, 166n2
  social, 3–4, 12, 14–15, 22, 48,
    50, 97
legalization of, 52, 162, 173n69
  defined, 31
  effect of, 9, 12, 16, 55, 57, 157,
    171n43, 174n80
  and liberalism, 5, 162
  opposition to, 6–8, 46
  paternalistic reasons against,
    31, 79, 94, 157, 162

and stigma, 17–18, 21–22
male, 12–13
morality of, 21, 45–46, 57–58,
    62–64, 162, 175n1,
    178n44
nontolerance of, 58–59
as oldest profession, 17
prohibition of, 12, 30–31, 36, 127,
    179n28
  costs of, 31–35
  defined, 28–29, 172n62
  effects of, 31–32, 173n72
  motives for, 63–64
  objections to, 31–32
  of safety, 35, 118
  and paternalism, 33, 36, 63, 119
  and rights of prostitutes, 115,
    118–119, 124–125, 131, 158
  and sexual autonomy, 4, 33–35,
    68–69, 114–118, 158
  in United States, 31–32, 39,
    64, 85
regulation of, 12, 28, 31, 86, 95,
    127, 133, 179n15
  vs. abolition, 36–44, 121–122,
    172n64
  arguments for, 8–9
  defined, 29–30
  effectiveness of, 118–119
  and individuality, 85
  and liberalism, 159
  and Mill's principle, 81–83
  in Netherlands, 14, 18, 39,
    42–43, 174n83, 179n15
  and neutrality, 153
  in Nevada, 29, 175n95
  objections to, 37–38, 165n14
  and paternalism, 68–70, 74, 79,
    86, 107, 148
  and rights of clients, 122–126,
    128, 132
  and rights of prostitutes,
    119–120, 131
  safety argument for, 41–42
  and stigma, 18, 170n33
  in U.K., 172n64
  in U.S., 58
in San Francisco, 168n11

prostitution (*continued*)
  sex positive view of, 25, 85
  as the social evil, 61, 177n26, 177n31
  stigma of, 14–15, 17–19, 21–23, 31, 48, 51, 53, 89, 93, 95, 171n49
    in Germany, 18, 170n33
    in Italy, 170n33
    in Netherlands, 14, 18, 170n33
    in Nevada, 170n33
    in Taiwan, 170n33
    in Yugoslavia, 170n33
  in Taiwan, 168n11
  as therapy, 168n18
  tolerance of, 9, 133
  underage, 37, 39–40, 43, 98, 121, 124
  as victimless crime, 3
  as violence against women, 8, 46, 64, 120–121, 155
  as voluntary, 3, 5–8, 115, 163–164n1
prostitution laws
  arguments for, 3–4, 7
  in Australia, 174n80
  benefit of, 16, 35, 119, 123
  in Canada, 64
  effectiveness of, 16–17, 23, 39, 174n80, 177n42
  in Germany, 9, 18, 30, 37, 42–43, 127, 170n33
  in Italy, 170n33
  justice of, 57
  as moralistic, 5, 55–64, 107, 121, 133, 157, 162, 177n42
  in Netherlands, 9, 14, 18, 30, 37, 39, 42–43, 127, 170n33, 174n83, 175n92, 179n15
  in Nevada, 29, 31, 170n33, 175n95
  nonpaternalistic arguments for, 8–9
  paternalistic argument for, 4, 7, 10, 12–13, 17, 22–23, 27–28, 31, 33, 35, 43–45, 47, 49–52, 55–58, 64–65, 73–74, 85, 94, 149–151, 178n4
  paternalistic function of, 35–36
  in Portugal, 170n33
  primary goal of, 43
  in Sweden, 29, 37–40, 43, 48, 64, 69, 84, 122, 174n87
  in Taiwan, 170n33
  in U.K., 29, 37, 43, 155, 172n64, 173n65, 173n66
  in U.S., 29, 31–32, 64, 85, 172n63
    history of, 58–62
    motives for, 62–64, 178n44
  in Yugoslavia, 170n33
puritanism, 56–57

rape, 8, 19, 46, 50–51, 53
  statutory, 26–27, 170n37
Rawls, John
  on basic liberty, 109–110, 181n5
  contractualism of, 99–104
  on degradation, 49–53, 136
  and democracy, 158
  liberalism of, 57
  and original position, 99–101, 103, 112
  on paternalism, 99–101, 103–104, 137, 149
  and perfectionism, 151–153
  and priority of liberty, 109
  and veil of ignorance, 100, 112
Raymond, Janice, 174n83
Raz, Joseph, 137–138
reasons
  impersonal, 142–143, 183n16
  moralistic, 47, 53–64, 140, 156, 159
  neutral, 134–136, 138–141, 149, 183n15
  nonmoralistic, 57–58, 63
  nonneutral, 134–142, 149, 183n15
  nonpaternalistic, 67, 78–79
  paternalistic, 55–64, 134, 138–139, 141, 149, 156
    defined, 79
  perfectionist, 149–150
  personal, 113, 142–143, 183n16
  religious, 54, 57
regulation. *See* prostitution, regulation of

Richards, David A.J., 56, 66, 92, 96–99, 101–102
rights, 63, 90, 107–133, 158
  of customers, 120–124
  and function of government, 103, 155
  liberal theories of, 4, 57, 112
  to liberty, 10–11
  and paternalism, 10, 36, 44, 104, 128–132
  theory of, 114, 140
  respect for, 7, 65
  to sexual freedom, 4–5, 114, 120, 125
  of sex workers, 114–120

San Francisco, 24, 123
Scalia, Antonin, 47, 158
Scanlon, T. M., 101–104, 142, 160–161, 183n17
scarlet letter syndrome, 168n13
seat belt laws, 72
self-enslavement, 38
sex
  anonymous, 45, 48
  commercial, 50, 59
  function of, 104
  with minors, 26–27
  nonmarital, 45, 47, 55, 61
  nonprocreative, 45, 104
  recreational, 45, 56
sexual abuse, 8, 36, 46
  of minors, 19, 46, 98, 173n78, 180n50
sexual consent, 6–7
  legal age of, 18, 30, 82, 179n15
  of minors, 6–7, 26
sexual labor, 57–58
sex work. *See* prostitution
Sex Worker Burnout Syndrome, 25
sex workers. *See* prostitutes
shoplifting, 33, 118–119
Shrage, Laurie, 172n61
Silbert, Mimi H., 168n11, 168n12, 173n78
slavery, 59, 111–112
  black, 172n64
  sexual, 6
  white, 172–173n64
Slavery of Prostitution, 59
sodomy, 67, 91, 104, 137
sodomy laws, 34, 49, 67, 90–91, 137
speed limits, 72, 77–78, 113
Sprinkle, Annie, 25, 69, 85
Steinberg, Ellen. *See* Sprinkle, Annie
St. James, Margo, 24, 42
street solicitation. *See* streetwalking
streetwalkers, 31, 41, 123–124
streetwalking, 8, 28–29, 32, 41, 58, 168–169n20
suicide, 100–101, 137
Sweden, 69

Theory of Justice, 49, 137
trafficking, 37–40, 121, 174n83, 174n84, 174n88, 175n92

Ulysses, 100, 181n56
United Kingdom, 9, 69
United States, 9, 69, 172n64
U.S. Constitution, 105
U.S. Supreme Court, 75, 108, 155–157
utilitarianism, 83–84, 111–112, 127, 146–147
Utlitarianism, 60, 83–84

Vice Commission of Chicago, 60, 168n11
  report of, 60–61
vice commissions, 59–61
volenti maxim, 75
vote selling, 34–35

well-being, 71, 148, 154–155
  objective list account of, 68, 110, 147–148, 150
  substantive good account of, 68, 110, 147–148, 150
WHISPER, 166n2
Wynter, Sarah. *See* Evelina Giobbe

zoning laws, 8–9, 29, 108, 120, 123

www.ingramcontent.com/pod-product-compliance
Ingram Content Group UK Ltd.
Pitfield, Milton Keynes, MK11 3LW, UK
UKHW022231230426
12048UKWH00016BA/1188